𝔉𝔯𝔬𝔫𝔱𝔢𝔫𝔞𝔠 𝔈𝔡𝔦𝔱𝔦𝔬𝔫

———

FRANCIS PARKMAN'S WORKS

VOLUME TEN

Frontenac Edition

A Half-Century

of

Conflict

*[France and England in North America
Part Sixth]*

BY

FRANCIS PARKMAN

IN TWO VOLUMES

VOLUME TWO

BOSTON

LITTLE, BROWN, AND COMPANY

1907

Printers

S. J. PARKHILL & CO., BOSTON, U. S. A.

CONTENTS.

———◆———

CHAPTER XXII.
1745–1747.
ACADIAN CONFLICTS.

CHAPTER XXIII.
1740–1747.
WAR AND POLITICS.

CHAPTER XXIV.
1745–1748.
FORT MASSACHUSETTS.

APPENDIX.

Illustrations

VOLUME II.

A HALF-CENTURY OF CONFLICT.

A HALF-CENTURY OF CONFLICT.

CHAPTER XVI.

1716–1761.

SEARCH FOR THE PACIFIC.

THE WESTERN SEA. — SCHEMES FOR REACHING IT. — JOURNEY
OF CHARLEVOIX. — THE SIOUX MISSION. — VARENNES DE LA
VÉRENDRYE : HIS ENTERPRISE ; HIS DISASTERS ; VISITS THE
MANDANS ; HIS SONS ; THEIR SEARCH FOR THE WESTERN
SEA ; THEIR ADVENTURES. — THE SNAKE INDIANS.— A GREAT
WAR-PARTY. — THE ROCKY MOUNTAINS. — A PANIC. — RETURN
OF THE BROTHERS ; THEIR WRONGS AND THEIR FATE.

IN the disastrous last years of Louis XIV. the
court gave little thought to the New World; but
under the regency of the Duke of Orléans interest in
American affairs revived. Plans for reaching the
Mer de l'Ouest, or Pacific Ocean, were laid before
the Regent in 1716. It was urged that the best hope
was in sending an expedition across the continent,
seeing that every attempt to find a westward passage
by Hudson Bay had failed. As starting-points and
bases of supply for the expedition, it was proposed to
establish three posts, one on the north shore of Lake
Superior, at the mouth of the river Kaministiguia,

another at Lac des Cristineaux, now called Lake of
the Woods, and the third at Lake Winnipeg, — the
last being what in American phrase is called the
"jumping-off place," or the point where the expedition was to leave behind the last trace of civilization.
These posts were to cost the Crown nothing; since
by a device common in such cases, those who built
and maintained them were to be paid by a monopoly
of the fur-trade in the adjacent countries. It was
admitted, however, that the subsequent exploration
must be at the charge of the government, and would
require fifty good men, at three hundred francs a
year each, besides equipment and supplies. All
things considered, it was reckoned that an overland
way to the Pacific might be found for about fifty
thousand francs, or ten thousand dollars.[1]

The Regent approved the scheme so far as to order
the preliminary step to be taken by establishing the
three posts, and in this same year, Lieutenant La
Noue, of the colony troops, began the work by building a stockade at the mouth of the Kaministiguia.
Little more was done in furtherance of the exploration till three years later, when the celebrated Jesuit,
Charlevoix, was ordered by the Duke of Orléans to
repair to America and gain all possible information
concerning the Western Sea and the way to it.[2]

In the next year he went to the Upper Lakes,

[1] *Mémoire fait et arresté par le Conseil de Marine,* 3 *Février,* 1717 ;
Mémoire du Roy, 26 *Juin,* 1717.

[2] *Charlevoix au Comte de Morville,* 1 *Avril,* 1723.

and questioned missionaries, officers, *voyageurs*, and Indians. The results were not satisfactory. The missionaries and the officers had nothing to tell; the voyagers and Indians knew no more than they, but invented confused and contradictory falsehoods to hide their ignorance. Charlevoix made note of everything, and reported to the Comte de Toulouse that the Pacific probably formed the western boundary of the country of the Sioux, and that some Indians told him that they had been to its shores and found white men there different from the French.

Believing that these stories were not without foundation, Charlevoix reported two plans as likely to lead to the coveted discovery. One was to ascend the Missouri, "the source of which is certainly not far from the sea, as all the Indians I have met have unanimously assured me;" and the other was to establish a mission among the Sioux, from whom, after thoroughly learning their language, the missionaries could, as he thinks, gain all the desired information.[1]

The Regent approved the plan of the mission; but the hostile disposition of the Sioux and the Outagamies prevented its execution for several years. In

---

[1] The valuable journal of Charlevoix's western travels, written in the form of letters, was published in connection with his *Histoire de la Nouvelle France*. After his visit to the Lakes, he went to New Orleans, intending to return in the spring and continue his inquiries for the Western Sea; but being unable to do this, he went back to France at the end of 1722. The official report of his mission is contained in a letter to the Comte de Toulouse, 20 January, 1723.

1727 the scheme was revived, and the colonial minister at Versailles ordered the governor of Canada to
send two missionaries to the Sioux. But the mission
required money, and the King would not give it.
Hence the usual expedient was adopted. A company was formed, and invested with a monopoly of
the Sioux fur-trade, on condition of building a fort,
mission-house, and chapel, and keeping an armed
force to guard them. It was specially provided that
none but pious and virtuous persons were to be
allowed to join the Company, "in order," says the
document, "to attract the benediction of God upon
them and their business."[1] The prospects of the
Company were thought good, and the governor himself was one of the shareholders. While the mission
was given the most conspicuous place in the enterprise, its objects were rather secular than spiritual, —
to attach the Sioux to the French interest by the
double ties of religion and trade, and utilize their
supposed knowledge to reach the Pacific.[2]

Father Guignas was made the head of the mission,
and Boucher de la Perrière the military chief. The
party left Montreal in June, and, journeying to the
Mississippi by way of Michilimackinac, Green Bay,
Fox River, and the Wisconsin, went up the great
river to Lake Pepin, where the adventurous Nicolas
Perrot had built two trading-posts more than forty

[1] *Traité de la Compagnie des Sioux, 6 Juin,* 1727.

[2] On this scheme, *Vaudreuil et Bégon au Ministre,* 4 *Octobre,* 1723;
Longueuil et Bégon au Ministre, 31 *Octobre,* 1725; *Beauharnois et
Dupuy au Ministre,* 25 *Septembre,* 1727.

years before.   Even if his time-worn tenements were
still standing, La Perrière had no thought of occupy-
ing them.   On the north, or rather west, side of the
lake his men found a point of land that seemed fit
for their purpose, disembarked, cut down trees, and
made a square stockade enclosing the necessary buildings.   It was near the end of October before they
were all well housed.   A large band of Sioux presently appeared, and set up their teepees hard by.
When the birthday of the governor came, the party
celebrated it with a display of fireworks and vociferous
shouts of *Vive le Roi*, *Vive Charles de Beauharnois*,
while the Indians yelped in fright and amazement at
the pyrotechnics, or stood pressing their hands upon
their mouths in silent amazement.   The French
called their fort Fort Beauharnois, and invited the
aid of Saint Michael the Archangel by naming the
mission in his honor.   All went well till April, when
the water rose with the spring floods and filled fort,
chapel, and houses to the depth of nearly three feet,
ejecting the whole party, and forcing them to encamp
on higher ground till the deluge subsided.[1]

Worse enemies than the floods soon found them
out.   These were the irrepressible Outagamies, who
rose against the intruding French and incited the
Sioux to join them.   There was no profit for the
Company, and no safety for its agents.   The stock-
holders became discouraged, and would not support
the enterprise.   The fort was abandoned, till in 1731

[1] *Guignas à Beauharnois*, 28 *Mai*, 1728.

a new arrangement was made, followed by another attempt.[1] For a time a prosperous trade was carried on; but, as commonly happened in such cases, the adventurers seem to have thought more of utilizing their monopoly than of fulfilling the terms on which they had received it. The wild Sioux of the plains, instead of being converted and turned into Frenchmen, proved such dangerous neighbors that, in 1737, Legardeur de Saint-Pierre, who then commanded the post, found himself forced to abandon it.[2] The enterprise had failed in both its aims. The Western Sea was still a mystery, and the Sioux were not friends, but enemies. Legardeur de Saint-Pierre recommended that they should be destroyed, — benevolent advice easy to give, and impossible to execute.[3]

René Gaultier de Varennes, lieutenant in the regiment of Carignan, married at Three Rivers, in 1667, the daughter of Pierre Boucher, governor of that place; the age of the bride, Demoiselle Marie Boucher, being twelve years, six months, and eighteen days. Varennes succeeded his father-in-law as governor of Three Rivers, with a salary of twelve hundred francs, to which he added the profits of a farm of forty acres; and on these modest resources, reinforced by an illicit trade in furs, he made shift to

[1] *Beauharnois et Hocquart au Ministre*, 25 *Octobre*, 1729; *Idem*, 12 *Octobre*, 1731.

[2] *Relation du Sieur de Saint-Pierre*, 14 *Octobre*, 1737.

[3] " Cet officier_[Saint-Pierre] a ajouté qu'il seroit avantageux de détruire cette nation." — *Mémoire de Beauharnois*, 1738.

sustain the dignity of his office. His wife became
the mother of numerous offspring, among whom was
Pierre, born in 1685, — an active and hardy youth,
who, like the rest of the poor but vigorous Canadian
noblesse, seemed born for the forest and the fur-trade.
When, however, the War of the Spanish Succession
broke out, the young man crossed the sea, obtained
the commission of lieutenant, and was nearly killed
at the battle of Malplaquet, where he was shot
through the body, received six sabre-cuts, and was
left for dead on the field. He recovered, and returned
to Canada, when, finding his services slighted, he
again took to the woods. He had assumed the
designation of La Vérendrye, and thenceforth his
full name was Pierre Gaultier de Varennes de la
Vérendrye.[1]

In 1728, he was in command of a small post on
Lake Nipigon, north of Lake Superior. Here an
Indian chief from the river Kaministiguia told him
of a certain great lake which discharged itself by a
river flowing westward. The Indian further declared
that he had descended this river till he reached water
that ebbed and flowed, and, terrified by the strange
phenomenon, had turned back, though not till he had
heard of a great salt lake, bordered with many villages. Other Indians confirmed and improved the
story. "These people," said La Vérendrye to the

---

[1] M. Benjamin Sulte has traced out the family history of the
Varennes in the parish registers of Three Rivers and other trustworthy sources. See *Revue Canadienne*, x. 781, 849, 935.

Jesuit Degonnor, "are great liars, but now and then they tell the truth."[1] It seemed to him likely that their stories of a western river flowing to a western sea were not totally groundless, and that the true way to the Pacific was not, as had been supposed, through the country of the Sioux, but farther northward, through that of the Cristineaux and Assiniboins, or, in other words, through the region now called Manitoba. In this view he was sustained by his friend Degonnor, who had just returned from the ill-starred Sioux mission.

La Vérendrye, fired with the zeal of discovery, offered to search for the Western Sea if the King would give him one hundred men and supply canoes, arms, and provisions.[2] But, as was usual in such cases, the King would give nothing; and though the governor, Beauharnois, did all in his power to promote the enterprise, the burden and the risk were left to the adventurer himself. La Vérendrye was authorized to find a way to the Pacific at his own expense, in consideration of a monopoly of the fur-trade in the regions north and west of Lake Superior. This vast and remote country was held by tribes who were doubtful friends of the French, and perpetual enemies of each other. The risks of the trade were as great as its possible profits, and, to reap these, vast outlays must first be made: forts must be built,

[1] *Relation du Père Degonnor, Jésuite, Missionnaire des Sioux, adressée à M. le Marquis de Beauharnois.*

[2] *Relation de Degonnor; Beauharnois au Ministre,* 1 *Octobre,* 1731.

manned, provisioned, and stocked with goods brought
through two thousand miles of difficult and perilous
wilderness. There were other dangers, more insidious,
and perhaps greater. The exclusive privileges granted
to La Vérendrye would inevitably rouse the intensest
jealousy of the Canadian merchants, and they would
spare no effort to ruin him. Intrigue and calumny
would be busy in his absence. If, as was likely, his
patron, Beauharnois, should be recalled, the new
governor might be turned against him, his privileges
might be suddenly revoked, the forts he had built
passed over to his rivals, and all his outlays turned
to their profit, as had happened to La Salle on the
recall of his patron, Frontenac. On the other hand,
the country was full of the choicest furs, which the
Indians had hitherto carried to the English at Hudson
Bay, but which the proposed trading-posts would
secure to the French. La Vérendrye's enemies pretended that he thought of nothing but beaver-skins,
and slighted the discovery which he had bound himself to undertake; but his conduct proves that he
was true to his engagements, and that ambition to
gain honorable distinction in the service of the King
had a large place among the motives that impelled
him.

As his own resources were of the smallest, he took
a number of associates on conditions most unfavorable
to himself. Among them they raised money enough
to begin the enterprise, and on the eighth of June,
1731, La Vérendrye and three of his sons, together

with his nephew, La Jemeraye, the Jesuit Messager, and a party of Canadians, set out from Montreal. It was late in August before they reached the great portage of Lake Superior, which led across the height of land separating the waters of that lake from those flowing to Lake Winnipeg. The way was long and difficult. The men, who had perhaps been tampered with, mutinied, and refused to go farther.[1] Some of them, with much ado, consented at last to proceed, and, under the lead of La Jemeraye, made their way by an intricate and broken chain of lakes and streams to Rainy Lake, where they built a fort and called it Fort St. Pierre. La Vérendrye was forced to winter with the rest of the party at the river Kaministiguia, not far from the great portage. Here months were lost, during which a crew of useless mutineers had to be fed and paid; and it was not till the next June that he could get them again into motion towards Lake Winnipeg.

This ominous beginning was followed by a train of disasters. His associates abandoned him; the merchants on whom he depended for supplies would not send them, and he found himself, in his own words, "destitute of everything." His nephew, La Jemeraye, died. The Jesuit Auneau, bent on returning to Michilimackinac, set out with La Vérendrye's eldest son and a party of twenty Canadians. A few days later, they were all found on an island in the Lake of

[1] *Mémoire du Sieur de la Vérendrye du Sujet des Établissements pour parvenir à la Découverte de la Mer de l'Ouest*, in Margry, vi. 585.

the Woods, murdered and mangled by the Sioux.[1]
The Assiniboins and Cristineaux, mortal foes of that
fierce people, offered to join the French and avenge
the butchery; but a war with the Sioux would have
ruined La Vérendrye's plans of discovery, and exposed
to torture and death the French traders in their
country. Therefore he restrained himself and declined the proffered aid, at the risk of incurring the
contempt of those who offered it.

Beauharnois twice appealed to the court to give La
Vérendrye some little aid, urging that he was at the
end of his resources, and that a grant of thirty thousand francs, or six thousand dollars, would enable him
to find a way to the Pacific. All help was refused,
but La Vérendrye was told that he might let out his
forts to other traders, and so raise means to pursue
the discovery.

In 1740 he went for the third time to Montreal,
where, instead of aid, he found a lawsuit. "In
spite," he says, "of the derangement of my affairs,
the envy and jealousy of various persons impelled
them to write letters to the court insinuating that I
thought of nothing but making my fortune. If more
than forty thousand livres of debt which I have on
my shoulders are an advantage, then I can flatter
myself that I am very rich. In all my misfortunes, I
have the consolation of seeing that M. de Beauharnois

---

[1] *Beauharnois au Ministre,* 14 *Octobre,* 1736; *Relation du Massacre
au Lac des Bois, en Juin,* 1736; *Journal de la Vérendrye, joint à la
lettre de M. de Beauharnois du — Octobre,* 1737.

enters into my views, recognizes the uprightness of my intentions, and does me justice in spite of opposition." [1]

Meanwhile, under all his difficulties, he had explored a vast region hitherto unknown, diverted a great and lucrative fur-trade from the English at Hudson Bay, and secured possession of it by six fortified posts, — Fort St. Pierre, on Rainy Lake; Fort St. Charles, on the Lake of the Woods; Fort Maurepas, at the mouth of the river Winnipeg; Fort Bourbon, on the eastern side of Lake Winnipeg; Fort La Reine, on the Assiniboin; Fort Dauphin, on Lake Manitoba. Besides these he built another post, called Fort Rouge, on the site of the city of Winnipeg; and, some time after, another, at the mouth of the river Poskoiac, or Saskatchewan, neither of which, however, was long occupied. These various forts were only stockade works flanked with block-houses; but the difficulty of building and maintaining them in this remote wilderness was incalculable. [2]

---

[1] *Mémoire du Sieur de la Vérendrye au Sujet des Établissements pour parvenir à la Découverte de la Mer de l'Ouest.*

[2] *Mémoire en abrégé de la Carte qui représente les Établissements faits par le Sieur de la Vérendrye et ses Enfants* (Margry, vi. 616); *Carte des Nouvelles Découvertes dans l'Ouest du Canada dressée sur les Mémoires du M*^r. *de la Vérandrie et donnée au Dépôt de la Marine par M. de la Galissonnière,* 1750; Bellin, *Remarques sur la Carte de l'Amérique,* 1755; Bougainville, *Mémoire sur l'État de la Nouvelle France,* 1757.

Most of La Vérendrye's forts were standing during the Seven Years' War, and were known collectively as *Postes de la Mer de l'Ouest.*

He had inquired on all sides for the Pacific. The Assiniboins could tell him nothing. Nor could any information be expected from them, since their relatives and mortal enemies, the Sioux, barred their way to the West. The Cristineaux were equally ignorant; but they supplied the place of knowledge by invention, and drew maps, some of which seem to have been made with no other intention than that of amusing themselves by imposing on the inquirer. They also declared that some of their number had gone down a river called White River, or River of the West, where they found a plant that shed drops like blood, and saw serpents of prodigious size. They said further that on the lower part of this river were walled towns, where dwelt white men who had knives, hatchets, and cloth, but no firearms.[1]

Both Assiniboins and Cristineaux declared that there was a distant tribe on the Missouri, called Mantannes (Mandans), who knew the way to the Western Sea, and would guide him to it. Lured by this assurance, and feeling that he had sufficiently secured his position to enable him to begin his western exploration, La Vérendrye left Fort La Reine in October, 1738, with twenty men, and pushed up the river Assiniboin till its rapids and shallows threatened his bark canoes with destruction. Then, with a band of Assiniboin Indians who had joined him, he struck across the prairie for the Mandans, his

[1] *Journal de la Vérendrye joint à la Lettre de M. de Beauharnois du — Octobre,* 1737.

Indian companions hunting buffalo on the way. They approached the first Mandan village on the afternoon of the third of December, displaying a French flag and firing three volleys as a salute. The whole population poured out to see the marvellous visitors, who were conducted through the staring crowd to the lodge of the principal chief, — a capacious structure so thronged with the naked and greasy savages that the Frenchmen were half smothered. What was worse, they lost the bag that held all their presents for the Mandans, which was snatched away in the confusion, and hidden in one of the *caches*, called cellars by La Vérendrye, of which the place was full. The chief seemed much discomposed at this mishap, and explained it by saying that there were many rascals in the village. The loss was serious, since without the presents nothing could be done. Nor was this all; for in the morning La Vérendrye missed his interpreter, and was told that he had fallen in love with an Assiniboin girl and gone off in pursuit of her. The French were now without any means of communicating with the Mandans, from whom, however, before the disappearance of the interpreter, they had already received a variety of questionable information, chiefly touching white men cased in iron who were said to live on the river below at the distance of a whole summer's journey. As they were impervious to arrows, — so the story ran, — it was necessary to shoot their horses, after which, being too heavy to run, they were easily

caught.   This was probably suggested by the armor
of the Spaniards, who had more than once made
incursions as far as the lower Missouri; but the nar-
rators drew on their imagination for various additional
particulars.

The Mandans seem to have much declined in numbers during the century that followed this visit of
La Vérendrye.   He says that they had six villages
on or near the Missouri, of which the one seen by
him was the smallest, though he thinks that it contained a hundred and thirty houses.[1]   As each of
these large structures held a number of families, the
population must have been considerable.   Yet when
Prince Maximilian visited the Mandans in 1833, he
found only two villages, containing jointly two hundred and forty warriors and a total population of
about a thousand souls.   Without having seen the
statements of La Vérendrye, he speaks of the population as greatly reduced by wars and the small-pox,
— a disease which a few years later nearly extermi-
nated the tribe.[2]

[1] *Journal de La Vérendrye*, 1738, 1739.   This journal, which is ill-
written and sometimes obscure, is printed in Brymner, *Report on
Canadian Archives*, 1889.

[2] Le Prince Maximilien de Wied-Neuwied, *Voyage dans l'Intérieur
de l'Amérique du Nord*, ii. 371, 372 (Paris, 1843).   When Captains
Lewis and Clark visited the Mandans in 1804, they found them in
two villages, with about three hundred and fifty warriors.   They
report that, about forty years before, they lived in nine villages,
the ruins of which the explorers saw about eighty miles below the
two villages then occupied by the tribe.   The Mandans had moved
up the river in consequence of the persecutions of the Sioux and

La Vérendrye represents the six villages as surrounded with ditches and stockades, flanked by a sort of bastion, — defences which, he says, had nothing savage in their construction. In later times the fortifications were of a much ruder kind, though Maximilian represents them as having pointed salients to serve as bastions. La Vérendrye mentions some peculiar customs of the Mandans which answer exactly to those described by more recent observers.

He had intended to winter with the tribe; but the loss of the presents and the interpreter made it useless to stay, and, leaving two men in the village to learn the language, he began his return to Fort La Reine. "I was very ill," he writes, "but hoped to get better on the way. The reverse was the case, for it was the depth of winter. It would be impossible to suffer more than I did. It seemed that nothing but death could release us from such miseries." He reached Fort La Reine on the eleventh of February, 1739.

His iron constitution seems to have been severely shaken; but he had sons worthy of their father. The two men left among the Mandans appeared at Fort La Reine in September. They reported that they had been well treated, and that their hosts had parted from them with regret. They also declared

the small-pox, which had made great havoc among them. *Expedition of Lewis and Clark,* i. 129 (ed. Philadelphia, 1814). These nine villages seem to have been above Cannon-ball River, a tributary of the Missouri.

that at the end of spring several Indian tribes, all
well supplied with horses, had come, as was their
yearly custom, to the Mandan villages to barter
embroidered buffalo hides and other skins for corn
and beans; that they had encamped, to the number
of two hundred lodges, on the farther side of the
Missouri, and that among them was a band said to
have come from a distant country towards the sunset,
where there were white men who lived in houses
built of bricks and stones.

The two Frenchmen crossed over to the camp of
these western strangers, among whom they found a
chief who spoke, or professed to speak, the language
of the mysterious white men, which to the two
Frenchmen was unintelligible. Fortunately, he also
spoke the language of the Mandans, of which the
Frenchmen had learned a little during their stay,
and hence were able to gather that the white men in
question had beards, and that they prayed to the
Master of Life in great houses, built for the purpose,
holding books, the leaves of which were like husks
of Indian corn, singing together and repeating *Jésus,
Marie*. The chief gave many other particulars,
which seemed to show that he had been in contact
with Spaniards, — probably those of California; for
he described their houses as standing near the great
lake, of which the water rises and falls and is not fit
to drink. He invited the two Frenchmen to go
with him to this strange country, saying that it could
be reached before winter, though a wide circuit must

be made, to avoid a fierce and dangerous tribe called
Snake Indians (*Gens du Serpent*).[1]

On hearing this story, La Vérendrye sent his eldest
son, Pierre, to pursue the discovery with two men,
ordering him to hire guides among the Mandans and
make his way to the Western Sea. But no guides
were to be found, and in the next summer the young
man returned from his bootless errand.[2]

Undaunted by this failure, Pierre set out again in
the next spring, 1742, with his younger brother, the
Chevalier de la Vérendrye. Accompanied only by two
Canadians, they left Fort La Reine on the twenty-
ninth of April, and following, no doubt, the route of
the Assiniboin and Mouse River, reached the chief
village of the Mandans in about three weeks.

Here they found themselves the welcome guests of
this singularly interesting tribe, ruined by the small-
pox nearly half a century ago, but preserved to
memory by the skilful pencil of the artist Charles
Bodmer, and the brush of the painter George Catlin,
both of whom saw them at a time when they were
little changed in habits and manners since the visit
of the brothers La Vérendrye.[3]

[1] *Journal du Sieur de la Vérendrye*, 1740, in Archives de la Marine.
[2] *Mémoire du Sieur de la Vérendrye, joint à sa lettre du 31 Octobre*,
1744.
[3] Prince Maximilian spent the winter of 1832–33 near the Mandan villages. His artist, with the instinct of genius, seized the
characteristics of the wild life before him, and rendered them with
admirable vigor and truth. Catlin spent a considerable time
among the Mandans soon after the visit of Prince Maximilian, and
had unusual opportunities of studying them. He was an indiffer-

Thus, though the report of the two brothers is too concise and brief, we know what they saw when they entered the central area, or public square, of the village. Around stood the Mandan lodges, looking like round flattened hillocks of earth, forty or fifty feet wide. On examination they proved to be framed of strong posts and poles, covered with a thick matting of intertwined willow-branches, over which was laid a bed of well-compacted clay or earth two or three feet thick. This heavy roof was supported by strong interior posts.[1] The open place which the dwellings enclosed served for games, dances, and the ghastly religious or magical ceremonies practised by the tribe. Among the other structures was the sacred "medicine lodge," distinguished by three or four tall poles planted before it, each surmounted by an effigy looking much like a scarecrow, and meant as an offering to the spirits.

If the two travellers had been less sparing of words, they would doubtless have told us that as they entered the village square the flattened earthen domes that surrounded it were thronged with squaws

ent painter, a shallow observer, and a garrulous and windy writer; yet his enthusiastic industry is beyond praise, and his pictures are invaluable as faithful reflections of aspects of Indian life which are gone forever.

Beauharnois calls the Mandans *Blancs Barbus*, and says that they have been hitherto unknown. *Beauharnois au Ministre*, 14 *Août*, 1739. The name Mantannes, or Mandans, is that given them by the Assiniboins.

[1] The Minnetarees and other tribes of the Missouri built their lodges in a similar way.

and children, — for this was always the case on occasions of public interest, — and that they were forced to undergo a merciless series of feasts in the lodges of the chiefs. Here, seated by the sunken hearth in the middle, under the large hole in the roof that served both for window and chimney, they could study at their ease the domestic economy of their entertainers. Each lodge held a *gens*, or family connection, whose beds of raw buffalo hide, stretched on poles, were ranged around the circumference of the building, while by each stood a post on which hung shields, lances, bows, quivers, medicine-bags, and masks formed of the skin of a buffalo's head, with the horns attached, to be used in the magic buffalo dance.

Every day had its sports to relieve the monotony of savage existence, the game of the stick and the rolling ring, the archery practice of boys, horse-racing on the neighboring prairie, and incessant games of chance; while every evening, in contrast to these gayeties, the long, dismal wail of women rose from the adjacent cemetery, where the dead of the village, sewn fast in buffalo hides, lay on scaffolds above the reach of wolves.

The Mandans did not know the way to the Pacific, but they told the brothers that they expected a speedy visit from a tribe or band called Horse Indians, who could guide them thither. It is impossible to identify this people with any certainty.[1] The two travellers

1 The Cheyennes have a tradition that they were the first tribe of this region to have horses. This may perhaps justify a conjec-

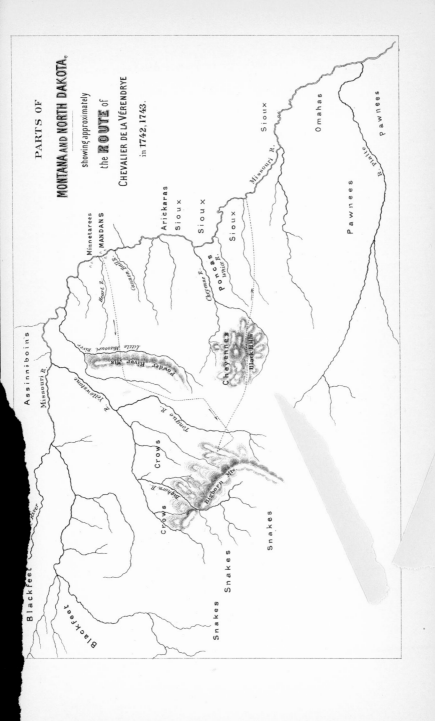

PARTS OF
MONTANA AND NORTH DAKOTA,
showing approximately
the **ROUTE** of
CHEVALIER DE LA VÉRENDRYE
in 1742, 1743.

waited for them in vain till after midsummer, and then, as the season was too far advanced for longer delay, they hired two Mandans to conduct them to their customary haunts.

They set out on horseback, their scanty baggage and their stock of presents being no doubt carried by pack-animals. Their general course was west-south-west, with the Black Hills at a distance on their left, and the upper Missouri on their right. The country was a rolling prairie, well covered for the most part with grass, and watered by small alkaline streams creeping towards the Missouri with an opaque, whitish current. Except along the watercourses, there was little or no wood. "I noticed," says the Chevalier de la Vérendrye, "earths of different colors, blue, green, red, or black, white as chalk, or yellowish like ochre." This was probably in the "bad lands" of the Little Missouri, where these colored earths form a conspicuous feature in the bare and barren bluffs, carved into fantastic shapes by the storms.[1]

For twenty days the travellers saw no human being, so scanty was the population of these plains. Game, however, was abundant. Deer sprang from the tall, reedy grass of the river bottoms; buffalo

ture that the northern division of this brave and warlike people were the Horse Indians of La Vérendrye; though an Indian tradi-tion, unless backed by well-established facts, can never be accepted as substantial evidence.

[1] A similar phenomenon occurs farther west on the face of the perpendicular bluffs that, in one place, border the valley of the river Rosebud.

tramped by in ponderous columns, or dotted the swells of the distant prairie with their grazing thousands; antelope approached, with the curiosity of their species, to gaze at the passing horsemen, then fled like the wind; and as they neared the broken uplands towards the Yellowstone, they saw troops of elk and flocks of mountain-sheep. Sometimes, for miles together, the dry plain was studded thick with the earthen mounds that marked the burrows of the curious marmots, called prairie-dogs, from their squeaking bark. Wolves, white and gray, howled about the camp at night, and their cousin, the coyote, seated in the dusk of evening upright on the grass, with nose turned to the sky, saluted them with a complication of yelpings, as if a score of petulant voices were pouring together from the throat of one small beast.

On the eleventh of August, after a march of about three weeks, the brothers reached a hill, or group of hills, apparently west of the Little Missouri, and perhaps a part of the Powder River Range. It was here that they hoped to find the Horse Indians, but nobody was to be seen. Arming themselves with patience, they built a hut, made fires to attract by the smoke any Indians roaming near, and went every day to the tops of the hills to reconnoitre. At length, on the fourteenth of September, they descried a spire of smoke on the distant prairie.

One of their Mandan guides had left them and gone back to his village. The other, with one of the

Frenchmen, went towards the smoke, and found a camp of Indians, whom the journal calls Les Beaux Hommes, and who were probably Crows, or Apsaroka, a tribe remarkable for stature and symmetry, who long claimed that region as their own.   They treated the visitors well, and sent for the other Frenchmen to come to their lodges, where they were received with great rejoicing.   The remaining Mandan, however, became frightened, — for the Beaux Hommes were enemies of his tribe, — and he soon followed his companion on his solitary march homeward.

The brothers remained twenty-one days in the camp of the Beaux Hommes, much perplexed for want of an interpreter.   The tribes of the plains have in common a system of signs by which they communicate with each other, and it is likely that the brothers had learned it from the Sioux or Assiniboins, with whom they had been in familiar intercourse.   By this or some other means they made their hosts understand that they wished to find the Horse Indians; and the Beaux Hommes, being soothed by presents, offered some of their young men as guides.   They set out on the ninth of October, following a south-southwest course.[1]

In two days they met a band of Indians, called by

[1] *Journal du Voyage fait par le Chevalier de la Vérendrye en* 1742. The copy before me is from the original in the Dépôt des Cartes de la Marine.   A duplicate, in the Archives des Affaires Étrangères, is printed by Margry.   It gives the above date as November 9 instead of October 9.   The context shows the latter to be correct.

them the Little Foxes, and on the fifteenth and seventeenth two villages of another unrecognizable horde, named Pioya. From La Vérendrye's time to our own, this name "villages" has always been given to the encampments of the wandering people of the plains. All these nomadic communities joined them, and they moved together southward, till they reached at last the lodges of the long-sought Horse Indians. They found them in the extremity of distress and terror. Their camp resounded with howls and wailings; and not without cause, for the Snakes, or Shoshones, — a formidable people living farther westward, — had lately destroyed most of their tribe. The Snakes were the terror of that country. The brothers were told that the year before they had destroyed seventeen villages, killing the warriors and old women, and carrying off the young women and children as slaves.

None of the Horse Indians had ever seen the Pacific; but they knew a people called Gens de l'Arc, or Bow Indians, who, as they said, had traded not far from it. To the Bow Indians, therefore, the brothers resolved to go, and by dint of gifts and promises they persuaded their hosts to show them the way. After marching southwestward for several ̄ they saw the distant prairie covered with the ̄ buffalo-skin lodges of a great Indian camp. ̄ was that of the Bow Indians, who may have been one of the bands of the western Sioux, — the predominant race in this region. Few or none of them could ever have seen a white man, and we may imagine their amazement at the arrival of the strangers, who, followed by staring crowds, were conducted to the lodge of the chief. "Thus far," says La Vérendrye, "we had been well received in all the villages we had passed; but this was nothing compared with the courteous manners of the great chief of the Bow Indians, who, unlike the others, was not self-interested in the least, and who took excellent care of everything belonging to us."

The first inquiry of the travellers was for the Pacific; but neither the chief nor his tribesmen knew anything of it, except what they had heard from Snake prisoners taken in war. The Frenchmen were surprised at the extent of the camp, which consisted of many separate bands. The chief explained that they had been summoned from far and near for a grand war-party against that common foe of all, — the Snakes.[1] In fact, the camp resounded with war-songs and war-dances. "Come with us," said their host; "we are going towards the mountains, where you can see the great water that you are looking for."

At length the camp broke up. The squaws took down the lodges, and the march began over prairies

[1] The enmity between the Sioux and the Snakes lasted to our own time. When the writer lived among the western Sioux, one of their chiefs organized a war-party against the Snakes, and numerous bands came to join the expedition from a distance in some cases of three hundred miles. Quarrels broke out among them, and the scheme was ruined.

dreary and brown with the withering touch of autumn.
The spectacle was such as men still young have seen
in these western lands, but which no man will see
again. The vast plain swarmed with the moving
multitude. The tribes of the Missouri and the
Yellowstone had by this time abundance of horses,
the best of which were used for war and hunting, and
the others as beasts of burden. These last were
equipped in a peculiar manner. Several of the long
poles used to frame the teepees, or lodges, were
secured by one end to each side of a rude saddle,
while the other end trailed on the ground. Crossbars
lashed to the poles just behind the horse kept them
three or four feet apart, and formed a firm support,
on which was laid, compactly folded, the buffalo-skin
covering of the lodge. On this, again, sat a mother
with her young family, sometimes stowed for safety
in a large open willow basket, with the occasional
addition of some domestic pet, — such as a tame
raven, a puppy, or even a small bear-cub. Other
horses were laden in the same manner with wooden
bowls, stone hammers, and other utensils, along with
stores of dried buffalo-meat packed in cases of raw-
hide whitened and painted. Many of the innumerable
dogs — whose manners and appearance strongly suggested their relatives the wolves, to whom, however,
they bore a mortal grudge — were equipped in a
similar way, with shorter poles and lighter loads.
Bands of naked boys, noisy and restless, roamed the
prairie, practising their bows and arrows on any small

animal they might find.   Gay young squaws — adorned
on each cheek with a spot of ochre or red clay, and
arrayed in tunics of fringed buckskin embroidered
with porcupine quills — were mounted on ponies,
astride like men; while lean and tattered hags — the
drudges of the tribe, unkempt and hideous — scolded
the lagging horses, or screeched at the disorderly
dogs, with voices not unlike the yell of the great
horned owl.   Most of the warriors were on horseback, armed with round white shields of bull-hide,
feathered lances, war-clubs, bows, and quivers filled
with stone-headed arrows; while a few of the elders,
wrapped in robes of buffalo-hide, stalked along in
groups with a stately air, chatting, laughing, and
exchanging unseemly jokes.[1]

"We continued our march," says La Vérendrye,
"sometimes south-southwest, and now and then northwest; our numbers constantly increasing by villages
of different tribes which joined us."   The variations
of their course were probably due to the difficulties of the country, which grew more rugged as they
advanced, with broken hills, tracts of dingy green
sage-bushes, and bright, swift streams, edged with
cottonwood and willow, hurrying northward to join
the Yellowstone.   At length, on the first of January,
1743, they saw what was probably the Bighorn Range

[1] The above descriptive particulars are drawn from repeated
observation of similar scenes at a time when the primitive condition of these tribes was essentially unchanged, though with the
difference that the concourse of savages counted by hundreds, and
not by thousands.

of the Rocky Mountains, a hundred and twenty miles east of the Yellowstone Park.

A council of all the allied bands was now called, and the Frenchmen were asked to take part in it. The questions discussed were how to dispose of the women and children, and how to attack the enemy. Having settled their plans, the chiefs begged their white friends not to abandon them; and the younger of the two, the Chevalier, consented to join the warriors, and aid them with advice, though not with arms.

The tribes of the western plains rarely go on war-parties in winter, and this great expedition must have been the result of unusual exasperation. The object was to surprise the Snakes in the security of their winter camp, and strike a deadly blow, which would have been impossible in summer.

On the eighth of January the whole body stopped to encamp, choosing, no doubt, after the invariable winter custom of western Indians, a place sheltered from wind, and supplied with water and fuel. Here the squaws and children were to remain, while most of the warriors advanced against the enemy. By pegging the lower edge of the lodge-skin to the ground, and piling a ridge of stones and earth upon it to keep out the air, fastening with wooden skewers the flap of hide that covered the entrance, and keeping a constant fire, they could pass a winter endurable to Indians, though smoke, filth, vermin, bad air, the crowd, and the total absence of privacy, would make it a purgatory to any civilized white man.

The Chevalier left his brother to watch over the baggage of the party, which was stored in the lodge of the great chief, while he himself, with his two Canadians, joined the advancing warriors. They were on horseback, marching with a certain order, and sending watchmen to reconnoitre the country from the tops of the hills.[1] Their movements were so slow that it was twelve days before they reached the foot of the mountains, which, says La Vérendrye, "are for the most part well wooded, and seem very high."[2] He longed to climb their great snow-encumbered peaks, fancying that he might then see the Pacific, and never dreaming that more than eight hundred miles of mountains and forests still lay between him and his goal.

Through the whole of the present century the villages of the Snakes were at a considerable distance west of the Bighorn Range, and some of them were even on the upper waters of the Pacific slope. It is likely that they were so in 1743, in which case the war-party would not have only reached the Bighorn Mountains, but have pushed farther on to within sight of the great Wind River Range. Be this as it may, their scouts reached the chief winter camp of

[1] At least this was done by a band of Sioux with whom the writer once traversed a part of the country ranged by these same Snakes, who had lately destroyed an entire Sioux village.

[2] The Bighorn Range, below the snow line, is in the main well timbered with pine, fir, oak, and juniper.

the Snakes, and found it abandoned, with lodges still
standing, and many household possessions left behind.
The enemy had discovered their approach, and fled.
Instead of encouraging the allies, this news filled
them with terror, for they feared that the Snake
warriors might make a circuit to the rear, and fall
upon the camp where they had left their women and
children. The great chief spent all his eloquence in
vain, nobody would listen to him; and with charac-
teristic fickleness they gave over the enterprise, and
retreated in a panic. "Our advance was made in
good order; but not so our retreat," says the Chevalier's journal. "Everybody fled his own way. Our
horses, though good, were very tired, and got little
to eat." The Chevalier was one day riding with his
friend, the great chief, when, looking behind him,
he missed his two French attendants. Hastening
back in alarm, he found them far in the rear, quietly
feeding their horses under the shelter of a clump of
trees. He had scarcely joined them when he saw a
party of fifteen hostile Indians stealthily creeping
forward, covered by their bull-hide shields. He and
his men let them approach, and then gave them a
few shots; on which they immediately ran off, firearms being to them an astounding novelty.

The three Frenchmen now tried to rejoin the great
chief and his band, but the task was not easy. The
prairie, bare of snow and hard as flint, showed no
trace of foot or hoof; and it was by rare good fortune
that they succeeded, on the second day, not in over-

taking the chief, but in reaching the camp where the women and children had been left. They found them all in safety; the Snakes had not attacked them, and the panic of the warriors was needless. It was the ninth of February. They were scarcely housed when a blizzard set in, and on the night of the tenth the plains were buried in snow. The great chief had not appeared. With such of his warriors as he could persuade to follow him, he had made a wide circuit to find the trail of the lost Frenchmen, but, to his great distress, had completely failed. It was not till five days after the arrival of the Chevalier and his men that the chief reached the camp, "more dead than alive," in the words of the journal. All his hardships were forgotten when he found his white friends safe, for he had given them up for lost. "His sorrow turned to joy, and he could not give us attention and caresses enough."

The camp broke up, and the allied bands dispersed. The great chief and his followers moved slowly through the snowdrifts towards the east-southeast, accompanied by the Frenchmen. Thus they kept on till the first of March, when the two brothers, learning that they were approaching the winter village of a people called Gens de la Petite Cerise, or Choke-Cherry Indians, sent one of their men, with a guide, to visit them. The man returned in ten days, bringing a message from the Choke-Cherry Indians, inviting the Frenchmen to their lodges.

The great chief of the Bow Indians, who seems to

have regarded his young friends with mingled affection, respect, and wonder, was grieved at the thought
of losing them, but took comfort when they promised
to visit him again, provided that he would make his
abode near a certain river which they pointed out.
To this he readily agreed, and then, with mutual
regret, they parted.[1]   The Frenchmen repaired to the
village of the Choke-Cherry Indians, who, like the
Bow Indians, were probably a band of Sioux.[2]   Hard
by their lodges, which stood near the Missouri, the
brothers buried a plate of lead graven with the royal
arms, and raised a pile of stones in honor of the governor of Canada.   They remained at this place till
April; then, mounting their horses again, followed
the Missouri upward to the village of the Mandans,
which they reached on the eighteenth of May.   After
spending a week here, they joined a party of
Assiniboins, journeyed with them towards Fort La
Reine, and reached it on the second of July, — to the

[1] The only two tribes of this region who were a match for the
Snakes were the Sioux and the Blackfeet. It is clear that the Bow
Indians could not have been Blackfeet, as in that case, after the war-
party broke up, they would have moved northward towards their
own country, instead of east-southeast into the country of their
enemies. Hence I incline to think the Bow Indians a band of Si___
or Dakota, — a people then, as since, predominant i_
  The banks of the Missouri, in the part which
would have reached in following an east-southea_____ _ere
occupied by numerous bands or sub-tribes of Sioux, such as the
Minneconjou, Yankton, Oncpapa, Brulé, and others, friends and
relatives of the Bow Indians, supposing these to have been Sioux.

[2] The Sioux, Cheyennes, and other prairie tribes use the small
astringent wild cherry for food. The squaws pound it, stones and
all, and then dry it for winter use.

great relief of their father, who was waiting in suspense, having heard nothing of them for more than a year.

Sixty-two years later, when the vast western regions then called Louisiana had just been ceded to the United States, Captains Lewis and Clark left the Mandan villages with thirty-two men, traced the Missouri to the mountains, penetrated the wastes beyond, and made their way to the Pacific. The first stages of that remarkable exploration were anticipated by the brothers La Vérendrye. They did not find the Pacific, but they discovered the Rocky Mountains, or at least the part of them to which the name properly belongs; for the southern continuation of the great range had long been known to the Spaniards. Their bold adventure was achieved, not at the charge of a government, but at their own cost and that of their father, — not with a band of well-equipped men, but with only two followers.

The fur-trading privilege which was to have been their compensation had proved their ruin. They were still pursued without ceasing by the jealousy of rival traders and the ire of disappointed partners. "Here in Canada more than anywhere else," the Chevalier wrote, some years after his return, "envy is the passion à la mode, and there is no escaping it." [1] It was the story of La Salle repeated. Beauharnois, however, still stood by them, encouraged and defended them, and wrote in their favor to the colonial minis-

[1] *Le Chevalier de la Vérendrye au Ministre*, 30 *Septembre*, 1750.

ter.[1] It was doubtless through his efforts that the elder La Vérendrye was at last promoted to a captaincy in the colony troops. Beauharnois was succeeded in the government by the sagacious and able Galissonière, and he too befriended the explorers. "It seems to me," he wrote to the minister, "that what you have been told touching the Sieur de la Vérendrye, to the effect that he has been more busy with his own interests than in making discoveries, is totally false, and, moreover, that any officers employed in such work will always be compelled to give some of their attention to trade, so long as the King allows them no other means of subsistence. These discoveries are very costly, and more fatiguing and dangerous than open war."[2] Two years later, the elder La Vérendrye received the cross of the Order of St. Louis, — an honor much prized in Canada, but which he did not long enjoy; for he died at Montreal in the following December, when on the point of again setting out for the West.

His intrepid sons survived, and they were not idle. One of them, the Chevalier, had before discovered the river Saskatchewan, and ascended it as far as the forks.[3] His intention was to follow it to the mountains, build a fort there, and thence push westward in another search for the Pacific; but a disastrous

[1] *La Vérendrye père au Ministre*, 1 *Novembre*, 1746, in Margry, vi. 611.

[2] *La Galissonière au Ministre*, 23 *Octobre*, 1747.

[3] *Mémoire en abrégé des Établissements et Découvertes faits Sieur de la Vérendrye et ses Enfants.*

event ruined all his hopes. La Galissonière returned to France, and the Marquis de la Jonquière succeeded him, with the notorious François Bigot as intendant. Both were greedy of money, — the one to hoard, and the other to dissipate it. Clearly there was money to be got from the fur-trade of Manitoba, for La Vérendrye had made every preparation and incurred every expense. It seemed that nothing remained but to reap where he had sown. His commission to find the Pacific, with the privileges connected with it, was refused to his sons, and conferred on a stranger. La Jonquière wrote to the minister: "I have charged M. de Saint-Pierre with this business. He knows these countries better than any officer in all the colony."[1] On the contrary, he had never seen them. It is difficult not to believe that La Jonquière, Bigot, and Saint-Pierre were partners in a speculation of which all three were to share the profits.

The elder La Vérendrye, not long before his death, had sent a large quantity of goods to his trading-forts. The brothers begged leave to return thither and save their property from destruction. They declared themselves happy to serve under the orders of Saint-Pierre, and asked for the use of only a single fort of all those which their father had built at his own cost. The answer was a flat refusal. In short, they were shamefully robbed. The Chevalier writes: "M. le Marquis de la Jonquière, being pushed hard, and as I thought even touched, by my representations, told

[1] *La Jonquière au Ministre,* 27 *Février,* 1750.

me at last that M. de Saint-Pierre wanted nothing to do with me or my brothers." "I am a ruined man," he continues. "I am more than two thousand livres in debt, and am still only a second ensign. My elder brother's grade is no better than mine. My younger brother is only a cadet. This is the fruit of all that my father, my brothers, and I have done. My other brother, whom the Sioux murdered some years ago, was not the most unfortunate among us. We must lose all that has cost us so much, unless M. de Saint-Pierre should take juster views, and prevail on the Marquis de la Jonquière to share them. To be thus shut out from the West is to be most cruelly robbed of a sort of inheritance which we had all the pains of acquiring, and of which others will get all the profit." [1]

His elder brother writes in a similar strain: "We spent our youth and our property in building up establishments so advantageous to Canada; and, after all, we were doomed to see a stranger gather the fruit we had taken such pains to plant." And he complains that their goods left in the trading-posts were wasted, their provisions consumed, and the men in their pay used to do the work of others. [2]

They got no redress. Saint-Pierre, backed by the governor and the intendant, remained master of the position. The brothers sold a small piece of land,

---

[1] *Le Chevalier de la Vérendrye au Ministre,* 30 *Septembre,* 1750.

[2] *Mémoire des Services de Pierre Gautier de la Vérendrye l'aisné, présenté à Mgr. Rouillé, ministre et secrétaire d'État.*

their last remaining property, to appease their most pressing creditors.[1]

Saint-Pierre set out for Manitoba on the fifth of June, 1750. Though he had lived more or less in the woods for thirty-six years, and though La Jonquière had told the minister that he knew the countries to which he was bound better than anybody else, it is clear from his own journal that he was now visiting them for the first time. They did not please him. "I was told," he says, "that the way would grow harder and more dangerous as we advanced, and I found, in fact, that one must risk life and property every moment." Finding himself and his men likely to starve, he sent some of them, under an ensign named Niverville, to the Saskatchewan. They could not reach it, and nearly perished on the way. "I myself was no more fortunate," says Saint-Pierre. "Food was so scarce that I sent some of my people into the woods among the Indians, — which did not save me from a fast so rigorous that it deranged my health and put it out of my power to do anything towards accomplishing my mission. Even if I had had strength enough, the war that broke out among the Indians would have made it impossible to proceed."

Niverville, after a winter of misery, tried to fulfil

[1] Legardeur de Saint-Pierre, in spite of his treatment of the La Vérendrye brothers, had merit as an officer. It was he who received Washington at Fort Le Bœuf in 1754. He was killed in 1755, at the battle of Lake George. See "Montcalm and Wolfe," i. 315.

an order which he had received from his commander.
When the Indians guided the two brothers La
Vérendrye to the Rocky Mountains, the course they
took tended so far southward that the Chevalier
greatly feared it might lead to Spanish settlements;
and he gave it as his opinion that the next attempt to
find the Pacific should be made farther towards the
north. . Saint-Pierre had agreed with him, and had
directed Niverville to build a fort on the Saskatchewan,
three hundred leagues above its mouth.   Therefore,
at the end of May, 1751, Niverville sent ten men in
two canoes on this errand, and they ascended the
Saskatchewan to what Saint-Pierre calls the "Rock
Mountain."   Here they built a small stockade fort
and called it Fort La Jonquière.   Niverville was to
have followed them; but he fell ill, and lay helpless
at the mouth of the river in such a condition that he
could not even write to his commander.

Saint-Pierre set out in person from Fort La Reine
for Fort La Jonquière, over ice and snow, for it was
late in November.   Two Frenchmen from Niverville
met him on the way, and reported that the Assiniboins
had slaughtered an entire band of friendly Indians
on whom Saint-Pierre had relied to guide him.   On
hearing this he gave up the enterprise, and returned
to Fort La Reine.   Here the Indians told him idle
stories about white men and a fort in some remote
place towards the west; but, he observes, "nobody
could reach it without encountering an infinity of
tribes more savage than it is possible to imagine."

He spent most of the winter at Fort La Reine. Here, towards the end of February, 1752, he had with him only five men, having sent out the rest in search of food. Suddenly, as he sat in his chamber, he saw the fort full of armed Assiniboins, extremely noisy and insolent. He tried in vain to quiet them, and they presently broke into the guard-house and seized the arms. A massacre would have followed, had not Saint-Pierre, who was far from wanting courage, resorted to an expedient which has more than once proved effective on such occasions. He knocked out the heads of two barrels of gunpowder, snatched a firebrand, and told the yelping crowd that he would blow up them and himself together. At this they all rushed in fright out of the gate, while Saint-Pierre ran after them, and bolted it fast. There was great anxiety for the hunters, but they all came back in the evening, without having met the enemy. The men, however, were so terrified by the adventure that Saint-Pierre was compelled to abandon the fort, after recommending it to the care of other band of Assiniboins, who had professed great friend-ship. Four days after he was gone they burned to the ground.

He soon came to the conclusion that farther discovery was impossible, because the English of Hudson Bay had stirred up the western tribes to oppose it. Therefore he set out for the settlements, and, reach-ing Quebec in the autumn of 1753, placed the journal of his futile enterprise in the hands of Duquesne, the new governor.[1]

Canada was approaching her last agony. In the death-struggle of the Seven Years' War there was no time for schemes of western discovery. The brothers La Vérendrye sank into poverty and neglect. A little before the war broke out, we find the eldest at the obscure Acadian post of Beauséjour, where he wrote to the colonial minister a statement of his services, which appears to have received no attention. After the fall of Canada, the Chevalier de la Vérendrye, he whose eyes first beheld the snowy peaks of the Rocky Mountains, perished in the wreck of the ship "Auguste," on the coast of Cape Breton, in November, 1761.[2]

---

[1] *Journal sommaire du Voyage de Jacques Legardeur de Saint-Pierre, chargé de la Découverte de la Mer de l'Ouest* (British Museum).

[2] The above narrative rests mainly on contemporary documents, official in character, of which the originals are preserved in the archives of the French Government. These papers have recently been printed by M. Pierre Margry, late custodian of the Archives of the Marine and Colonies at Paris, in the sixth volume of his *Découvertes et Établissements des Français dans l'Amérique Septentrionale*, — a documentary collection of great value, published at the expense of the American Government. It was M. Margry who first drew attention to the achievements of the family of La Vérendrye, by an article in the *Moniteur* in 1852. I owe to his kindness the opportunity of using the above-mentioned documents in advance of publication. I obtained copies from duplicate originals of some of the principal among them from the Dépôt des Cartes de la Marine, in 1872. These answer closely, with rare and trivial variations, to the same documents as printed from other sources by M. Margry. Some additional papers preserved in the Archives of the Marine and Colonies have also been used.

My friends, Hon. William C. Endicott, then Secretary of War, and Captain John G. Bourke, Third Cavalry, U. S. A., kindly placed in my hands a valuable collection of Government maps and surveys of the country between the Missouri and the Rocky Mountains visited by the brothers La Vérendrye ; and I have received from Captain Bourke, and also from Mr. E. A. Snow, formerly of the Third Cavalry, much information concerning the same region, repeatedly traversed by them in peace and war.

CHAPTER XVII.

1700–1750.

THE CHAIN OF POSTS.

WE have seen that the contest between France and England in America divided itself, after the Peace of Utrecht, into three parts, — the Acadian contest; the contest for northern New England; and last, though greatest, the contest for the West. Nothing is more striking than the difference, or rather contrast, in the conduct and methods of the rival claimants to this wild but magnificent domain. Each was strong in its own qualities, and utterly wanting in the qualities that marked its opponent.

On maps of British America in the earlier part of the eighteenth century, one sees the eastern shore, from Maine to Georgia, garnished with ten or twelve colored patches, very different in shape and size, and defined, more or less distinctly, by dividing-lines which, in some cases, are prolonged westward till they touch the Mississippi, or even cross it and stretch indefinitely towards the Pacific. These patches are the British provinces, and the westward prolongation of their boundary lines represents their several claims to vast interior tracts, founded on ancient grants, but not made good by occupation, or vindicated by any exertion of power.

These English communities took little thought of the region beyond the Alleghanies. Each lived a life of its own, shut within its own limits, not dreaming of a future collective greatness to which the possession of the West would be a necessary condition. No conscious community of aims and interests held them together, nor was there any authority capable of uniting their forces and turning them to a common object. Some of the servants of the Crown had urged the necessity of joining them all under a strong central government, as the only means of making them loyal subjects and arresting the encroachments of France; but the scheme was plainly impracticable. Each province remained in jealous isolation, busied with its own work, growing in strength, in the capacity of self-rule and the spirit of independence, and stubbornly resisting all exercise of authority from without. If the English-speaking populations flowed westward, it was in obedience to natural laws, for King did not aid the movement, the royal government had no authority to do so, and the colonial assemblies were too much engrossed with immediate local interests. The power of these colonies was that of a rising flood slowly invading and conquering, by the unconscious force of its own growing volume, unless means be found to hold it back by dams and embankments within appointed limits.

In the French colonies all was different. Here the representatives of the Crown were men bred in an atmosphere of broad ambition and masterful and far-reaching enterprise. Achievement was demanded of them. They recognized the greatness of the prize, studied the strong and weak points of their rivals, and with a cautious forecast and a daring energy set themselves to the task of defeating them.

If the English colonies were comparatively strong in numbers, their numbers could not be brought into action; while if the French forces were small, they were vigorously commanded, and always ready at a word. It was union confronting division, energy confronting apathy, military centralization opposed to industrial democracy; and, for a time, the advantage was all on one side.

The demands of the French were sufficiently comprehensive. They repented of their enforced concessions at the Treaty of Utrecht, and in spite of that compact, maintained that, with a few local and trivial exceptions, the whole North American continent, except Mexico, was theirs of right; while their opponents seemed neither to understand the situation, nor see the greatness of the stakes at issue.

In 1720 Father Bobé, priest of the Congregation of

Missions, drew up a paper in which he sets forth the claims of France with much distinctness, beginning with the declaration that "England has usurped from France nearly everything that she possesses in America," and adding that the plenipotentiaries at Utrecht did not know what they were about when they made such concessions to the enemy; that, among other blunders, they gave Port Royal to England when it belonged to France, who should "insist vigorously" on its being given back to her.

He maintains that the voyages of Verrazzano and Ribaut made France owner of the whole continent, from Florida northward; that England was an interloper in planting colonies along the Atlantic coast, and will admit as much if she is honest, since all that country is certainly a part of New France. In this modest assumption of the point at i 1e, he ignores John Cabot and his son Sebastian, w   discovered North America more than twenty-five   rs before the voyage of Verrazzano, and more than   ty years before that of Ribaut.

When the English, proceeds Father Bo   have restored Port Royal to us, which they are b   ' to do, though we ceded it by the treaty, a French   -ernor should be at once set over it, with a commis to command as far as Cape Cod, which would inclu Boston. We should also fortify ourselves, "in a wa, to stop the English, who have long tried to seize on French America, of which they know the importance, and of which," he observes with much candor, "they

would make a better use than the French do.[1] . . .
The Atlantic coast, as far as Florida, was usurped
from the French, to whom it belonged then, and to
whom it belongs now." England, as he thinks, is
bound in honor to give back these countries to their
true owner; and it is also the part of wisdom to do
so, since by grasping at too much, one often loses
all. But France, out of her love of peace, will cede
to England the countries along the Atlantic, from
the Kennebec in New France to the Jordan[2] in
Carolina, on condition that England will restore to
her all that she gave up by the Treaty of Utrecht.
When this is done, France, always generous, will
consent to accept as boundary a line drawn from the
mouth of the Kennebec, passing thence midway
between Schenectady and Lake Champlain and along
the ridge of the Alleghanies to the river Jordan, the
country between this line and the sea to belong to
England, and the rest of the continent to France.

If England does not accept this generous offer,
she is to be told that the King will give to the
Compagnie des Indes (Law's Mississippi Company)
full authority to occupy "all the countries which the
English have usurped from France;" and, pursues

1 "De manière qu'on puisse arrêter les Anglois, qui depuis
longtems tachent de s'emparer de l'Amérique françoise, dont ils
conoissent l'importance et dont ils feroient un meillieur usage que
celuy qui les françois en font."

2 On the river Jordan, so named by Vasquez de Ayllon, see
"Pioneers of France in the New World," i. 11, 39, note. It was
probably the broad river of South Carolina.

Father Bobé, "it is certain that the fear of having to do with so powerful a company will bring the English to our terms." The company that was thus to strike the British heart with terror was the same which all the tonics and stimulants of the government could not save from predestined ruin. But, concludes this ingenious writer, whether England accepts our offers or not, France ought not only to take a high tone (*parler avec hauteur*), but also to fortify diligently, and make good her right by force of arms.[1]

Three years later we have another document, this time of an official character, and still more radical in its demands. It admits that Port Royal and a part of the Nova Scotian peninsula, under the name of Acadia, were ceded to England by the treaty, and consents that she shall keep them, but requires her to restore the part of New France that she has wrongfully seized, — namely, the whole Atlantic coast from the Kennebec to Florida; since France never gave England this country, which is hers by the discovery of Verrazzano in 1524. Here, again, the voyages of the Cabots, in 1497 and 1498, are completely ignored.

"It will be seen," pursues this curious document, "that our kings have always preserved sovereignty over the countries between the thirtieth and the fiftieth degrees of north latitude. A time will come when

---

[1] *Second Mémoire concernant les Limites des Colonies présenté en 1720 par Bobé, prêtre de la Congrégation de la Mission* (Archives Nationales).

they will be in a position to assert their rights, and
then it will be seen that the dominions of a king of
France cannot be usurped with impunity. What we
demand now is that the English make immediate
restitution." No doubt, the paper goes on to say,
they will pretend to have prescriptive rights, because
they have settled the country and built towns and
cities in it; but this plea is of no avail, because all
that country is a part of New France, and because
England rightfully owns nothing in America except
what we, the French, gave her by the Treaty of
Utrecht, which is merely Port Royal and Acadia.
She is bound in honor to give back all the vast
countries she has usurped; but, continues the paper,
"the King loves the English nation too much, and
wishes too much to do her kindness, and is too
generous to exact such a restitution. Therefore,
provided that England will give us back Port Royal,
Acadia, and everything else that France gave her by
the Treaty of Utrecht, the King will forego his rights,
and grant to England the whole Atlantic coast from
the thirty-second degree of latitude to the Kennebec,
to the extent inland of twenty French leagues [about
fifty miles], on condition that she will solemnly bind
herself never to overstep these limits or encroach in
the least on French ground."

Thus, through the beneficence of France, England,
provided that she renounced all pretension to the
rest of the continent, would become the rightful
owner of an attenuated strip of land reaching south-

ward from the Kennebec along the Atlantic seaboard. The document containing this magnanimous proposal was preserved in the Château St. Louis at Quebec till the middle of the eighteenth century, when, the boundary dispute having reached a crisis, and commissioners of the two powers having been appointed to settle it, a certified copy of the paper was sent to France for their instruction.[1]

Father Bobé had advised that France should not trust solely to the justice of her claims, but should back right with might, and build forts on the Niagara, the Ohio, the Tennessee, and the Alabama, as well as at other commanding points, to shut out the English from the West. Of these positions, Niagara was the most important, for the possession of it would close the access to the Upper Lakes, and stop the western tribes on their way to trade at Albany. The Five Nations and the governor of New York were jealous of the French designs, which, however, were likely enough to succeed, through the prevailing apathy and divisions in the British colonies. "If those not immediately concerned," writes a member of the New York council, "only stand gazing on while the wolff is murthering other parts of the flock, it will come to every one's turn at last." The warning was well founded, but it was not heeded. Again: "It is the policy of the French to attack one colony at a time, and the others are so besotted as to sit still."[2]

---

[1] *Demandes de la France,* 1723 (Archives des Affaires Étrangères).
[2] *Colonel Heathcote to Governor Hunter,* 8 *July,* 1715. *Ibid. to Townshend,* 12 *July,* 1715.

For gaining the consent of the Five Nations to the building of a French fort at Niagara, Vaudreuil trusted chiefly to his agent among the Senecas, the bold, skilful, and indefatigable Joncaire, who was naturalized among that tribe, the strongest of the confederacy. Governor Hunter of New York sent Peter Schuyler and Philip Livingston to counteract his influence. The Five Nations, who, conscious of declining power, seemed ready at this time to be all things to all men, declared that they would prevent the French from building at Niagara, which, as they said, would "shut them up as in a prison."[1] Not long before, however, they had sent a deputation to Montreal to say that the English made objection to Joncaire's presence among them, but that they were masters of their land, and hoped that the French agent would come as often as he pleased; and they begged that the new King of France would take them under his protection.[2] Accordingly, Vaudreuil sent them a present, with a message to the effect that they might plunder such English traders as should come among them.[3]

Yet so jealous were the Iroquois of a French fort at Niagara that they sent three Seneca chiefs to see what was going on *. The chiefs found a few Frenchmen ir blockhouse, or loopholed store-house. ney had just built near Lewiston

at of Schuyler and Livingston, 1720.
audreuil au Conseil de Marine, 24 Octobre, 1717.
  [3] Vaudreuil et Bégon au Conseil de Marine, 26 Octobre, 1719.

Heights. The three Senecas requested them to demolish it and go away, which the Frenchmen refused to do; on which the Senecas asked the English envoys, Schuyler and Livingston, to induce the governor of New York to destroy the obnoxious building. In short, the Five Nations wavered incessantly between their two European neighbors, and changed their minds every day. The skill and perseverance of the French emissaries so far prevailed at last that the Senecas consented to the building of a fort at the mouth of the Niagara, where Denonville had built one in 1687; and thus that important pass was made tolerably secure.

Meanwhile the English of New York, or rather Burnet, their governor, were not idle. Burnet was on ill terms with his assembly, which grudged him all help in serving the province whose interests it was supposed to represent. Burnet's plan was to build a fortified trading-house at Oswego, on Lake Ontario, in the belief that the western Indians, who greatly preferred English goods and English prices, would pass Niagara and bring their furs to the new post. He got leave from the Five Nations to execute his plan, bought canoes, hired men, and built a loopholed house of stone on the site of the present city of Oswego. As the Assembly would give no money, Burnet furnished it himself; and though the object was one of the greatest importance to the province, he was never fully repaid.[1] A small garrison for the

---

[1] "I am ashamed to confess that he built the fort at his private expense, and that a balance of above £56 remains due to his

new post was drawn from the four independent companies maintained in the province at the charge of the Crown.

The establishment of Oswego greatly alarmed and incensed the French, and a council of war at Quebec resolved to send two thousand men against it; but Vaudreuil's successor, the Marquis de Beauharnois, learning that the court was not prepared to provoke a war, contented himself with sending a summons to the commanding officer to abandon and demolish the place within a fortnight.[1] To this no attention was given; and as Burnet had foreseen, Oswego became the great centre of Indian trade, while Niagara, in spite of its more favorable position, was comparatively slighted by the western tribes. The chief danger rose from the obstinate prejudice of the Assembly, which, in its disputes with the Royal Governor, would give him neither men nor money to defend the new post.

The Canadian authorities, who saw in Oswego an intrusion on their domain and a constant injury and menace, could not attack it without bringing on a war, and therefore tried to persuade the Five Nations to destroy it, — an attempt which completely failed.[2]

estate to this very day." — Smith, *History of New York*, 267 (ed. 1814).

[1] *Mémoire de Dupuy*, 1728. Dupuy was intendant of Canada. The King approved the conduct of Beauharnois in not using force. *Dépêche du Roy*, 14 *Mai*, 1728.

[2] When urged by the younger Longueuil to drive off the English from Oswego, the Indians replied, "Drive them off thyself" ("*Chassez-les toi-même*"). *Longueuil fils au Ministre*, 19 *Octobre*, 1728.

They then established a trading-post at Toronto, in the vain hope of stopping the northern tribes on their way to the more profitable English market, and they built two armed vessels at Fort Frontenac to control the navigation of Lake Ontario.

Meanwhile, in another quarter the French made an advance far more threatening to the English colonies than Oswego was to their own. They had already built a stone fort at Chambly, which covered Montreal from any English attack by way of Lake Champlain. As that lake was the great highway between the rival colonies, the importance of gaining full mastery of it was evident. It was rumored in Canada that the English meant to seize and fortify the place called Scalp Point (*Pointe à la Chevelure*) by the French, and Crown Point by the English, where the lake suddenly contracts to the proportions of a river, so that a few cannon would stop the passage.

As early as 1726 the French made an attem to establish themselves on the east side of the lake o site Crown Point, but were deterred by the opposit of Massachusetts. This eastern shore was, howeve claimed not only by Massachusetts, but by her neighbor, New Hampshire, with whom she presently fell into a dispute about the ownership, and, as a writer of the time observes, "while they were quarrelling for the bone, the French ran away with it."[1]

At length, in 1731, the French took post on the western side of the lake, and began to intrench them-

---

[1] Mitchell, *Contest in America*, 22.

selves at Crown Point, which was within the bounds
claimed by New York; but that province, being then
engrossed, not only by her chronic dispute with her
governor, but by a quarrel with her next neighbor,
New Jersey, slighted the danger from the common
enemy, and left the French to work their will. It
was Saint-Luc de la Corne, Lieutenant du Roy at
Montreal, who pointed out the necessity of fortifying
this place,[1] in order to anticipate the English, who,
as he imagined, were about to do so, — a danger which
was probably not imminent, since the English colonies,
as a whole, could not and would not unite for such a
purpose, while the individual provinces were too
much absorbed in their own internal affairs and their
own jealousies and disputes to make the attempt. La
Corne's suggestion found favor at court, and the governor of Canada was ordered to occupy Crown Point.
The Sieur de la Fresnière was sent thither with troops
and workmen, and a fort was built, and named Fort
Frédéric. It contained a massive stone tower, mounted
with cannon to command the lake, which is here but
a musket-shot wide. Thus was established an advanced post of France, — a constant menace to New
York and New England, both of which denounced
it as an outrageous encroachment on British territory,
but could not unite to rid themselves of it.[2]

[1] *La Corne au Ministre,* 15 *Octobre,* 1730.

[2] On the establishment of Crown Point, *Beauharnois et Hocquart
au Roy,* 10 *Octobre,* 1731; *Beauharnois et Hocquart au Ministre,* 14
Novembre, 1731.

While making this bold push against their neighbors of the South, the French did not forget the
West; and towards the middle of the century they
had occupied points controlling all the chief water-
ways between Canada and Louisiana. Niagara held
the passage from Lake Ontario to Lake Erie. Detroit
closed the entrance to Lake Huron, and Michilimackinac guarded the point where Lake Huron is
joined by Lakes Michigan and Superior; while the
fort called La Baye, at the head of Green Bay,
stopped the way to the Mississippi by Marquette's old
route of Fox River and the Wisconsin. Another
route to the Mississippi was controlled by a post on
the Maumee to watch the carrying-place between that
river and the Wabash, and by another on the Wabash
where Vincennes now stands. La Salle's route, by
way of the Kankakee and the Illinois, was barred by
a fort on the St. Joseph; and even if, in spite of
these obstructions, an enemy should reach the Mississippi by any of its northern affluents, the cannon of
Fort Chartres would prevent him from descending it.

These various western forts, except Fort Chartres
and Fort Niagara, which were afterwards rebuilt, the
one in stone and the other in earth, were stockades
of no strength against cannon. Slight as they were,
their establishment was costly; and as the King, to
whom Canada was a yearly loss, grudged every franc
spent upon it, means were contrived to make them
self-supporting. Each of them was a station of the
fur-trade, and the position of most of them had been

determined more or less with a view to that traffic.
Hence they had no slight commercial value.   In some
of them the Crown itself carried on trade through
agents who usually secured a lion's share of the
profits.   Others were farmed out to merchants at a
fixed sum.   In others, again, the commanding officer
was permitted to trade on condition of maintaining
the post, paying the soldiers, and supporting a missionary; while in one case, at least, he was subjected
to similar obligations, though not permitted to trade
himself, but only to sell trading licenses to merchants.
These methods of keeping up forts and garrisons were
of course open to prodigious abuses, and roused end-
less jealousies and rivalries.

France had now occupied the valley of the Mississippi, and joined with loose and uncertain links her
two colonies of Canada and Louisiana.   But the
strength of her hold on these regions of unkempt
savagery bore no proportion to the vastness of her
claims or the growing power of the rivals who were
soon to contest them.[1]

[1] On the claim of France that all North America, except the
Spanish colonies of Mexico and Florida, belonged to her, see
Appendix A.

CHAPTER XVIII.

1744, 1745.

A MAD SCHEME.

War of the Austrian Succession. — The French seize Canseau and attack Annapolis. — Plan of Reprisal. — William Vaughan. — Governor Shirley: he advises an Attack on Louisbourg. — The Assembly refuses, but at last consents. — Preparation. — William Pepperrell. — George Whitefield. — Parson Moody. — The Soldiers. — The Provincial Navy. — Commodore Warren. — Shirley as an Amateur Soldier. — The Fleet sails.

THE Peace of Utrecht left unsettled the perilous questions of boundary between the rival powers in North America, and they grew more perilous every day. Yet the quarrel was not yet quite ripe; and though the French governor, Vaudreuil, and perhaps also his successor, Beauharnois, seemed willing to precipitate it, the courts of London and Versailles still hesitated to appeal to the sword. Now as before, it was a European, and not an American, quarrel that was to set the world on fire. The war of the Austrian Succession broke out in 1744. When Frederic of Prussia seized Silesia and began that bloody conflict, it meant that packs of howling savages would again spread fire and carnage along the New England border.

News of the declaration of war reached Louisbourg some weeks before it reached Boston, and the French military governor, Duquesnel, thought he saw an opportunity to strike an unexpected blow for the profit of France and his own great honor.

One of the French inhabitants of Louisbourg has left us a short sketch of Duquesnel, whom he calls "capricious, of an uncertain temper, inclined to drink, and when in his cups neither reasonable or civil."[1] He adds that the governor had offended nearly every officer in the garrison, and denounces him as the "chief cause of our disasters." When Duquesnel heard of the declaration of war, his first thought was to strike some blow before the English were warned. The fishing-station of Canseau was a tempting prize, being a near and an inconvenient neighbor, at the southern end of the Strait of Canseau, which separates the Acadian peninsula from the island of Cape Breton, or Isle Royale, of which Louisbourg was the place of strength. Nothing was easier than to seize Canseau, which had no defence but a wooden redoubt built by the fishermen, and occupied by about eighty Englishmen thinking no danger. Early in May, Duquesnel sent Captain Duvivier against it, with six hundred, or, as the English say, nine hundred soldiers and sailors, escorted by two small armed vessels. The English surrendered, on condition of being sent to Boston,

---

[1] *Lettre d'un Habitant de Louisbourg contenant une Relation exacte et circonstanciée de la Prise de l'Isle Royale par les Anglois.*

and the miserable hamlet, with its wooden citadel, was burned to the ground.

Thus far successful, the governor addressed himself to the capture of Annapolis, — which meant the capture of all Acadia. Duvivier was again appointed to the command. His heart was in the work, for he was a descendant of La Tour, feudal claimant of Acadia in the preceding century. Four officers and ninety regular troops were given him,[1] and from three to four hundred Micmac and Malicite Indians joined him on the way. The Micmacs, under command, it is said, of their missionary, Le Loutre, had already tried to surprise the English fort, but had only succeeded in killing two unarmed stragglers in the adjacent garden.[2]

Annapolis, from the neglect and indifference of the British ministry, was still in such a state of dilapidation that its sandy ramparts were crumbling into the ditches, and the cows of the garrison walked over them at their pleasure. It was held by about a hundred effective men under Major Mascarene, a French Protestant whose family had been driven to exile by the persecutions that followed the revocation of the Edict of Nantes. Shirley, governor of Massachusetts, sent him a small reinforcement of militia, but as most of these came without arms, and as

---

[1] *Lettre d'un Habitant de Louisbourg.*

[2] *Mascarene to the Besiegers,* 3 *July,* 1744. Duquesnel had written to all the missionaries "d'engager les sauvages à faire quelque coup important sur le fort" (Annapolis). *Duquesnel à Beauharnois,* 1 *Juin,* 1744.

Mascarene had few or none to give them, they proved of doubtful value.

Duvivier and his followers, white and red, appeared before the fort in August, made their camp behind the ridge of a hill that overlooked it, and marched towards the rampart; but being met by a discharge of cannon-shot, they gave up all thoughts of an immediate assault, began a fusillade under cover of darkness, and kept the garrison on the alert all night.

Duvivier had looked for help from the Acadians of the neighboring village, who were French in blood, faith, and inclination. They would not join him openly, fearing the consequences if his attack should fail; but they did what they could without committing themselves, and made a hundred and fifty scaling-ladders for the besiegers. Duvivier now returned to his first plan of an assault, which, if made with vigor, could hardly have failed. Before attempting it, he sent Mascarene a flag of truce to tell him that he hourly expected two powerful armed ships from Louisbourg, besides a reinforcement of two hundred and fifty regulars, with cannon, mortars, and other enginery of war. At the same time he proposed favorable terms of capitulation, not to take effect till the French war-ships should have appeared. Mascarene refused all terms, saying that when he saw the French ships, he would consider what to do, and meanwhile would defend himself as he could.

The expected ships were the "Ardent" and the "Caribou," then at Louisbourg. A French writer says that when Duquesnel directed their captains to sail for Annapolis and aid in its capture, they refused, saying that they had no orders from the court.[1] Duvivier protracted the parley with Mascarene, and waited in vain for the promised succor. At length the truce was broken off, and the garrison, who had profited by it to get rest and sleep, greeted the renewal of hostilities with three cheers.

Now followed three weeks of desultory attacks; but there was no assault, though Duvivier had boasted that he had the means of making a successful one. He waited for the ships which did not come, and kept the Acadians at work in making ladders and fire-arrows. At length, instead of aid from Louisbourg, two small vessels appeared from Boston, bringing Mascarene a reinforcement of fifty Indian rangers. This discouraged the besiegers, and towards the end of September they suddenly decamped and vanished. "The expedition was a failure," writes the *Habitant de Louisbourg*, "though one might have bet everything on its success, so small was the force that the enemy had to resist us."

This writer thinks that the seizure of Canseau and the attack of Annapolis were sources of dire calamity to the French. "Perhaps," he says, "the English would have let us alone if we had not first insulted them. It was the interest of the people of New England to live at peace with us, and they would no doubt have done so, if we had not taken it into our

[1] *Lettre d'un Habitant de Louisbourg.*

heads to waken them from their security. They expected that both parties would merely stand on the defensive, without taking part in this cruel war that has set Europe in a blaze."

Whatever might otherwise have been the disposition of the "Bastonnais," or New England people, the attacks on Canseau and Annapolis alarmed and exasperated them, and engendered in some heated brains a project of wild audacity. This was no less than the capture of Louisbourg, reputed the strongest fortress, French or British, in North America, with the possible exception of Quebec, which owed its chief strength to nature, and not to art.

Louisbourg was a standing menace to all the northern British colonies. It was the only French naval station on the continent, and was such a haunt of privateers that it was called the American Dunkirk. It commanded the chief entrance of Canada, and threatened to ruin the fisheries, which were nearly as vital to New England as was the fur-trade to New France. The French government had spent twenty-five years in fortifying it, and the cost of its powerful defences — constructed after the system of Vauban — was reckoned at thirty million livres.

This was the fortress which William Vaughan of Damariscotta advised Governor Shirley to attack with fifteen hundred raw New England militia.[1]

---

[1] Smollett says that the proposal came from Robert Auchmuty, judge of admiralty in Massachusetts. Hutchinson, Douglas, Belknap, and other well-informed writers ascribe the scheme to Vaughan, while Pepperrell says that it originated with Colonel John Brad-

Vaughan was born at Portsmouth in 1703, and graduated at Harvard College nineteen years later. His father, also a graduate of Harvard, was for a time lieutenant-governor of New Hampshire. Soon after leaving college, the younger Vaughan — a youth of restless and impetuous activity — established a fishing-station on the island of Matinicus, off the coast of Maine, and afterwards became the owner of most of the land on both sides of the little river Damariscotta, where he built a garrison-house, or wooden fort, established a considerable settlement, and carried on an extensive trade in fish and timber. He passed for a man of ability and force, but was accused of a headstrong rashness, a self-confidence that hesitated at nothing, and a harebrained contempt of every obstacle in his way. Once, having fitted out a number of small vessels at Portsmouth for his fishing at Matinicus, he named a time for sailing. It was a gusty and boisterous March day, the sea was rough, and old sailors told him that such craft could not carry sail. Vaughan would not listen, but went on board and ordered his men to follow. One vessel was wrecked at the mouth of the river; the rest, after severe buffeting, came safe, with their owner, to Matinicus.

Being interested in the fisheries, Vaughan was

street. In the Public Record Office there is a letter from Bradstreet, written in 1753, but without address, in which he declares that he not only planned the siege, but "was the Principal Person in conducting it," — assertions which may pass for what they are worth, Bradstreet being much given to self-assertion.

doubly hostile to Louisbourg, — their worst enemy. He found a willing listener in the governor, William Shirley. Shirley was an English barrister who had come to Massachusetts in 1731 to practise his profession and seek his fortune. After filling various offices with credit, he was made governor of the province in 1741, and had discharged his duties with both tact and talent. He was able, sanguine, and a sincere well-wisher to the province, though gnawed by an insatiable hunger for distinction. He thought himself a born strategist, and was possessed by a propensity for contriving military operations, which finally cost him dear. Vaughan, who knew something of Louisbourg, told him that in winter the snow-drifts were often banked so high against the rampart that it could be mounted readily, if the assailants could but time their arrival at the right moment. This was not easy, as that rocky and tempestuous coast was often made inaccessible by fogs and surf; Shirley therefore preferred a plan of his own contriving. But nothing could be done without first persuading his Assembly to consent.

On the ninth of January the General Court of Massachusetts — a convention of grave city merchants and solemn rustics from the country villages — was astonished by a message from the governor to the effect that he had a communication to make, so critical that he wished the whole body to swear secrecy. The request was novel, but being then on good terms with Shirley, the representatives con-

sented, and took the oath.   Then, to their amazement, the governor invited them to undertake
forthwith the reduction of Louisbourg.   The idea of
an attack on that redoubtable fortress was not new.
Since the autumn, proposals had been heard to petition the British ministry to make the attempt, under
a promise that the colonies would give their best aid.
But that Massachusetts should venture it alone, or
with such doubtful help as her neighbors might give,
at her own charge and risk, though already insolvent,
without the approval or consent of the ministry, and
without experienced officers or trained soldiers, was
a startling suggestion to the sober-minded legislators
of the General Court.   They listened, however, with
respect to the governor's reasons, and appointed a
committee of the two houses to consider them.   The
committee deliberated for several days, and then
made a report adverse to the plan, as was also the
vote of the Court.

Meanwhile, in spite of the oath, the secret had
escaped.   It is said that a country member, more
pious than discreet, prayed so loud and fervently, at
his lodgings, for light to guide him on the moment-
ous question, that his words were overheard, and the
mystery of the closed doors was revealed.   The news
flew through the town, and soon spread through all
the province.

After his defeat in the Assembly, Shirley returned,
vexed and disappointed, to his house in Roxbury.   A
few days later, James Gibson, a Boston merchant,

says that he saw him "walking slowly down King Street, with his head bowed down, as if in a deep study." "He entered my counting-room," pursues the merchant, "and abruptly said, ' Gibson, do you feel like giving up the expedition to Louisbourg?'" Gibson replied that he wished the House would reconsider their vote. "You are the very man I want!" exclaimed the governor.[1] They then drew up a petition for reconsideration, which Gibson signed, promising to get also the signatures of merchants, not only of Boston, but of Salem, Marblehead, and other towns along the coast. In this he was completely successful, as all New England merchants looked on Louisbourg as an arch-enemy.

The petition was presented, and the question came again before the Assembly. There had been much intercourse between Boston and Louisbourg, which had largely depended on New England for provisions.[2] The captured militiamen of Canseau, who, after some delay, had been sent to Boston, according to the terms of surrender, had used their opportunities to the utmost, and could give Shirley much information concerning the fortress. It was reported that the garrison was mutinous, and that provisions were fallen short, so that the place could not hold out without supplies from France. These, however, could be cut off only by blockading the harbor with a stronger naval force than all the colonies together

---

[1] Gibson, *Journal of the Siege of Louisbourg.*
[2] *Lettre d'un Habitant de Louisbourg.*

could supply. The Assembly had before reached the reasonable conclusion that the capture of Louisbourg was beyond the strength of Massachusetts, and that the only course was to ask the help of the mother-country.[1]

The reports of mutiny, it was urged, could not be depended on; raw militia in the open field were no match for disciplined troops behind ramparts; the expense would be enormous, and the credit of the province, already sunk low, would collapse under it; we should fail, and instead of sympathy, get nothing but ridicule. Such were the arguments of the opposition, to which there was little to answer, except that if Massachusetts waited for help from England, Louisbourg would be reinforced and the golden opportunity lost. The impetuous and irrepressible Vaughan put forth all his energy; the plan was carried by a single vote. And even this result was said to be due to the accident of a member in opposition falling and breaking a leg as he was hastening to the House.

The die was cast, and now doubt and hesitation vanished. All alike set themselves to push on the work. Shirley wrote to all the colonies, as far south as Pennsylvania, to ask for co-operation. All excused themselves except Connecticut, New Hampshire, and Rhode Island, and the whole burden fell on the four New England colonies. These, and Massachusetts above all, blazed with pious zeal; for as the enter-

[1] *Report of Council*, 12 *January*, 1745.

prise was directed against Roman Catholics, it was supposed in a peculiar manner to commend itself to Heaven. There were prayers without ceasing in churches and families, and all was ardor, energy, and confidence; while the other colonies looked on with distrust, dashed with derision. When Benjamin Franklin, in Philadelphia, heard what was afoot, he wrote to his brother in Boston, "Fortified towns are hard nuts to crack, and your teeth are not accustomed to it; but some seem to think that forts are as easy taken as snuff." [1] It has been said of Franklin that while he represented some of the New England qualities, he had no part in that enthusiasm of which our own time saw a crowning example when the cannon opened at Fort Sumter, and which pushes to its end without reckoning chances, counting costs, or heeding the scoffs of ill-wishers.

The prevailing hope and faith were, it is true, born largely of ignorance, aided by the contagious zeal of those who first broached the project; for as usual in such cases, a few individuals supplied the initiate force of the enterprise. Vaughan the indefatigable rode express to Portsmouth with a letter from Shirley to Benning Wentworth, governor of New Hampshire. That pompous and self-important personage admired the Massachusetts governor, who far surpassed him in talents and acquirements, and who at the same time knew how to soothe his vanity. Wentworth was ready to do his part, but his province

---

[1] Sparks, *Works of Franklin*, vii. 16.

had no money, and the King had ordered him to permit the issue of no more paper currency. The same prohibition had been laid upon Shirley; but he, with sagacious forecast, had persuaded his masters to relent so far as to permit the issue of £50,000 in what were called bills of credit to meet any pressing exigency of war. He told this to Wentworth, and succeeded in convincing him that his province might stretch her credit like Massachusetts, in case of similar military need. New Hampshire was thus enabled to raise a regiment of five hundred men out of her scanty population, with the condition that a hundred and fifty of them should be paid and fed by Massachusetts.[1]

Shirley was less fortunate in Rhode Island. The governor of that little colony called Massachusetts "our avowed enemy, always trying to defame us."[2] There was a grudge between the neighbors, due partly to notorious ill-treatment by the Massachusetts Puritans of Roger Williams, founder of Rhode Island, and partly to one of those boundary disputes which often produced ill-blood among the colonies. The representatives of Rhode Island, forgetting past differences, voted to raise a hundred and fifty men for the expedition, till, learning that the project was neither ordered nor approved by the Home

---

[1] Correspondence of Shirley and Wentworth, in *Belknap Papers*. *Provincial Papers of New Hampshire*, v.

[2] *Governor Wanton to the Agent of Rhode Island*, 20 *December,* 1745, in *Colony Records of Rhode Island*, v.

Government, they prudently reconsidered their
action. They voted, however, that the colony
sloop " Tartar," carrying fourteen cannon and twelve
swivels, should be equipped and manned for the service, and that the governor should be instructed to
find and commission a captain and a lieutenant to
command her.[1]

Connecticut promised five hundred and sixteen
men and officers, on condition that Roger Wolcott,
their commander, should have the second rank in the
expedition. Shirley accordingly commissioned him
as major-general. As Massachusetts was to supply
above three thousand men, or more than three quarters
of the whole force, she had a natural right to name a
commander-in-chief.

It was not easy to choose one. The colony had
been at peace for twenty years, and except some
grizzled Indian fighters of the last war, and some
survivors of the Carthagena expedition, nobody had
seen service. Few knew well what a fortress was,
and nobody knew how to attack one. Courage,
energy, good sense, and popularity were the best
qualities to be hoped for in the leader. Popularity
was indispensable, for the soldiers were all to be
volunteers, and they would not enlist under a commander whom they did not like. Shirley's choice
was William Pepperrell, a merchant of Kittery.
Knowing that Benning Wentworth thought himself
the man for the place, he made an effort to placate

[1] *Colony Records of Rhode Island*, v. (*February*, 1745).

Sir William Pepperrell.

him, and wrote that he would gladly have given him
the chief command, but for his gouty legs.   Wentworth took fire at the suggestion, forgot his gout,
and declared himself ready to serve his country and
assume the burden of command.   The position was
awkward, and Shirley was forced to reply, " On communicating your offer to two or three gentlemen in
whose judgment I most confide, I found them clearly
of opinion that any alteration of the present command
would be attended with great risk, both with respect
to our Assembly and the soldiers being entirely
disgusted." [1]

The painter Smibert has left us a portrait of
Pepperrell,— a good bourgeois face, not without
dignity, though with no suggestion of the soldier.
His spacious house at Kittery Point still stands,
sound and firm, though curtailed in some of its proportions.   Not far distant is another noted relic of
colonial times, the not less spacious mansion built
by the disappointed Wentworth at Little Harbor.   I
write these lines at a window of this curious old
house, and before me spreads the scene familiar to
Pepperrell from childhood.   Here the river Piscataqua
widens to join the sea, holding in its gaping mouth
the large island of Newcastle, with attendant groups
of islets and island rocks, battered with the rack of
ages, studded with dwarf savins, or half clad with
patches of whortleberry bushes, sumach, and the shin-
ing wax-myrtle, green in summer, red with the touch

[1] *Shirley to Wentworth,* 16 *February,* 1745.

of October. The flood tide pours strong and full around them, only to ebb away and lay bare a desolation of rocks and stones buried in a shock of brown drenched seaweed, broad tracts of glistening mud, sand-banks black with mussel-beds, and half-submerged meadows of eel-grass, with myriads of minute shell-fish clinging to its long lank tresses. Beyond all these lies the main, or northern channel, more than deep enough, even when the tide is out, to float a line-of-battle-ship. On its farther bank stands the old house of the Pepperrell, wearing even now an air of dingy respectability. Looking through its small, quaint window-panes, one could see across the water the rude dwellings of fishermen along the shore of Newcastle, and the neglected earthwork called Fort William and Mary, that feebly guarded the river's mouth. In front, the Piscataqua, curving southward, widened to meet the Atlantic between rocky headlands and foaming reefs, and in dim distance the Isles of Shoals seemed floating on the pale gray sea.

Behind the Pepperrell house was a garden, probably more useful than ornamental, and at the foot of it were the owner's wharves, with storehouses for salt-fish, naval stores, and imported goods for the country trade.

Pepperrell was the son of a Welshman [1] who

[1] "A native of Ravistock Parish, in Wales." Parsons, *Life of Pepperrell*. Mrs. Adelaide Cilley Waldron, a descendant of Pepperrell, assures me, however, that his father, the emigrant, came, not from Wales, but from Devonshire.

migrated in early life to the Isles of Shoals, and thence to Kittery, where, by trade, ship-building, and the fisheries, he made a fortune, most of which he left to his son William. The young Pepperrell learned what little was taught at the village school, supplemented by a private tutor, whose instructions, however, did not perfect him in English grammar. In the eyes of his self-made father, education was valuable only so far as it could make a successful trader; and on this point he had reason to be satisfied, as his son passed for many years as the chief merchant in New England. He dealt in ships, timber, naval stores, fish, and miscellaneous goods brought from England; and he also greatly prospered by successful land purchases, becoming owner of the greater part of the growing towns of Saco and Scarborough. When scarcely twenty-one, he was made justice of the peace, on which he ordered from London what his biographer calls a law library, consisting of a law dictionary, Danvers' "Abridgment of the Common Law," the "Complete Solicitor," and several other books. In law as in war, his best qualities were good sense and good-will. About the time when he was made a justice, he was commissioned captain of militia, then major, then lieutenant-colonel, and at last colonel, commanding all the militia of Maine. The town of Kittery chose him to represent her in the General Court, Maine being then a part of Massachusetts. Finally, he was made a member of the Governor's Council, — a post which he held for thirty-two years, during eighteen of which he was president of the board.

These civil dignities served him as educators better than tutor or village school; for they brought him into close contact with the chief men of the province; and in the Massachusetts of that time, so different from our own, the best education and breeding were found in the official class. At once a provincial magnate and the great man of a small rustic village, his manners are said to have answered to both positions, — certainly they were such as to make him popular. But whatever he became as a man, he learned nothing to fit him to command an army and lay siege to Louisbourg. Perhaps he felt this, and thought, with the governor of Rhode Island, that "the attempt to reduce that prodigiously strong town was too much for New England, which had not one officer of experience, nor even an engineer."[1] Moreover, he was unwilling to leave his wife, children, and business. He was of a religious turn of mind, and partial to the clergy, who, on their part, held him in high favor. One of them, the famous preacher, George Whitefield, was a guest at his house when he heard that Shirley had appointed him to command the expedition against Louisbourg. Whitefield had been the leading spirit in the recent religious fermentation called the Great Awakening, which, though it produced bitter quarrels among

[1] *Governor Wanton to the Agent of Rhode Island in London,* 20 *December,* 1745.

the ministers, besides other undesirable results, was imagined by many to make for righteousness. So thought the Rev. Thomas Prince, who mourned over the subsiding delirium of his flock as a sign of backsliding. "The heavenly shower was over," he sadly exclaims; "from fighting the devil they must turn to fighting the French." Pepperrell, always inclined to the clergy, and now in great perplexity and doubt, asked his guest Whitefield whether or not he had better accept the command. Whitefield gave him cold comfort, told him that the enterprise was not very promising, and that if he undertook it, he must do so "with a single eye," prepared for obloquy if he failed, and envy if he succeeded.[1]

Henry Sherburn, commissary of the New Hampshire regiment, begged Whitefield to furnish a motto for the flag. The preacher, who, zealot as he was, seemed unwilling to mix himself with so madcap a business, hesitated at first, but at length consented, and suggested the words, *Nil desperandum Christo duce*, which, being adopted, gave the enterprise the air of a crusade. It had, in fact, something of the character of one. The cause was imagined to be the cause of Heaven, crowned with celestial benediction. It had the fervent support of the ministers, not only by prayers and sermons, but, in one case, by counsels wholly temporal. A certain pastor, much esteemed for benevolence, proposed to Pepperrell, who had at last accepted the command, a plan,

---

[1] Parsons, *Life of Pepperrell*, 51.

unknown to Vauban, for confounding the devices of
the enemy. He advised that two trustworthy persons
should cautiously walk together along the front of
the French ramparts under cover of night, one of
them carrying a mallet, with which he was to hammer
the ground at short intervals. The French sentinels,
it seems to have been supposed, on hearing this
mysterious thumping, would be so bewildered as to
give no alarm. While one of the two partners was
thus employed, the other was to lay his ear to the
ground, which, as the adviser thought, would return
a hollow sound if the artful foe had dug a mine under
it; and whenever such secret danger was detected, a
mark was to be set on the spot, to warn off the
soldiers.[1]

Equally zealous, after another fashion, was the
Rev. Samuel Moody, popularly known as Father
Moody, or Parson Moody, minister of York and
senior chaplain of the expedition. Though about
seventy years old, he was amazingly tough and
sturdy. He still lives in the traditions of York as
the spiritual despot of the settlement and the uncom-
promising guardian of its manners and doctrine, pre-
dominating over it like a rough little village pope.
The comparison would have kindled his burning
wrath, for he abhorred the Holy Father as an
embodied Antichrist. Many are the stories told of
him by the descendants of those who lived under his
rod, and sometimes felt its weight; for he was known

---

[1] Belknap, *Hist. New Hampshire*, ii. 208.

to have corrected offending parishioners with his
cane.[1] When some one of his flock, nettled by his
strictures from the pulpit, walked in dudgeon towards
the church door, Moody would shout after him,
"Come back, you graceless sinner, come back!" or if
any ventured to the alehouse of a Saturday night,
the strenuous pastor would go in after them, collar
them, drag them out, and send them home with rous-
ing admonition.[2] Few dared gainsay him, by reason
both of his irritable temper and of the thick-skinned
insensibility that encased him like armor of proof.
And while his pachydermatous nature made him
invulnerable as a rhinoceros, he had at the same time
a rough and ready humor that supplied keen weapons
for the warfare of words and made him a formidable
antagonist. This commended him to the rude bor-
derers, who also relished the sulphurous theology of
their spiritual dictator, just as they liked the raw
and fiery liquors that would have scorched more sus-
ceptible stomachs. What they did not like was the
pitiless length of his prayers, which sometimes kept
them afoot above two hours shivering in the polar
cold of the unheated meeting-house, and which were
followed by sermons of equal endurance; for the old
man's lungs were of brass, and his nerves of ham-
mered iron. Some of the sufferers ventured to remon-
strate; but this only exasperated him, till one

[1] Tradition told me at York by Mr. N. Marshall.
[2] Lecture of Ralph Waldo Emerson, quoted by Cabot, *Memoir
of Emerson*, i. 10.

parishioner, more worldly wise than the rest, accompanied his modest petition for mercy with the gift of a barrel of cider, after which the parson's ministrations were perceptibly less exhausting than before. He had an irrepressible conscience and a highly aggressive sense of duty, which made him an intolerable meddler in the affairs of other people, and which, joined to an underlying kindness of heart, made him so indiscreet in his charities that his wife and children were often driven to vain protest against the excesses of his almsgiving. The old Puritan fanaticism was rampant in him; and when he sailed for Louisbourg, he took with him an axe, intended, as he said, to hew down the altars of Antichrist and demolish his idols.[1]

Shirley's choice of a commander was perhaps the best that could have been made; for Pepperrell joined to an unusual popularity as little military incompetency as anybody else who could be had. Popularity, we have seen, was indispensable, and even company officers were appointed with an eye to it. Many of these were well-known men in rustic neighborhoods, who had raised companies in the hope of being commissioned to command them. Others were militia officers recruiting under orders of the governor. Thus, John Storer, major in the Maine

[1] Moody found sympathizers in his iconoclastic zeal. Deacon John Gray of Biddeford wrote to Pepperrell: " Oh that I could be with you and dear Parson Moody in that church [at Louisbourg] to destroy the images there set up, and hear the true Gospel of our Lord and Saviour there preached!"

militia, raised in a single day, it is said, a company
of sixty-one, the eldest being sixty years old, and the
youngest sixteen.[1]   They formed about a quarter of
the fencible population of the town of Wells, one of
the most exposed places on the border.   Volunteers
offered themselves readily everywhere; though the
pay was meagre, especially in Maine and Massachusetts, where in the new provincial currency it was
twenty-five shillings a month, — then equal to fourteen shillings sterling, or less than sixpence a day,[2]
the soldier furnishing his own clothing and bringing
his own gun.   A full third of the Massachusetts
contingent, or more than a thousand men, are reported
to have come from the hardy population of Maine,
whose entire fighting force, as shown by the muster-
rolls, was then but 2,855.[3]   Perhaps there was not
one officer among them whose experience of war
extended beyond a drill on muster day and the sham
fight that closed the performance, when it generally
happened that the rustic warriors were treated with
rum at the charge of their captain, to put them in
good humor, and so induce them to obey the word of
command.

As the three provinces contributing soldiers recognized no common authority nearer than the King,
Pepperrell received three several commissions as

---

[1] Bourne, *Hist. of Wells and Kennebunk*, 371.

[2] Gibson, *Journal*; *Records of Rhode Island*, v.   Governor Wanton of that province says, with complacency, that the pay of Rhode
Island was twice that of Massachusetts.

[3] Parsons, *Life of Pepperrell*, 54.

lieutenant-general, — one from the governor of Massachusetts, and the others from the governors of Connecticut and New Hampshire; while Wolcott, commander of the Connecticut forces, was commissioned as major-general by both the governor of his own province and that of Massachusetts.   When the levies were complete, it was found that Massachusetts had contributed about 3,300 men, Connecticut 516, and New Hampshire 304 in her own pay, besides 150 paid by her wealthier neighbor.[1]   Rhode Island had lost faith and disbanded her 150 men; but afterwards raised them again, though too late to take part in the siege.

Each of the four New England colonies had a little navy of its own, consisting of from one to three or four small armed vessels; and as privateering — which was sometimes a euphemism for piracy where Frenchmen and Spaniards were concerned — was a favorite occupation, it was possible to extemporize an additional force in case of need.   For a naval commander, Shirley chose Captain Edward Tyng, who had signalized himself in the past summer by capturing a French privateer of greater strength than his own.   Shirley authorized him to buy for the province the best ship he could find, equip her for fighting, and take command of her.   Tyng soon found a brig to his mind, on the stocks nearly ready

---

[1] Of the Massachusetts contingent, three hundred men were raised and maintained at the charge of the merchant James Gibson.

for launching. She was rapidly fitted for her new destination, converted into a frigate, mounted with 24 guns, and named the "Massachusetts." The rest of the naval force consisted of the ship "Cæsar," of 20 guns; a vessel called the "Shirley," commanded by Captain Rous, and also carrying 20 guns; another, of the kind called a "snow," carrying 16 guns; one sloop of 12 guns, and two of 8 guns each; the "Boston Packet," of 16 guns; two sloops from Connecticut of 16 guns each; a privateer hired in Rhode Island, of 20 guns; the government sloop "Tartar," of the same colony, carrying 14 carriage guns and 12 swivels; and, finally, the sloop of 14 guns which formed the navy of New Hampshire.[1]

It was said, with apparent reason, that one or two heavy French ships-of-war — and a number of such was expected in the spring — would outmatch the whole colonial squadron, and, after mastering it, would hold all the transports at mercy; so that the troops on shore, having no means of return and no hope of succor, would be forced to surrender or starve. The danger was real and serious, and Shirley felt the necessity of help from a few British ships-of-war. Commodore Peter Warren was then with a small squadron at Antigua. Shirley sent an express boat to him with a letter stating the situation and asking his aid. Warren, who had married an American woman and who owned large tracts of land on the Mohawk, was known to be a warm friend

---

[1] The list is given by Williamson, ii. 227.

to the provinces. It is clear that he would gladly have complied with Shirley's request; but when he laid the question before a council of officers, they were of one mind that without orders from the Admiralty he would not be justified in supporting an attempt made without the approval of the King.[1] He therefore saw no choice but to decline. Shirley, fearing that his refusal would be too discouraging, kept it secret from all but Pepperrell and General Wolcott, or, as others say, Brigadier Waldo. He had written to the Duke of Newcastle in the preceding autumn that Acadia and the fisheries were in great danger, and that ships-of-war were needed for their protection. On this, the duke had written to Warren, ordering him to sail for Boston and concert measures with Shirley "for the annoyance of the enemy, and his Majesty's service in North America."[2] Newcastle's letter reached Warren only two or three days after he had sent back his refusal of Shirley's request. Thinking himself now sufficiently authorized to give the desired aid, he made all sail for Boston with his three ships, the "Superbe," "Mermaid," and "Launceston." On the way he met a schooner from Boston, and learned from its officers that the expedition had already sailed; on which, detaining the master as a pilot, he changed his course and made directly for Canseau, — the place of rendezvous of the expedition, — and at the same time

---

[1] *Memoirs of the Principal Transactions of the Last War,* 44.
[2] *Ibid.,* 46. *Letters of Shirley* (Public Record Office).

sent orders by the schooner that any king's ships that might arrive at Boston should immediately join him.

Within seven weeks after Shirley issued his proclamation for volunteers, the preparations were all made, and the unique armament was afloat. Transports, such as they were, could be had in abundance; for the harbors of Salem and Marblehead were full of fishing-vessels thrown out of employment by the war. These were hired and insured by the province for the security of the owners. There was a great dearth of cannon. The few that could be had were too light, the heaviest being of twenty-two-pound calibre. New York lent ten eighteen-pounders to the expedition. But the adventurers looked to the French for their chief supply. A detached work near Louisbourg, called the Grand, or Royal, Battery, was known to be armed with thirty heavy pieces; and these it was proposed to capture and turn against the town, — which, as Hutchinson remarks, was "like selling the skin of the bear before catching him."

It was clear that the expedition must run for luck against risks of all kinds. Those whose hopes were highest, based them on a belief in the special and direct interposition of Providence; others were sanguine through ignorance and provincial self-conceit. As soon as the troops were embarked, Shirley wrote to the ministers of what was going on, telling them that, accidents apart, four thousand New England men would land on Cape Breton in April, and that,

even should they fail to capture Louisbourg, he
would answer for it that they would lay the town in
ruins, retake Canseau, do other good service to his
Majesty, and then come safe home.[1] On receiving
this communication, the government resolved to aid
the enterprise if there should yet be time, and
accordingly ordered several ships-of-war to sail for
Louisbourg.

The sarcastic Dr. Douglas, then living at Boston,
writes that the expedition had a lawyer for contriver,
a merchant for general, and farmers, fishermen, and
mechanics for soldiers. In fact, it had something of
the character of broad farce, to which Shirley himself, with all his ability and general good sense, was
a chief contributor. He wrote to the Duke of Newcastle that though the officers had no experience and
the men no discipline, he would take care to provide
against these defects, — meaning that he would give
exact directions how to take Louisbourg. Accordingly, he drew up copious instructions to that effect.
These seem to have undergone a process of evolution,
for several distinct drafts of them are preserved.[2]

[1] *Shirley to Newcastle,* 24 *March,* 1745. The ministry was not
wholly unprepared for this announcement, as Shirley had before
reported to it the vote of his Assembly consenting to the expedition. *Shirley to Newcastle,* 1 *February,* 1745.

[2] The first draft of Shirley's instructions for taking Louisbourg
is in the large manuscript volume entitled *Siege of Louisbourg,* in
the library of the Massachusetts Historical Society. The document
is called *Memo for the attacking of Louisbourg this Spring by Surprise.*
After giving minute instructions for every movement, it goes on to
say that, as the surprise may possibly fail, it will be necessary to

The complete and final one is among the Pepperrell Papers, copied entire in the neat, commercial hand of the general himself.[1] It seems to assume that Providence would work a continued miracle, and on every occasion supply the expedition with weather precisely suited to its wants. "It is thought," says this singular document, "that Louisbourg may be surprised if they [the French] have no advice of your coming. To effect it you must time your arrival about nine of the clock in the evening, taking care that the fleet be far enough in the offing to prevent their being seen from the town in the daytime." He then goes on to prescribe how the troops are to land, after dark, at a place called Flat Point Cove, in four divisions, three of which are to march to the back of certain hills a mile and a half west of the town, where two of the three "are to halt and keep a profound silence;" the third continuing its march "under cover of the said hills," till it comes opposite the Grand Battery, which it will attack at a concerted signal; while one of the two divisions behind the hills assaults the west gate, and the other moves up to support the attack.

send two small mortars and twelve cannon carrying nine-pound balls, "so as to bombard them and endeavour to make Breaches in their walls and then to Storm them." Shirley was soon to discover the absurdity of trying to breach the walls of Louisbourg with nine-pounders.

[1] It is printed in the first volume of the *Collections of the Massachusetts Historical Society*. Shirley was so well pleased with it that he sent it to the Duke of Newcastle enclosed in his letter of 1 February, 1745 (Public Record Office).

While this is going on, the soldiers of the fourth division are to march with all speed along the shore till they come to a certain part of the town wall, which they are to scale; then proceed "as fast as can be" to the citadel and "secure the windows of the governor's apartments." After this follow page after page of complicated details which must have stricken the general with stupefaction. The rocks, surf, fogs, and gales of that tempestuous coast are all left out of the account; and so, too, is the nature of the country, which consists of deep marshes, rocky hills, and hollows choked with evergreen thickets. Yet a series of complex and mutually dependent operations, involving long marches through this rugged and pathless region, was to be accomplished, in the darkness of one April night, by raw soldiers who knew nothing of the country. This rare specimen of amateur soldiering is redeemed in some measure by a postscript in which the governor sets free the hands of the general, thus: "Notwithstanding the instructions you have received from me, I must leave you to act, upon unforeseen emergencies, according to your best discretion."

On the twenty-fourth of March, the fleet, consisting of about ninety transports, escorted by the provincial cruisers, sailed from Nantasket Roads, followed by prayers and benedictions, and also by toasts drunk with cheers, in bumpers of rum punch.[1]

[1] The following letter from John Payne of Boston to Colonel Robert Hale, of the Essex regiment, while it gives no sign of the

prevailing religious feeling, illustrates the ardor of the New England people towards their rash adventure : —

BOSTON, Apr. 24, 1745.

SIR, — I hope this will find you at Louisbourg with a Bowl of Punch a Pipe and a P — k of C — ds in your hand and whatever else you desire (I had forgot to mention a Pretty French Madammoselle). We are very Impatiently expecting to hear from you, your Friend Luke has lost several Beaver Hatts already concerning the Expedition, he is so very zealous about it that he has turned Poor Boutier out of his House for saying he believed you would not Take the Place. —— Damn his Blood says Luke, let him be an Englishman or a Frenchman and not pretend to be an Englishman when he is a Frenchman in his Heart. If drinking to your success would Take Cape Briton, you must be in Possession of it now, for it's a standing Toast. I think the least thing you Military Gentn can do is to send us some arrack when you take ye Place to celebrate your Victory and not to force us to do it in Rum Punch or Luke's bad wine or sour cyder.

To Collonell Robert Hale
    at (or near) Louisbourg.

I am indebted for a copy of this curious letter to Robert Hale Bancroft, Esq., a descendant of Colonel Hale.

CHAPTER XIX.

1745.

LOUISBOURG BESIEGED.

On board one of the transports was Seth Pomeroy, gunsmith at Northampton, and now major of Willard's Massachusetts regiment. He had a turn for soldiering, and fought, ten years later, in the battle of Lake George. Again, twenty years later still, when Northampton was astir with rumors of war from Boston, he borrowed a neighbor's horse, rode a hundred miles, reached Cambridge on the morning of the battle of Bunker Hill, left his borrowed horse out of the way of harm, walked over Charlestown Neck, then swept by the fire of the ships-of-war, and reached the scene of action as the British were forming for the attack. When Israel Putnam, his comrade in the last war, saw from the rebel breastwork the old man striding, gun in hand, up the hill, he shouted,

"By God, Pomeroy, you here! A cannon-shot would waken you out of your grave!"

But Pomeroy, with other landsmen, crowded in the small and 'malodorous fishing-vessels that were made to serve as transports, was now in the gripe of the most unheroic of maladies. "A terrible northeast storm" had fallen upon them, and, he says, "we lay rolling in the seas, with our sails furled, among prodigious waves." "Sick, day and night," writes the miserable gunsmith, "so bad that I have not words to set it forth." [1] The gale increased and the fleet was scattered, there being, as a Massachusetts private soldier writes in his diary, "a very fierse Storm of Snow, som Rain and very Dangerous weather to be so nigh ye Shore as we was; but we escaped the Rocks, and that was all." [2]

On Friday, April 5, Pomeroy's vessel entered the harbor of Canseau, about fifty miles from Louisbourg. Here was the English fishing-hamlet, the seizure of which by the French had first provoked the expedition. The place now quietly changed hands again. Sixty-eight of the transports lay here at anchor, and the rest came dropping in from day to day, sorely buffeted, but all safe. On Sunday there was a great concourse to hear Parson Moody preach an open-air sermon from the text, "Thy people shall be willing

[1] Diary of Major Seth Pomeroy. I owe the copy before me to the kindness of his descendant, Theodore Pomeroy, Esq.

[2] Diary of a Massachusetts soldier in Captain Richardson's company (Papers of Dr. Belknap).

in the day of thy power," concerning which occasion the soldier diarist observes, — "Several sorts of
Busnesses was Going on, Som a Exercising, Som
a Hearing Preaching." The attention of Parson
Moody's listeners was, in fact, distracted by shouts
of command and the awkward drill of squads of
homespun soldiers on the adjacent pasture.

Captain Ammi Cutter, with two companies, was
ordered to remain at Canseau and defend it from
farther vicissitudes; to which end a blockhouse was
also built, and mounted with eight small cannon.
Some of the armed vessels had been set to cruise off
Louisbourg, which they did to good purpose, and
presently brought in six French prizes, with supplies
for the fortress. On the other hand, they brought
the ominous news that Louisbourg and the adjoining
bay were so blocked with ice that landing was
impossible. This was a serious misfortune, involving
long delay, and perhaps ruin to the expedition, as
the expected ships-of-war might arrive meanwhile
from France. Indeed, they had already begun to
appear. On Thursday, the eighteenth, heavy can-
nonading was heard far out at sea, and again on
Friday "the cannon," says Pomeroy, "fired at a
great rate till about 2 of the clock." It was the
provincial cruisers attacking a French frigate, the
"Renommée," of thirty-six guns. As their united
force was too much for her, she kept up a running
fight, outsailed them, and escaped after a chase of
more than thirty hours, being, as Pomeroy quaintly

observes, "a smart ship." She carried despatches to
the governor of Louisbourg, and being unable to
deliver them, sailed back for France to report what
she had seen.

On Monday, the twenty-second, a clear, cold,
windy day, a large ship, under British colors, sailed
into the harbor, and proved to be the frigate
"Eltham," escort to the annual mast fleet from New
England. On orders from Commander Warren she
had left her charge in waiting, and sailed for
Canseau to join the expedition, bringing the unexpected and welcome news that Warren himself would
soon follow. On the next day, to the delight of all,
he appeared in the ship "Superbe," of sixty guns,
accompanied by the "Launceston" and the "Mermaid," of forty guns each. Here was force enough
to oppose any ships likely to come to the aid of
Louisbourg; and Warren, after communicating with
Pepperrell, sailed to blockade the port, along with
the provincial cruisers, which, by order of Shirley,
were placed under his command.

The transports lay at Canseau nearly three weeks,
waiting for the ice to break up. The time was
passed in drilling the raw soldiers and forming them
into divisions of four and six hundred each, according
to the directions of Shirley. At length, on Friday,
the twenty-seventh, they heard that Gabarus Bay
was free from ice, and on the morning of the twenty-
ninth, with the first fair wind, they sailed out of
Canseau harbor, expecting to reach Louisbourg at

nine in the evening, as prescribed in the governor's receipt for taking Louisbourg "while the enemy were asleep."[1] But a lull in the wind defeated this plan; and after sailing all day, they found themselves becalmed towards night. It was not till the next morning that they could see the town, — no very imposing spectacle, for the buildings, with a few exceptions, were small, and the massive ramparts that belted them round rose to no conspicuous height.

Louisbourg stood on a tongue of land which lay between its harbor and the sea, and the end of which was prolonged eastward by reefs and shoals that partly barred the entrance to the port, leaving a navigable passage not half a mile wide. This passage was commanded by a powerful battery called the "Island Battery," being upon a small rocky island at the west side of the channel, and was also secured by another detached work called the "Grand," or "Royal Battery," which stood on the shore of the harbor, opposite the entrance, and more than a mile from the town. Thus a hostile squadron trying to force its way in would receive a flank fire from the one battery, and a front fire from the other. The strongest line of defence of the fortress was drawn across the base of the tongue of land from the harbor on one side to the sea on the other, — a distance of about twelve hundred yards. The ditch was eighty feet wide and from thirty to thirty-six feet deep; and the rampart, of earth faced with masonry, was about

[1] The words quoted are used by General Wolcott in his journal.

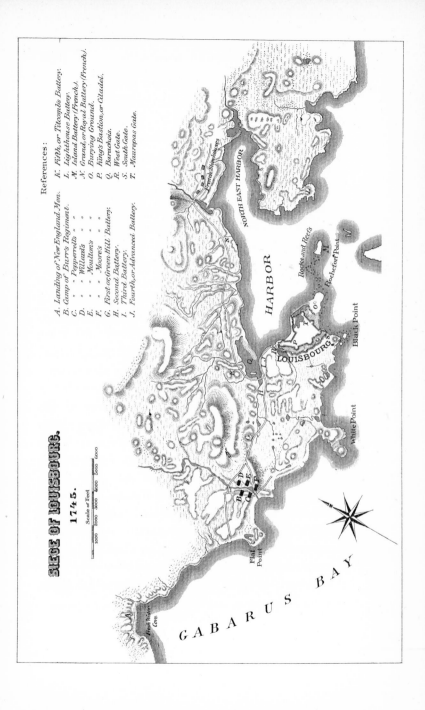

SIEGE OF LOUISBOURG.

1745.

Scale of Feet

1000 2000 3000 4000 5000 6000

References :

A. Landing of New England Men.
B. Camp of Burr's Regiment.
C.   "   " Pepperrell's   "   :
D.   "   " Willard's   "   :
E.   "   " Moulton's   "   :
F.   "   " Moore's   "   :
G. First or Green Hill Battery.
H. Second Battery.
I. Third Battery.
J. Fourth, or Advanced Battery.

K. Fifth, or Titcomb's Battery.
L. Lighthouse Battery.
M. Island Battery (French).
N. Grand, or Royal Battery (French).
O. Burying Ground.
P. King's Bastion, or Citadel.
Q. Barrachois.
R. West Gate.
S. South Gate.
T. Maurepas Gate.

NORTH EAST HARBOR

French Store-houses

HARBOR

Rocks and Reefs

Rochefort Point

LOUISBOURG

Black Point

White Point

Flat Point

Fresh Water Cove

GABARUS BAY

sixty feet thick. The glacis sloped down to a vast
marsh, which formed one of the best defences of the
place. The fortress, without counting its outworks,
had embrasures for one hundred and forty-eight
cannon; but the number in position was much less,
and is variously stated. Pomeroy says that at the
end of the siege a little above ninety were found,
with "a great number of swivels;" others say seventy-
six.[1] In the Grand and Island batteries there were
sixty heavy pieces more. Against this formidable
armament the assailants had brought thirty-four
cannon and mortars, of much inferior weight, to be
used in bombarding the fortress, should they chance
to fail of carrying it by surprise, "while the enemy
were asleep."[2] Apparently they distrusted the
efficacy of their siege-train, though it was far stronger
than Shirley had at first thought sufficient; for they
brought with them good store of balls of forty-two
pounds, to be used in French cannon of that calibre
which they expected to capture, their own largest
pieces being but twenty-two-pounders.

According to the *Habitant de Louisbourg*, the garrison consisted of five hundred and sixty regular
troops, of whom several companies were Swiss,
besides some thirteen or fourteen hundred militia,
inhabitants partly of the town, and partly of neigh-

---

[1] Brown, *Cape Breton*, 183. Parsons, *Life of Pepperrell*, 103. An
anonymous letter, dated Louisbourg, 4 July, 1745, says that eighty-
five cannon and six mortars have been found in the town.

[2] *Memoirs of the Principal Transactions of the Last War*, 40.

boring settlements.[1] The regulars were in bad condition. About the preceding Christmas they had broken into mutiny, being discontented with their rations and exasperated with getting no extra pay for work on the fortifications. The affair was so serious that though order was restored, some of the officers lost all confidence in the soldiers; and this distrust proved most unfortunate during the siege. The governor, Chevalier Duchambon, successor of Duquesnel, who had died in the autumn, was not a man to grapple with a crisis, being deficient in decision of character, if not in capacity.

He expected an attack. "We were informed of the preparations from the first," says the *Habitant de Louisbourg*. Some Indians, who had been to Boston, carried to Canada the news of what was going on there; but it was not believed, and excited no alarm.[2] It was not so at Louisbourg, where, says the French writer just quoted, "we lost precious moments in useless deliberations and resolutions no sooner made than broken. Nothing to the purpose was done, so that we were as much taken by surprise as if the enemy had pounced upon us unawares."

[1] "On fit venir cinq ou six cens Miliciens aux Habitans des environs; ce que, avec ceux de la Ville, pouvoit former treize à quatorze cens hommes." — *Lettre d'un Habitant de Louisbourg*. This writer says that three or four hundred more might have been had from Niganiche and its neighborhood, if they had been summoned in time. The number of militia just after the siege is set by English reports at 1,310. Parsons, 103.

[2] *Shirley to Newcastle*, 17 *June*, 1745, citing letters captured on board a ship from Quebec.

It was about the twenty-fifth of March[1] when the garrison first saw the provincial cruisers hovering off the mouth of the harbor. They continued to do so at intervals till daybreak of the thirtieth of April, when the whole fleet of transports appeared standing towards Flat Point, which projects into Gabarus Bay, three miles west of the town.[2] On this, Duchambon sent Morpain, captain of a privateer, or "corsair," to oppose the landing. He had with him eighty men, and was to be joined by forty more, already on the watch near the supposed point of disembarkation.[3] At the same time cannon were fired and alarm bells rung in Louisbourg, to call in the militia of the neighborhood.

Pepperrell managed the critical work of landing with creditable skill. The rocks and the surf were more dangerous than the enemy. Several boats, filled with men, rowed towards Flat Point; but on a signal from the flagship "Shirley," rowed back again, Morpain flattering himself that his appearance had frightened them off. Being joined by several other boats, the united party, a hundred men in all, pulled for another landing-place called Fresh-water Cove, or Anse de la Cormorandière, two miles farther up Gabarus Bay. Morpain and his party ran to meet them; but the boats were first in the race, and as

---

[1] 14 March, old style.

[2] Gabarus Bay, sometimes called "Chapeau Rouge" Bay, is a spacious outer harbor, immediately adjoining Louisbourg.

[3] *Bigot au Ministre*, 1 *Août*, 1745.

soon as the New England men got ashore, they rushed upon the French, killed six of them, captured as many more, including an officer named Boularderie, and put the rest to flight, with the loss, on their own side, of two men slightly wounded.[1] Further resistance to the landing was impossible, for a swarm of boats pushed against the rough and stony beach, the men dashing through the surf, till before night about two thousand were on shore.[2] The rest, or about two thousand more, landed at their leisure on the next day.

On the second of May Vaughan led four hundred men to the hills near the town, and saluted it with three cheers, — somewhat to the discomposure of the French, though they described the unwelcome visitors as a disorderly crowd. Vaughan's next proceeding pleased them still less. He marched behind the hills, in rear of the Grand Battery, to the northeast arm of the harbor, where there were extensive magazines of naval stores. These his men set on fire, and the pitch, tar, and other combustibles made a prodigious smoke. He was returning, in the morning, with a small party of followers behind the hills, when coming opposite the Grand Battery, and observing it from the ridge, he saw neither flag on the flagstaff,

---

[1] *Pepperrell to Shirley*, 12 *May*, 1745. *Shirley to Newcastle*, 28 *October*, 1745. *Journal of the Siege*, attested by Pepperrell and four other chief officers (London, 1746).

[2] Bigot says six thousand, or two thousand more than the whole New England force, which was constantly overestimated by the French.

nor smoke from the barrack chimneys. One of his party was a Cape Cod Indian. Vaughan bribed him with a flask of brandy which he had in his pocket, — though, as the clerical historian takes pains to assure us, he never used it himself,— and the Indian, pretending to be drunk, or, as some say, mad, staggered towards the battery to reconnoitre.[1] All was quiet. He clambered in at an embrasure, and found the place empty. The rest of the party followed, and one of them, William Tufts, of Medford, a boy of eighteen, climbed the flagstaff, holding in his teeth his red coat, which he made fast at the top, as a substitute for the British flag, — a proceeding that drew upon him a volley of unsuccessful cannon-shot from the town batteries.[2]

Vaughan then sent this hasty note to Pepperrell: "May it please your Honour to be informed that by the grace of God and the courage of 13 men, I entered the Royal Battery about 9 o'clock, and am waiting for a reinforcement and a flag." Soon after, four boats, filled with men, approached from the town to reoccupy the battery, — no doubt in order to save the munitions and stores, and complete the destruction of the cannon. Vaughan and his thirteen men, standing on the open beach, under the fire of the town and the Island Battery, plied the boats with

[1] Belknap, ii.

[2] John Langdon Sibley, in *N. E. Hist. and Gen. Register*, xxv. 377. The *Boston Gazette* of 3 June, 1771, has a notice of Tufts' recent death, with an exaggerated account of his exploit, and an appeal for aid to his destitute family.

musketry, and kept them from landing, till Lieutenant-Colonel Bradstreet appeared with a reinforcement, on which the French pulled back to
Louisbourg.[1]

The English supposed that the French in the
battery, when the clouds of smoke drifted over them
from the burning storehouses, thought that they
were to be attacked in force, and abandoned their
post in a panic. This was not the case. "A detachment of the enemy," writes the *Habitant de Louisbourg*, "advanced to the neighborhood of the Royal
Battery." This was Vaughan's four hundred on
their way to burn the storehouses. "At once we
were all seized with fright," pursues this candid
writer, "and on the instant it was proposed to
abandon this magnificent battery, which would have
been our best defence, if one had known how to use
it. Various councils were held, in a tumultuous
way. It would be hard to tell the reasons for such a
strange proceeding. Not one shot had yet been fired
at the battery, which the enemy could not take,
except by making regular approaches, as if against
the town itself, and by besieging it, so to speak, in
form. Some persons remonstrated, but in vain; and
so a battery of thirty cannon, which had cost the
King immense sums, was abandoned before it was
attacked."

Duchambon says that soon after the English landed,

---

[1] Vaughan's party seems to have consisted in all of sixteen men,
three of whom took no part in this affair.

he got a letter from Thierry, the captain in command
of the Royal Battery, advising that the cannon should
be spiked and the works blown up. It was then,
according to the governor, that the council was called,
and a unanimous vote passed to follow Thierry's
advice, on the ground that the defences of the battery
were in bad condition, and that the four hundred
men posted there could not stand against three or
four thousand.[1] The engineer, Verrier, opposed the
blowing up of the works, and they were therefore left
untouched. Thierry and his garrison came off in
boats, after spiking the cannon in a hasty way, without stopping to knock off the trunnions or burn the
carriages. They threw their loose gunpowder into
the well, but left behind a good number of cannon
cartridges, two hundred and eighty large bombshells,
and other ordinance stores, invaluable both to the
enemy and to themselves. Brigadier Waldo was
sent to occupy the battery with his regiment, and
Major Seth Pomeroy, the gunsmith, with twenty
soldier-mechanics, was set at drilling out the spiked
touch-holes of the cannon. There were twenty-
eight forty-two-pounders, and two eighteen-pounders.[2]

[1] *Duchambon au Ministre*, 2 *Septembre*, 1745. This is the governor's official report. "Four hundred men," is perhaps a copyist's
error, the actual number in the battery being not above two
hundred.

[2] *Waldo to Shirley*, 12 *May*, 1745. Some of the French writers
say twenty-eight thirty-six pounders, while all the English call
them forty-twos, — which they must have been, as the forty-two-
pound shot brought from Boston fitted them.

Mr. Theodore Roosevelt draws my attention to the fact that can-

Several were ready for use the next morning, and immediately opened on the town, — which, writes a soldier in his diary, "damaged the houses and made the women cry." "The enemy," says the *Habitant de Louisbourg*, "saluted us with our own cannon, and made a terrific fire, smashing everything within range."

The English occupation of the Grand Battery may be called the decisive event of the siege. There seems no doubt that the French could have averted the disaster long enough to make it of little help to the invaders. The water-front of the battery was impregnable. The rear defences consisted of a loop-holed wall of masonry, with a ditch ten feet deep and twelve feet wide, and also a covered way and glacis, which General Wolcott describes as unfinished. In this he mistook. They were not unfinished, but had been partly demolished, with a view to reconstruction. The rear wall was flanked by two towers, which, says Duchambon, were demolished; but General Wolcott declares that swivels were still mounted on them,[1] and he adds that "two hundred men might hold the battery against five thousand without cannon." The English landed their cannon near Flat Point; and before they could be turned against the Grand Battery, they must be dragged four miles over hills and rocks, through spongy marshes and jungles

non were differently rated in the French and English navies of the seventeenth century, and that a French thirty-six carried a ball as large as an English forty-two, or even a little larger.

[1] *Journal of Major-General Wolcott.*

of matted evergreens. This would have required a week or more. The alternative was an escalade, in which the undisciplined assailants would no doubt have met a bloody rebuff. Thus this Grand Battery, which, says Wolcott, "is in fact a fort," might at least have been held long enough to save the munitions and stores, and effectually disable the cannon, which supplied the English with the only artillery they had, competent to the work before them. The hasty abandonment of this important post was not Duchambon's only blunder, but it was the worst of them all.

On the night after their landing, the New England men slept in the woods, wet or dry, with or without blankets, as the case might be, and in the morning set themselves to encamping with as much order as they were capable of. A brook ran down from the hills and entered the sea two miles or more from the town. The ground on each side, though rough, was high and dry, and here most of the regiments made their quarters, — Willard's, Moulton's, and Moore's on the east side, and Burr's and Pepperrell's on the west. Those on the east, in some cases, saw fit to extend themselves towards Louisbourg as far as the edge of the intervening marsh, but were soon forced back to a safer position by the cannon-balls of the fortress, which came bowling amongst them. This marsh was that green, flat sponge of mud and moss that stretched from this point to the glacis of Louisbourg.

There was great want of tents, for material to make

them was scarce in New England. Old sails were
often used instead, being stretched over poles, — perhaps after the fashion of a Sioux teepee. When these
could not be had, the men built huts of sods, with
roofs of spruce-boughs overlapping like a thatch; for
at that early season, bark would not peel from the
trees. The landing of guns, munitions, and stores
was a formidable task, consuming many days and
destroying many boats, as happened again when
Amherst landed his cannon at this same place. Large
flat boats, brought from Boston, were used for the
purpose, and the load; were carried ashore on the
heads of the men, wading through ice-cold surf to
the waist, after which, having no change of clothing,
they slept on the ground through the chill and foggy
nights, reckless of future rheumatisms.[1]

A worse task was before them. The cannon were
to be dragged over the marsh to Green Hill, a spur
of the line of rough heights that half encircled the
town and harbor. Here the first battery was to be
planted; and from this point other guns were to be
dragged onward to more advanced stations, — a distance in all of more than two miles, thought by the
French to be impassable. So, in fact, it seemed; for

---

[1] The author of *The Importance and Advantage of Cape Breton*
says: "When the hardships they were exposed to come to be considered, the behaviour of these men will hardly gain credit. They
went ashore wet, had no [dry] clothes to cover them, were exposed
in this condition to cold, foggy nights, and yet cheerfully under-
went these difficulties for the sake of executing a project they had
voluntarily undertaken."

at the first attempt, the wheels of the cannon sank to the hubs in mud and moss, then the carriage, and finally the piece itself slowly disappeared. Lieutenant-Colonel Meserve, of the New Hampshire regiment, a ship-builder by trade, presently overcame the difficulty. By his direction sledges of timber were made, sixteen feet long and five feet wide; a cannon was placed on each of these, and it was then dragged over the marsh by a team of two hundred men, harnessed with rope-traces and breast-straps, and wading to the knees. Horses or oxen would have foundered in the mire. The way had often to be changed, as the mossy surface was soon churned into a hopeless slough along the line of march. The work could be done only at night or in thick fog, the men being completely exposed to the cannon of the town. Thirteen years after, when General Amherst besieged Louisbourg again, he dragged his cannon to the same hill over the same marsh; but having at his command, instead of four thousand militiamen, eleven thousand British regulars, with all appliances and means to boot, he made a road, with prodigious labor, through the mire, and protected it from the French shot by an epaulement, or lateral earthwork.[1]

Pepperrell writes in ardent words of the cheerfulness of his men "under almost incredible hardships." Shoes and clothing failed, till many were in tatters and many barefooted;[2] yet they toiled on with uncon-

---

[1] See "Montcalm and Wolfe," chap. xix.
[2] *Pepperrell to Newcastle*, 28 *June*, 1745.

querable spirit, and within four days had planted a
battery of six guns on Green Hill, which was about
a mile from the King's Bastion of Louisbourg.   In
another week they had dragged four twenty-two-
pound cannon and ten coehorns — gravely called
"cowhorns" by the bucolic Pomeroy — six or seven
hundred yards farther, and planted them within easy
range of the citadel.   Two of the cannon burst, and
were replaced by four more and a large mortar, which
burst in its turn, and Shirley was begged to send
another.   Meanwhile a battery, chiefly of coehorns,
had been planted on a hillock four hundred and forty
yards from the West Gate, where it greatly annoyed
the French; and on the next night an advanced
battery was placed just opposite the same gate, and
scarcely two hundred and fifty yards from it.   This
West Gate, the principal gate of Louisbourg, opened
upon the tract of high, firm ground that lay on the
left of the besiegers, between the marsh and the
harbor, an arm of which here extended westward
beyond the town, into what was called the Barachois,
a salt pond formed by a projecting spit of sand.   On
the side of the Barachois farthest from the town was
a hillock on which stood the house of an *habitant*
named Martissan.   Here, on the twentieth of May,
a fifth battery was planted, consisting of two of
the French forty-two-pounders taken in the Grand
Battery, to which three others were afterwards added.
Each of these heavy pieces was dragged to its destination by a team of three hundred men over rough

and rocky ground swept by the French artillery. This fifth battery, called the Northwest, or Titcomb's, proved most destructive to the fortress.[1]

All these operations were accomplished with the utmost ardor and energy, but with a scorn of rule and precedent that astonished and bewildered the French. The raw New England men went their own way, laughed at trenches and zigzags, and persisted in trusting their lives to the night and the fog. Several writers say that the English engineer Bastide tried to teach them discretion, but this could hardly be, for Bastide, whose station was Annapolis, did not reach Louisbourg till the fifth of June, when the batteries were finished, and the siege was nearly ended. A recent French writer makes the curious assertion that it was one of the ministers, or army chaplains, who took upon him the vain task of instruction in the art of war on this occasion.[2]

This ignorant and self-satisfied recklessness might have cost the besiegers dear if the French, instead of being perplexed and startled at the novelty of their proceedings, had taken advantage of it; but Duchambon and some of his officers, remembering the mutiny of the past winter, feared to make sorties, lest the soldiers might desert or take part with the

[1] *Journal of the Siege*, appended to Shirley's report to Newcastle; *Duchambon au Ministre, 2 Septembre*, 1745; *Lettre d'un Habitant*; Pomeroy, etc.

[2] Ferland, *Cours d'Histoire du Canada*, ii. 477. "L'ennemi ne nous attaquoit point dans les formes, et ne pratiquoit point aucun retranchement pour se couvrir." — *Habitant de Louisbourg.*

enemy. The danger of this appears to have been small. Warren speaks with wonder in his letters of the rarity of desertions, of which there appear to have been but three during the siege, — one being that of a half-idiot, from whom no information could be got. A bolder commander would not have stood idle while his own cannon were planted by the enemy to batter down his walls; and whatever the risks of a sortie, the risks of not making one were greater. "Both troops and militia eagerly demanded it, and I believe it would have succeeded," writes the intendant, Bigot.[1] The attempt was actually made more than once in a half-hearted way, — notably on the eighth of May, when the French attacked the most advanced battery, and were repulsed, with little loss on either side.

The *Habitant de Louisbourg* says: "The enemy did not attack us with any regularity, and made no intrenchments to cover themselves." This last is not exact. Not being wholly demented, they made intrenchments, such as they were, — at least, at the advanced battery;[2] as they would otherwise have been swept out of existence, being under the concentred fire of several French batteries, two of which were within the range of a musket-shot.

The scarcity of good gunners was one of the chief difficulties of the besiegers. As privateering, and piracy also, against Frenchmen and Spaniards was a

---

[1] *Bigot au Ministre*, 1 *Août*, 1745.

[2] *Diary of Joseph Sherburn, Captain at the Advanced Battery.*

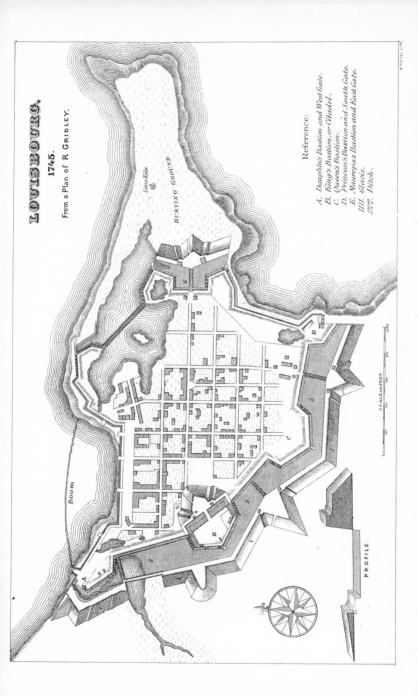

LOUISBOURG.
1745.
From a Plan of R. Gridley.

Reference:

A. Dauphin's Bastion and West Gate.
B. King's Bastion, or Citadel.
C. Queen's Bastion.
D. Princess's Bastion and South Gate.
E. Maurepas Bastion and East Gate.
IIII. Glacis.
ͻͻͻ. Ditch.

BURYING GROUND

Limekiln

Boom

PROFILE.

SCALE of FEET

favorite pursuit in New England, there were men in Pepperrell's army who knew how to handle cannon; but their number was insufficient, and the general sent a note to Warren, begging that he would lend him a few experienced gunners to teach their trade to the raw hands at the batteries. Three or four were sent, and they found apt pupils.

Pepperrell placed the advanced battery in charge of Captain Joseph[1] Sherburn, telling him to enlist as many gunners as he could. On the next day Sherburn reported that he had found six, one of whom seems to have been sent by Warren. With these and a number of raw men he repaired to his perilous station, where "I found," he says, "a very poor intrenchment. Our best shelter from the French fire, which was very hot, was hogsheads filled with earth." He and his men made the West Gate their chief mark; but before they could get a fair sight of it, they were forced to shoot down the fish-flakes, or stages for drying cod, that obstructed the view. Some of their party were soon killed, — Captain Pierce by a cannon-ball, Thomas Ash by a "bumb," and others by musketry. In the night they improved their defences, and mounted on them three more guns, one of eighteen-pound calibre, and the others of forty-two, — French pieces dragged from the Grand Battery, a mile and three quarters round the Barachois.

---

[1] He signs his name Jos. Sherburn; but in a list of the officers of the New Hampshire Regiment it appears in full as Joseph.

The cannon could be loaded only under a constant fire of musketry, which the enemy briskly returned. The French practice was excellent. A soldier who in bravado mounted the rampart and stood there for a moment was shot dead with five bullets. The men on both sides called to each other in scraps of bad French or broken English; while the French drank ironical healths to the New England men, and gave them bantering invitations to breakfast.

Sherburn continues his diary. "Sunday morning. Began our fire with as much fury as possible, and the French returned it as warmly from the Citidale [citadel], West Gate, and North East Battery with Cannon, Mortars, and continual showers of musket balls; but by 11 o'clock we had beat them all from their guns." He goes on to say that at noon his men were forced to stop firing from want of powder, that he went with his gunners to get some, and that while they were gone, somebody, said to be Mr. Vaughan, brought a supply, on which the men loaded the forty-two pounders in a bungling way, and fired them. One was dismounted, and the other burst; a barrel and a half-barrel of powder blew up, killed two men, and injured two more. Again: "Wednesday. Hot fire on both sides, till the French were beat from all their guns. May 29th went to 2 Gun [Titcomb's] Battery to give the gunners some directions; then returned to my own station, where I spent the rest of the day with pleasure, seeing our Shott Tumble down their walls and Flagg Staff."

The following is the intendant Bigot's account of the effect of the New England fire: "The enemy established their batteries to such effect that they soon destroyed the greater part of the town, broke the right flank of the King's Bastion, ruined the Dauphin Battery with its spur, and made a breach at the Porte Dauphine [West Gate], the neighboring wall, and the sort of redan adjacent."[1]   Duchambon says in addition that the cannon of the right flank of the King's Bastion could not be served, by reason of the continual fire of the enemy, which broke the embrasures to pieces; that when he had them repaired, they were broken to pieces (*démantibulés*) again, — and nobody could keep his ground behind the wall of the quay, which was shot through and through and completely riddled.[2]   The town was ploughed with cannon-balls, the streets were raked from end to end, nearly all the houses damaged, and the people driven for refuge into the stifling casemates.   The results were creditable to novices in gunnery.

The repeated accidents from the bursting of cannon were no doubt largely due to unskilful loading and the practice of double-shotting, to which the over-zealous artillerists are said to have often resorted.[3]

[1] *Bigot au Ministre,* 1 *Août,* 1745.

[2] *Duchambon au Ministre,* 2 *Septembre,* 1745.

[3] "Another forty-two pound gun burst at the Grand Battery. All the guns are in danger of going the same way, by double-shotting them, unless under better regulation than at present." — *Waldo to Pepperrell,* 20 *May,* 1745.

Waldo had written four days before : "Captain Hale, of my regiment, is dangerously hurt by the bursting of another gun.   He was

It is said, in proof of the orderly conduct of the men, that not one of them was punished during all the siege; but this shows the mild and conciliating character of the general quite as much as any peculiar merit of the soldiers. The state of things in and about the camp was compared by the caustic Dr. Douglas to "a Cambridge Commencement," which academic festival was then attended by much rough frolic and boisterous horseplay among the disorderly crowds, white and black, bond and free, who swarmed among the booths on Cambridge Common. The careful and scrupulous Belknap, who knew many who took part in the siege, says: "Those who were on the spot have frequently, in my hearing, laughed at the recital of their own irregularities, and expressed their admiration when they reflected on the almost miraculous preservation of the army from destruction." While the cannon bellowed in the front, frolic and confusion reigned at the camp, where the men raced, wrestled, pitched quoits, fired at marks, — though there was no ammunition to spare, — and ran after the French cannon-balls, which were carried to the batteries, to be returned to those who sent them. Nor were calmer recreations wanting. "Some of our men went a fishing, about 2 miles off," writes Lieutenant Benjamin Cleaves in his diary: "caught 6 Troutts." And, on the same day, "Our men went to catch Lobsters: caught 30." In view of this

our mainstay for gunnery since Captain Rhodes's misfortune" (also caused by the bursting of a cannon). *Waldo to Pepperrell,* 16 *May,* 1745.

truant disposition, it is not surprising that the
besiegers now and then lost their scalps at the hands
of prowling Indians who infested the neighborhood.
Yet through all these gambols ran an undertow of
enthusiasm, born in brains still fevered from the
"Great Awakening." The New England soldier, a
growth of sectarian hotbeds, fancied that he was
doing the work of God. The army was Israel, and
the French were Canaanitish idolaters. Red-hot
Calvinism, acting through generations, had modified
the transplanted Englishman; and the descendant of
the Puritans was never so well pleased as when
teaching their duty to other people, whether by pen,
voice, or bombshells. The ragged artillerymen, bat-
tering the walls of papistical Louisbourg, flattered
themselves with the notion that they were champions
of gospel truth.

Barefoot and tattered, they toiled on with indomi-
table pluck and cheerfulness, doing the work which
oxen could not do, with no comfort but their daily
dram of New England rum, as they plodded through
the marsh and over rocks, dragging the ponderous
guns through fog and darkness. Their spirit could
not save them from the effects of excessive fatigue
and exposure. They were ravaged with diarrhœa
and fever, till fifteen hundred men were at one time
on the sick-list, and at another, Pepperrell reported
that of the four thousand only about twenty-one
hundred were fit for duty.[1] Nearly all at last recov-

[1] *Pepperrell to Warren, 28 May, 1745.*

ered, for the weather was unusually good; yet the number fit for service was absurdly small. Pepperrell begged for reinforcements, but got none till the siege was ended.

It was not his nature to rule with a stiff hand, — and this, perhaps, was fortunate. Order and discipline, the sinews of an army, were out of the question; and it remained to do as well as might be without them, keep men and officers in good-humor, and avoid all that could dash their ardor. For this, at least, the merchant-general was well fitted. His popularity had helped to raise the army, and perhaps it helped now to make it efficient. His position was no bed of roses. Worries, small and great, pursued him without end. He made friends of his officers, kept a bountiful table at his tent, and labored to soothe their disputes and jealousies, and satisfy their complaints. So generous were his contributions to the common cause that according to a British officer who speaks highly of his services, he gave to it, in one form or another, £10,000 out of his own pocket.[1]

His letter-books reveal a swarm of petty annoyances, which may have tried his strength and patience as much as more serious cares. The soldiers complained that they were left without clothing, shoes, or rum; and when he implored the Committee of War to send them, Osborne, the chairman, replied with explanations why it could not be done. Letters

---

[1] *Letter from an Officer of Marines,* appended to *A particular Account of the Taking of Cape Breton* (London, 1745).

came from wives and fathers entreating that husbands and sons who had gone to the war should be sent back. At the end of the siege a captain "humble begs leave for to go home," because he lives in a very dangerous country, and his wife and children are "in a declining way" without him. Then two entire companies raised on the frontier offered the same petition on similar grounds. Sometimes Pepperrell was beset with prayers for favors and promotion; sometimes with complaints from one corps or another that an undue share of work had been imposed on it. One Morris, of Cambridge, writes a moving petition that his slave "Cuffee," who had joined the army, should be restored to him, his lawful master. One John Alford sends the general a number of copies of the Rev. Mr. Prentice's late sermon, for distribution, assuring him that "it will please your whole army of volunteers, as he has shown them the way to gain by their gallantry the hearts and affections of the Ladys." The end of the siege brought countless letters of congratulation, which, whether lay or clerical, never failed to remind him, in set phrases, that he was but an instrument in the hands of Providence.

One of his most persistent correspondents was his son-in-law, Nathaniel Sparhawk, a thrifty merchant, with a constant eye to business, who generally began his long-winded epistles with a bulletin concerning the health of " Mother Pepperrell," and rarely ended them without charging his father-in-law with some commission, such as buying for him the cargo of a French prize, if he could get it cheap. Or thus: "If you would procure for me a hogshead of the best Clarett, and a hogshead of the best white wine, at a reasonable rate, it would be very grateful to me." After pestering him with a few other commissions, he tells him that "Andrew and Bettsy [children of Pepperrell] send their proper compliments," and signs himself, with the starched flourish of provincial breeding, "With all possible Respect, Honoured Sir, Your Obedient Son and Servant." [1] Pepperrell was much annoyed by the conduct of the masters of the transports, of whom he wrote: "The unaccountable irregular behaviour of these fellows is the greatest fatigue I meet with;" but it may be doubted whether his son-in-law did not prove an equally efficient persecutor.

[1] *Sparhawk to Pepperrell,— June,* 1745.   This is but one of many letters from Sparhawk.

CHAPTER XX.

1745.

LOUISBOURG TAKEN.

A RASH RESOLUTION. — THE ISLAND BATTERY. — THE VOLUN-
TEERS. — THE ATTACK. — THE REPULSE. — CAPTURE OF THE
"VIGILANT." — A SORTIE. — SKIRMISHES. — DESPONDENCY OF
THE FRENCH. — ENGLISH CAMP THREATENED. — PEPPERRELL
AND WARREN. — WARREN'S PLAN. — PREPARATION FOR A GEN-
ERAL ATTACK. — FLAG OF TRUCE. — CAPITULATION. — STATE
OF THE FORTRESS. — PARSON MOODY. — SOLDIERS DISSATISFIED.
— DISORDERS. — ARMY AND NAVY. — REJOICINGS. — ENGLAND
REPAYS PROVINCIAL OUTLAYS.

FREQUENT councils of war were held in solemn
form at headquarters. On the seventh of May a
summons to surrender was sent to Duchambon, who
replied that he would answer with his cannon. Two
days after, we find in the record of the council the
following startling entry: "Advised unanimously
that the Town of Louisbourg be attacked by storm
this Night." Vaughan was a member of the board,
and perhaps his impetuous rashness had turned the
heads of his colleagues. To storm the fortress at
that time would have been a desperate attempt for
the best-trained and best-led troops. There was as
yet no breach in the walls, nor the beginning of one;
and the French were so confident in the strength of
their fortifications that they boasted that women alone

could defend them. Nine in ten of the men had no
bayonets,[1] many had no shoes, and it is said that the
scaling-ladders they had brought from Boston were
ten feet too short.[2] Perhaps it was unfortunate for
the French that the army was more prudent than its
leaders; and another council being called on the same
day, it was "Advised, That, inasmuch as there
appears a great Dissatisfaction in many of the officers
and Soldiers at the designed attack of the Town by
Storm this Night, the said Attack be deferred for the
present."[3]

Another plan was adopted, hardly less critical,
though it found favor with the army. This was the
assault of the Island Battery, which closed the
entrance of the harbor to the British squadron, and
kept it open to ships from France. Nobody knew
precisely how to find the two landing-places of this
formidable work, which were narrow gaps between
rocks lashed with almost constant surf; but Vaughan
would see no difficulties, and wrote to Pepperrell
that if he would give him the command and leave
him to manage the attack in his own way, he would
engage to send the French flag to headquarters within
forty-eight hours.[4] On the next day he seems to
have thought the command assured to him, and
writes from the Grand Battery that the carpenters

---

[1] *Shirley to Newcastle,* 7 *June,* 1745.
[2] Douglas, *Summary,* i. 347.
[3] *Record of the Council of War,* 9 *May,* **1745.**
[4] *Vaughan to Pepperrell,* 11 *May,* 1745.

are at work mending whale-boats and making paddles,
asking at the same time for plenty of pistols and one
hundred hand-grenades, with men who know how to
use them.[1] The weather proved bad, and the attempt
was deferred. This happened several times, till
Warren grew impatient, and offered to support the
attack with two hundred sailors.

At length, on the twenty-third, the volunteers for
the perilous enterprise mustered at the Grand Battery, whence the boats were to set out. Brigadier
Waldo, who still commanded there, saw them with
concern and anxiety, as they came dropping in, in
small squads, without officers, noisy, disorderly, and,
in some cases, more or less drunk. "I doubt," he
told the general, "whether straggling fellows, three,
four, or seven out of a company, ought to go on such
a service."[2] A bright moon and northern lights
again put off the attack. The volunteers remained
at the Grand Battery, waiting for better luck.
"They seem to be impatient for action," writes
Waldo. "If there were a more regular appearance,
it would give me greater sattysfaction."[3] On the
twenty-sixth their wish for action was fully gratified.
The night was still and dark, and the boats put out
from the battery towards twelve o'clock, with about
three hundred men on board.[4] These were to be

---

[1] *Vaughan to Pepperrell,* 12 *May,* 1745.

[2] *Waldo to Pepperrell,* 23 *May,* 1745.

[3] *Ibid.,* 26 *May,* 1745.

[4] "There is scarce three hundred men on this atact [attack], so

joined by a hundred or a hundred and fifty more
from Gorham's regiment, then stationed at Lighthouse Point. The commander was not Vaughan,
but one Brooks, — the choice of the men themselves,
as were also his subordinates.[1] They moved slowly,
the boats being propelled, not by oars, but by paddles,
which, if skilfully used, would make no noise. The
wind presently rose; and when they found a landing-
place, the surf was lashing the rocks with even more
than usual fury. There was room for but three
boats at once between the breakers on each hand.
They pushed in, and the men scrambled ashore with
what speed they might.

The Island Battery was a strong work, walled in
on all sides, garrisoned by a hundred and eighty
men, and armed with thirty cannon, seven swivels,
and two mortars.[2] It was now a little after mid-
night. Captain d'Aillebout, the commandant, was
on the watch, pacing the battery platform; but he
seems to have seen nothing unusual till about a hundred and fifty men had got on shore, when they had

there will be a sufficient number of Whail boats." — *Waldo to Pepperrell*, 26 *May*, 10½ *p. m.*

[1] The list of a company of forty-two "subscribers to go voluntarily upon an attack against the Island Battery" is preserved. It
includes a negro called "Ruben." The captain, chosen by the men,
was Daniel Bacon. The fact that neither this name nor that of
Brooks, the chief commander, is to be found in the list of commissioned officers of Pepperrell's little army (see Parsons, *Life of Pepperrell, Appendix*) suggests the conclusion that the "subscribers"
were permitted to choose officers from their own ranks. This list,
however, is not quite complete.

[2] *Journal of the Siege*, appended to Shirley's report.

the folly to announce their presence by three cheers.
Then, in the words of General Wolcott, the battery
"blazed with cannon, swivels, and small-arms." The
crowd of boats, dimly visible through the darkness,
as they lay just off the landing, waiting their turn to
go in, were at once the target for volleys of grape-
shot, langrage-shot, and musket-balls, of which the
men on shore had also their share. These succeeded,
however, in planting twelve scaling-ladders against
the wall.[1] It is said that some of them climbed into
the place, and the improbable story is told that
Brooks, their commander, was hauling down the
French flag when a Swiss grenadier cut him down
with a cutlass.[2] Many of the boats were shattered
or sunk, while those in the rear, seeing the state of
things, appear to have sheered off. The affair was
soon reduced to an exchange of shots between the
garrison and the men who had landed, and who,
standing on the open ground without the walls, were
not wholly invisible, while the French, behind their
ramparts, were completely hidden. "The fire of
the English," says Bigot, "was extremely obstinate,
but without effect, as they could not see to take aim."
They kept it up till daybreak, or about two hours
and a half; and then, seeing themselves at the mercy

[1] *Duchambon au Ministre, 2 Septembre,* 1745. *Bigot au Ministre,*
1 *Août,* 1745.

[2] The exploit of the boy William Tufts in climbing the French
flagstaff and hanging his red coat at the top as a substitute for the
British flag, has also been said to have taken place on this occasion.
It was, as before mentioned, at the Grand Battery.

of the French, surrendered to the number of one
hundred and nineteen, including the wounded, three
or more of whom died almost immediately. By the
most trustworthy accounts the English loss in killed,
drowned, and captured was one hundred and eighty-
nine; or, in the words of Pepperrell, "nearly half
our party."[1] Disorder, precipitation, and weak
leadership ruined what hopes the attempt ever had.

As this was the only French success during the
siege, Duchambon makes the most of it. He reports
that the battery was attacked by a thousand men,
supported by eight hundred more, who were afraid to
show themselves; and, farther, that there were
thirty-five boats, all of which were destroyed or
sunk,[2] — though he afterwards says that two of them
got away with thirty men, being all that were left of
the thousand. Bigot, more moderate, puts the number of assailants at five hundred, of whom he says
that all perished, except the one hundred and nineteen who were captured.[3]

At daybreak Louisbourg rang with shouts of
triumph. It was plain that a disorderly militia could
not capture the Island Battery. Yet captured or
silenced it must be; and orders were given to plant a

[1] Douglas makes it a little less. "We lost in this mad frolic
sixty men killed and drowned, and one hundred and sixteen prisoners." — *Summary*, i. 353.

[2] "Toutes les barques furent brisées ou coulées à fond; le feu
fut continuel depuis environ minuit jusqu'à trois heures du matin."
— *Duchambon au Ministre*, 2 *Septembre*, 1745.

[3] *Bigot au Ministre*, 1 *Août*, 1745.

battery against it at Lighthouse Point, on the eastern side of the harbor's mouth, at the distance of a short half-mile. The neighboring shore was rocky and almost inaccessible. Cannon and mortars were carried in boats to the nearest landing-place, hauled up a steep cliff, and dragged a mile and a quarter to the chosen spot, where they were planted under the orders of Colonel Gridley, who thirty years after directed the earthworks on Bunker Hill. The new battery soon opened fire with deadly effect.

The French, much encouraged by their late success, were plunged again into despondency by a disaster which had happened a week before the affair of the Island Battery, but did not come to their knowledge till some time after. On the nineteenth of May a fierce cannonade was heard from the harbor, and a large French ship-of-war was seen hotly engaged with several vessels of the squadron. She was the "Vigilant," carrying 64 guns and 560 men, and commanded by the Marquis de la Maisonfort. She had come from France with munitions and stores, when on approaching Louisbourg she met one of the English cruisers, — some say the "Mermaid," of 40 guns, and others the "Shirley," of 20. Being no match for her, the British or provincial frigate kept up a running fight and led her towards the English fleet. The "Vigilant" soon found herself beset by several other vessels, and after a gallant resistance and the loss of eighty men, struck her colors. Nothing could be more timely for the New England army, whose ammunition and provisions had sunk perilously low. The French prize now supplied their needs, and drew from the *Habitant de Louisbourg* the mournful comment, "We were victims devoted to appease the wrath of Heaven, which turned our own arms into weapons for our enemies."

Nor was this the last time when the defenders of Louisbourg supplied the instruments of their own destruction; for ten cannon were presently unearthed at low tide from the flats near the careening wharf in the northeast arm of the harbor, where they had been hidden by the French some time before. Most of them proved sound; and being mounted at Lighthouse Point, they were turned against their late owners at the Island Battery.

When Gorham's regiment first took post at Lighthouse Point, Duchambon thought the movement so threatening that he forgot his former doubts, and ordered a sortie against it, under the Sieur de Beaubassin. Beaubassin landed, with a hundred men, at a place called Lorembec, and advanced to surprise the English detachment; but was discovered by an outpost of forty men, who attacked and routed his party.[1] Being then joined by eighty Indians, Beaubassin had several other skirmishes with English scouting-parties, till, pushed by superior numbers, and their leader severely wounded, his men regained Louisbourg by sea, escaping with difficulty from the

[1] *Journal of the Siege,* appended to Shirley's report. Pomeroy, *Journal.*

guard-boats of the squadron. The Sieur de la
Vallière, with a considerable party of men, tried to
burn Pepperrell's storehouses, near Flat Point Cove;
but ten or twelve of his followers were captured, and
nearly all the rest wounded. Various other petty
encounters took place between English scouting-
parties and roving bands of French and Indians,
always ending, according to Pepperrell, in the dis-
comfiture of the latter. To this, however, there was
at least one exception. Twenty English were waylaid and surrounded near Petit Lorembec by forty or
fifty Indians, accompanied by two or three Frenchmen. Most of the English were shot down, several
escaped, and the rest surrendered on promise of life;
upon which the Indians, in cold blood, shot or speared
some of them, and atrociously tortured others.

This suggested to Warren a device which had two
objects, — to prevent such outrages in future, and to
make known to the French that the ship "Vigilant,"
the mainstay of their hopes, was in English hands.
The treatment of the captives was told to the Marquis
de la Maisonfort, late captain of the "Vigilant," now
a prisoner on board the ship he had commanded, and
he was requested to lay the facts before Duchambon.
This he did with great readiness, in a letter containing these words: "It is well that you should be
informed that the captains and officers of this squadron treat us, not as their prisoners, but as their good
friends, and take particular pains that my officers and
crew should want for nothing; therefore it seems to

me just to treat them in like manner, and to punish those who do otherwise and offer any insult to the prisoners who may fall into your hands."

Captain M'Donald, of the marines, carried this letter to Duchambon under a flag-of-truce. Though familiar with the French language, he spoke to the governor through an interpreter, so that the French officers present, who hitherto had only known that a large ship had been taken, expressed to each other without reserve their discouragement and dismay when they learned that the prize was no other than the "Vigilant." Duchambon replied to La Maison-fort's letter that the Indians alone were answerable for the cruelties in question, and that he would forbid such conduct for the future.[1]

The besiegers were now threatened by a new danger. We have seen that in the last summer the Sieur Duvivier had attacked Annapolis. Undaunted by ill-luck, he had gone to France to beg for help to attack it again; two thousand men were promised him, and in anticipation of their arrival the governor of Canada sent a body of French and Indians, under the noted partisan Marin, to meet and co-operate with them. Marin was ordered to wait at Les Mines till he heard of the arrival of the troops from France; but he grew impatient, and resolved to attack Annapolis without them. Accordingly, he laid siege to it with the six or seven hundred whites and

---

[1] *De la Maisonfort à Duchambon*, 18 *Juin* (new style), 1745. *Duchambon à De la Maisonfort*, 19 *Juin* (new style), 1745.

Indians of his party, aided by the so-called Acadian
neutrals. Mascarene, the governor, kept them at
bay till the twenty-fourth of May, when, to his surprise, they all disappeared. Duchambon had sent
them an order to make all haste to the aid of Louisbourg. As the report of this reached the besiegers,
multiplying Marin's force fourfold, they expected to
be attacked by numbers more than equal to those of
their own effective men. This wrought a wholesome
reform. Order was established in the camp, which
was now fenced with palisades and watched by sentinels and scouting-parties.

Another tribulation fell upon the general. Shirley
had enjoined it upon him to keep in perfect harmony
with the naval commander, and the injunction was
in accord with Pepperrell's conciliating temper.
Warren was no less earnest than he for the success of
the enterprise, lent him ammunition in time of need,
and offered every aid in his power, while Pepperrell
in letters to Shirley and Newcastle praised his colleague without stint. But in habits and character
the two men differed widely. Warren was in the
prime of life, and the ardor of youth still burned in
him. He was impatient at the slow movement of the
siege. Prisoners told him of a squadron expected
from Brest, of which the "Vigilant" was the fore-
runner; and he feared that even if it could not defeat
him, it might elude the blockade, and with the help
of the continual fogs, get into Louisbourg in spite of
him, thus making its capture impossible. Therefore

he called a council of his captains on board his flag-
ship, the "Superbe," and proposed a plan for taking
the place without further delay. On the same day
he laid it before Pepperrell. It was to the effect that
all the King's ships and provincial cruisers should
enter the harbor, after taking on board sixteen hundred of Pepperrell's men, and attack the town from
the water side, while what was left of the army
should assault it by land.[1] To accept the proposal
would have been to pass over the command to Warren,
only about twenty-one hundred of the New England
men being fit for service at the time, while of these
the general informs Warren that "six hundred are
gone in quest of two bodies of French and Indians,
who, we are informed, are gathering, one to the eastward, and the other to the westward."[2]

To this Warren replies, with some appearance of
pique, "I am very sorry that no one plan of mine,
though approved by all my captains, has been so fortunate as to meet your approbation or have any
weight with you." And to show his title to consideration, he gives an extract from a letter written
to him by Shirley, in which that inveterate flatterer
hints his regret that, by reason of other employments,
Warren could not take command of the whole expedition, — "which I doubt not," says the governor,

[1] *Report of a Consultation of Officers on board his Majesty's ship
"Superbe,"* enclosed in a letter of *Warren to Pepperrell,* 24 *May,*
1745.

[2] *Pepperrell to Warren,* 28 *May,* 1745.

"would be a most happy event for his Majesty's service."[1]

Pepperrell kept his temper under this thrust, and wrote to the commodore with invincible courtesy: ".Am extremely sorry the fogs prevent me from the pleasure of waiting on you on board your ship," adding that six hundred men should be furnished from the army and the transports to man the "Vigilant," which was now the most powerful ship in the squadron. In short, he showed every disposition to meet Warren halfway. But the commodore was beginning to feel some doubts as to the expediency of the bold action he had proposed, and informed Pepperrell that his pilots thought it impossible to go into the harbor until the Island Battery was silenced. In fact, there was danger that if the ships got in while that battery was still alive and active, they would never get out again, but be kept there as in a trap, under the fire from the town ramparts.

Gridley's artillery at Lighthouse Point had been doing its best, dropping bombshells with such precision into the Island Battery that the French soldiers were sometimes seen running into the sea to escape the explosions. Many of the Island guns were dismounted, and the place was fast becoming untenable. At the same time the English batteries on the land side were pushing their work of destruction with relentless industry, and walls and bastions crumbled under their fire. The French labored with energy

---

[1] *Warren to Pepperrell,* 29 *May,* 1745.

under cover of night to repair the mischief; closed the shattered West Gate with a wall of stone and earth twenty feet thick, made an epaulement to protect what was left of the formidable Circular Battery, — all but three of whose sixteen guns had been dismounted, — stopped the throat of the Dauphin's Bastion with a barricade of stone, and built a cavalier, or raised battery, on the King's Bastion, — where, however, the English fire soon ruined it. Against that near and peculiarly dangerous neighbor, the advanced battery, or, as they called it, the *Batterie de Francœur*, they planted three heavy cannon to take it in flank. "These," says Duchambon, "produced a marvellous effect, dismounted one of the cannon of the Bastonnais, and damaged all their embrasures, — which," concludes the governor, "did not prevent them from keeping up a constant fire; and they repaired by night the mischief we did them by day."[1]

Pepperrell and Warren at length came to an understanding as to a joint attack by land and water. The Island Battery was by this time crippled, and the town batteries that commanded the interior of the harbor were nearly destroyed. It was agreed that Warren, whose squadron was now increased by recent arrivals to eleven ships, besides the provincial cruisers, should enter the harbor with the first fair wind, cannonade the town and attack it in boats, while Pepperrell stormed it from the land side.

[1] *Duchambon au Ministre, 2 Septembre,* 1745.

Warren was to hoist a Dutch flag under his pennant, at his main-top-gallant mast-head, as a signal that he was about to sail in; and Pepperrell was to answer by three columns of smoke, marching at the same time towards the walls with drums beating and colors flying.[1]

The French saw with dismay a large quantity of fascines carried to the foot of the glacis, ready to fill the ditch, and their scouts came in with reports that more than a thousand scaling-ladders were lying behind the ridge of the nearest hill. Toil, loss of sleep, and the stifling air of the casemates, in which they were forced to take refuge, had sapped the strength of the besieged. The town was a ruin; only one house was untouched by shot or shell. "We could have borne all this," writes the intendant Bigot; "but the scarcity of powder, the loss of the 'Vigilant,' the presence of the squadron, and the absence of any news from Marin, who had been ordered to join us with his Canadians and Indians, spread terror among troops and inhabitants. The townspeople said that they did not want to be put to the sword, and were not strong enough to resist a general assault."[2] On the fifteenth of June they brought a petition to Duchambon, begging him to capitulate.[3]

On that day Captain Sherburn, at the advanced

[1] *Warren to Pepperrell*, 11 *June*, 1745. *Pepperrell to Warren*, 13 *June*, 1745.

[2] *Bigot au Ministre*, 1 *Août*, 1745.

[3] *Duchambon au Ministre*, 2 *Septembre*, 1745.

battery, wrote in his diary: "By 12 o'clock we had
got all our platforms laid, embrazures mended, guns
in order, shot in place, cartridges ready, dined, gunners quartered, matches lighted to return their last
favours, when we heard their drums beat a parley;
and soon appeared a flag of truce, which I received
midway between our battery and their walls, conducted the officer to Green Hill, and delivered him
to Colonel Richman [Richmond]."

La Perelle, the French officer, delivered a note
from Duchambon, directed to both Pepperrell and
Warren, and asking for a suspension of arms to
enable him to draw up proposals for capitulation.[1]
Warren chanced to be on shore when the note came;
and the two commanders answered jointly that it
had come in good time, as they had just resolved on
a general attack, and that they would give the governor till eight o'clock of the next morning to make
his proposals.[2]

They came in due time, but were of such a nature
that Pepperrell refused to listen to them, and sent
back Bonaventure, the officer who brought them,
with counter-proposals. These were the terms which
Duchambon had rejected on the seventh of May,
with added conditions; as, among others, that no
officer, soldier, or inhabitant of Louisbourg should
bear arms against the King of England or any of his
allies for the space of a year. Duchambon stipulated,

---

[1] *Duchambon à Pepperrell et Warren, 26 Juin* (new style), 1745.
[2] *Warren and Pepperrell to Duchambon, 15 June,* 1745.

as the condition of his acceptance, that his troops should march out of the fortress with their arms and colors.[1] To this both the English commanders consented, Warren observing to Pepperrell "the uncertainty of our affairs, that depend so much on wind and weather, makes it necessary not to stickle at trifles."[2] The articles were signed on both sides, and on the seventeenth the ships sailed peacefully into the harbor, while Pepperrell with a part of his ragged army entered the south gate of the town. "Never was a place more mal'd [mauled] with cannon and shells," he writes to Shirley; "neither have I red in History of any troops behaving with greater courage. We gave them about nine thousand cannon-balls and six hundred bombs."[3] Thus this unique military performance ended in complete and astonishing success.

According to English accounts, the French had lost about three hundred men during the siege; but their real loss seems to have been not much above a third of that number. On the side of the besiegers, the deaths from all causes were only a hundred and thirty, about thirty of which were from disease. The French used their muskets to good purpose; but their mortar practice was bad, and close as was the advanced battery to their walls, they often failed to hit it, while the ground on both sides of it looked

[1] *Duchambon à Warren et Pepperrell*, 27 *Juin* (new style), 1745.

[2] *Pepperrell to Warren*, 16 *June*, 1745. *Warren to Pepperrell*, 16 *June*, 1745.

[3] *Pepperrell to Shirley*, 18 *June* (old style), 1745. *Ibid.*, 4 *July*, 1745.

like a ploughed field, from the bursting of their shells. Their surrender was largely determined by want of ammunition, as, according to one account, the French had but thirty-seven barrels of gunpowder left,[1] — in which particular the besiegers fared little better.[2]

The New England men had been full of confidence in the result of the proposed assault, and a French writer says that the timely capitulation saved Louisbourg from a terrible catastrophe;[3] yet, ill-armed and disorderly as the besiegers were, it may be doubted whether the quiet ending of the siege was not as fortunate for them as for their foes. The discouragement of the French was increased by greatly exaggerated ideas of the force of the "Bastonnais." The *Habitant de Louisbourg* places the land-force alone at eight or nine thousand men, and Duchambon reports to the minister D'Argenson that he was attacked in all by thirteen thousand. His mortifying position was a sharp temptation to exaggerate; but his conduct can only be explained by a belief that the force of his enemy was far greater than it was in fact.

Warren thought that the proposed assault would succeed, and wrote to Pepperrell that he hoped they

[1] *Habitant de Louisbourg.*

[2] Pepperrell more than once complains of a total want of both powder and balls. Warren writes to him on May 29: "It is very lucky that we could spare you some powder; I am told you had not a grain left."

[3] "C'est par une protection visible de la Providence que nous avons prévenu une journée qui nous auroit été si funeste." — *Lettre d'un Habitant de Louisbourg.*

would "soon keep a good house together, and give the Ladys of Louisbourg a Gallant Ball." [1] During his visit to the camp on the day when the flag of truce came out, he made a speech to the New England soldiers, exhorting them to behave like true Englishmen; at which they cheered lustily. Making a visit to the Grand Battery on the same day, he won high favor with the regiment stationed there by the gift of a hogshead of rum to drink his health.

Whether Warren's "gallant ball" ever took place in Louisbourg does not clearly appear. Pepperrell, on his part, celebrated the victory by a dinner to the commodore and his officers. As the redoubtable Parson Moody was the general's chaplain and the oldest man in the army, he expected to ask a blessing at the board, and was, in fact, invited to do so, — to the great concern of those who knew his habitual prolixity, and dreaded its effect on the guests. At the same time, not one of them dared rasp his irritable temper by any suggestion of brevity; and hence they came in terror to the feast, expecting an invocation of a good half-hour, ended by open revolt of the hungry Britons; when, to their surprise and relief, Moody said: "Good Lord, we have so much to thank thee for, that time will be too short, and we must leave it for eternity. Bless our food and fellowship upon this joyful occasion, for the sake of Christ our Lord, Amen." And with that he sat down. [2]

---

[1] *Warren to Pepperrell,* 10 *June,* 1745.
[2] *Collections of Mass. Hist. Society,* i. 49.

It is said that he had been seen in the French church hewing at the altar and images with the axe that he had brought for that purpose; and perhaps this iconoclastic performance had eased the high pressure of his zeal.[1]

Amazing as their triumph was, Pepperrell's soldiers were not satisfied with the capitulation, and one of them utters his disapproval in his diary thus: "Sabbath Day, ye 16ᵗʰ June. They came to Termes for us to enter ye Sitty to morrow, and Poore Termes they Bee too."

The occasion of discontent was the security of property assured to the inhabitants, "by which means," says that dull chronicler, Niles, "the poor soldiers lost all their hopes and just demerit [desert] of plunder promised them." In the meagreness of their pay they thought themselves entitled to the plunder of Louisbourg, which they imagined to be a seat of wealth and luxury. Nathaniel Sparhawk, Pepperrell's thrifty son-in-law, shared this illusion, and begged the general to get for him (at a low price) a handsome service of silver plate. When the volunteers exchanged their wet and dreary camp for what they expected to be the comfortable quarters of the town, they were disgusted to see the houses still occupied by the owners, and to find themselves forced to stand guard at the doors, to protect them.[2]

---

[1] A descendant of Moody, at the village of York, told me that he was found in the church busy in the work of demolition.

[2] "Thursday, ye 21ˢᵗ Ye French keep possession yet, and we

"A great Noys and hubbub a mongst ye Solders a bout ye Plunder; Som Cursing, som a Swarein," writes one of the disgusted victors.

They were not, and perhaps could not be, long kept in order; and when, in accordance with the capitulation, the inhabitants had been sent on board vessels for transportation to France, discipline gave way, and General Wolcott records that, while Moody was preaching on a Sunday in the garrison-chapel, there was "excessive stealing in every part of the town." Little, however, was left to steal.

But if the army found but meagre gleanings, the navy reaped a rich harvest. French ships, instead of being barred out of the harbor, were now lured to enter it. The French flag was kept flying over the town, and in this way prizes were entrapped to the estimated value of a million sterling, half of which went to the Crown, and the rest to the British officers and crews, the army getting no share whatever.

Now rose the vexed question of the relative part borne by the colonies and the Crown, the army and the navy, in the capture of Louisbourg; and here it may be well to observe the impressions of a French witness of the siege. "It was an enterprise less of the English nation and its King than of the inhabitants of New England alone. This singular people have their own laws and adminis-

are forsed to stand at their Dores to gard them." — *Diary of a Soldier, anonymous.*

tration, and their governor plays the sovereign. Admiral [Commodore] Warren had no authority over the troops sent by the Governor of Boston, and he was only a spectator. . . . Nobody would have said that their sea and land forces were of the same nation and under the same prince. No nation but the English is capable of such eccentricities (*bizarreries*), — which, nevertheless, are a part of the precious liberty of which they show themselves so jealous."[1]

The French writer is correct when he says that the land and sea forces were under separate commands, and it is equally true that but for the conciliating temper of Pepperrell, harmony could not have been preserved between the two chiefs; but when he calls Warren a mere spectator, he does glaring injustice to that gallant officer, whose activity and that of his captains was incessant, and whose services were invaluable. They maintained, with slight lapses, an almost impossible blockade, without which the siege must have failed. Two or three small vessels got into the harbor; but the capture of the "Vigilant," more than any other event of the siege, discouraged the French and prepared them for surrender.

Several English writers speak of Warren and the navy as the captors of Louisbourg, and all New England writers give the chief honor to Pepperrell and the army. Neither army nor navy would have

[1] *Lettre d'un Habitant de Louisbourg.*

been successful without the other. Warren and his officers, in a council of war, had determined that so long as the Island Battery and the water batteries of the town remained in an efficient state, the ships could not enter the harbor; and Warren had personally expressed the same opinion.[1] He did not mean to enter till all the batteries which had made the attempt impracticable, including the Circular Battery, which was the most formidable of all, had been silenced or crippled by the army, and by the army alone. The whole work of the siege fell upon the land forces; and though it had been proposed to send a body of marines on shore, this was not done.[2] Three or four gunners, "to put your men in the way of loading cannon,"[3] was Warren's contribution to the operations of the siege; though the fear of attack

[1] *Report of Consultation on board the "Superbe,"* 7 *June*, 1745. "Commodore Warren did say publickly that before the Circular Battery was reduced he would not venture in here with three times ye sea force he had with him, and, through divine assistance, we tore that [battery] and this city almost to pieces." — *Pepperrell to Shirley,* 4 *July*, 1745.

[2] Warren had no men to spare. He says: "If it should be thought necessary to join your troops with any men from our ships, it should only be done for some sudden attack that may be executed in one day or night." — *Warren to Pepperrell,* 11 *May*, 1745. No such occasion arose.

[3] *Ibid.,* 13 *May*, 1745. On the nineteenth of May, 1746, Warren made a parting speech to the New England men at Louisbourg, in which he tells them that it was they who conquered the country, and expresses the hope that should the French try to recover it, "the same Spirit that induced you to make this Conquest will prompt you to protect it." See the speech in *Beamish-Murdoch,* ii. 100–102.

by the ships, jointly with the land force, no doubt hastened the surrender.   Beauharnois, governor of Canada, ascribes the defeat to the extreme activity with
which the New England men pushed their attacks.

The *Habitant de Louisbourg* says that each of the
two commanders was eager that the keys of the
fortress should be delivered to him, and not to his
colleague; that before the surrender, Warren sent an
officer to persuade the French that it would be for
their advantage to make their submission to him
rather than to Pepperrell; and that it was in fact so
made.   Wolcott, on the other hand, with the best
means of learning the truth, says in his diary that
Pepperrell received the keys at the South Gate.
The report that it was the British commodore, and
not their own general, to whom Louisbourg surrendered, made a prodigious stir among the inhabitants of New England, who had the touchiness
common to small and ambitious peoples; and as they
had begun the enterprise and borne most of its
burdens and dangers, they thought themselves entitled to the chief credit of it.   Pepperrell was blamed
as lukewarm for the honor of his country because he
did not demand the keys and reject the capitulation
if they were refused.   After all this ebullition it
appeared that the keys were in his hands, for when,
soon after the siege, Shirley came to Louisbourg,
Pepperrell formally presented them to him, in presence of the soldiers.

Warren no doubt thought that he had a right to

precedence, as being an officer of the King in regular
standing, while Pepperrell was but a civilian, clothed
with temporary rank by the appointment of a provincial governor. Warren was an impetuous sailor
accustomed to command, and Pepperrell was a merchant accustomed to manage and persuade. The
difference appears in their correspondence during the
siege. Warren is sometimes brusque and almost
peremptory; Pepperrell is forbearing and considerate to the last degree. He liked Warren, and, to
the last, continued to praise him highly in letters
to Shirley and other provincial governors;[1] while
Warren, on occasion of Shirley's arrival at Louisbourg, made a speech highly complimentary to both
the general and his soldiers.

The news that Louisbourg was taken, reached
Boston at one o'clock in the morning of the third of
July by a vessel sent express. A din of bells and
cannon proclaimed it to the slumbering townsmen,
and before the sun rose, the streets were filled with
shouting crowds. At night every window shone
with lamps, and the town was ablaze with fireworks
and bonfires. The next Thursday was appointed a
day of general thanksgiving for a victory believed to
be the direct work of Providence. New York and
Philadelphia also hailed the great news with illumi-
nations, ringing of bells, and firing of cannon.

[1] See extracts in Parsons, 105, 106. The *Habitant de Louisbourg*
extols Warren, but is not partial to Pepperrell, whom he calls, in-
correctly, " the son of a Boston shoemaker."

In England the tidings were received with astonishment and a joy that was dashed with reflections
on the strength and mettle of colonists supposed
already to aspire to independence. Pepperrell was
made a baronet, and Warren an admiral. The merchant soldier was commissioned colonel in the British
army; a regiment was given him, to be raised in
America and maintained by the King, while a similar
recognition was granted to the lawyer Shirley.[1]

A question vital to Massachusetts worried her in
the midst of her triumph. She had been bankrupt
for many years, and of the large volume of her out-
standing obligations, a part was not worth eight
pence in the pound. Added to her load of debt, she
had spent £183,649 sterling on the Louisbourg expedition. That which Smollett calls "the most important achievement of the war" would never have taken
place but for her, and Old England, and not New,
was to reap the profit; for Louisbourg, conquered by
arms, was to be restored by diplomacy. If the
money she had spent for the mother-country were
not repaid, her ruin was certain. William Bollan,
English by birth and a son-in-law of Shirley, was
sent out to urge the just claim of the province, and

[1] To Rous, captain of a provincial cruiser, whom Warren had
commended for conduct and courage, was given the command of a
ship in the royal navy.

"Tell your Council and Assembly, in his Majesty's name," writes
Newcastle to Shirley, "that their conduct will always entitle them,
in a particular manner, to his royal favor and protection." — *Newcastle to Shirley*, 10 *August*, 1745.

after long and vigorous solicitation, he succeeded. The full amount, in sterling value, was paid to Massachusetts, and the expenditures of New Hampshire, Connecticut, and Rhode Island were also reimbursed.[1] The people of Boston saw twenty-seven of those long unwieldy trucks which many elders of the place still remember as used in their youth, rumbling up King Street to the treasury, loaded with two hundred and seventeen chests of Spanish dollars, and a hundred barrels of copper coin. A pound sterling was worth eleven pounds of the old-tenor currency of Massachusetts, and thirty shillings of the new-tenor. Those beneficent trucks carried enough to buy in at a stroke nine-tenths of the old-tenor notes of the province, — nominally worth above two millions. A stringent tax, laid on by the Assembly, paid the remaining tenth, and Massachusetts was restored to financial health.[2]

[1] £183,649 to Massachusetts; £16,355 to New Hampshire; £28,863 to Connecticut; £6,332 to Rhode Island.

[2] Palfrey, *New England*, v. 101–109; Shirley, *Report to the Board of Trade. Bollan to Secretary Willard*, in *Coll. Mass. Hist. Soc.*, i. 53; Hutchinson, *Hist. Mass.*, ii. 391–395. *Letters of Bollan* in Massachusetts Archives.

It was through the exertions of the much-abused Thomas Hutchinson, Speaker of the Assembly and historian of Massachusetts, that the money was used for the laudable purpose of extinguishing the old debt.

Shirley did his utmost to support Bollan in his efforts to obtain compensation, and after highly praising the zeal and loyalty of the people of his province, he writes to Newcastle: " Justice, as well as the affection which I bear to 'em, constrains me to beseech your Grace to recommend their Case to his Majesty's paternal Care &

Tenderness in the Strongest manner." — *Shirley to Newcastle,* 6 *November,* 1745.

The English documents on the siege of Louisbourg are many and voluminous. The Pepperrell Papers and the Belknap Papers, both in the library of the Massachusetts Historical Society, afford a vast number of contemporary letters and documents on the subject. The large volume entitled *Siege of Louisbourg,* in the same repository, contains many more, including a number of autograph diaries of soldiers and others. To these are to be added the journals of General Wolcott, James Gibson, Benjamin Cleaves, Seth Pomeroy, and several others, in print or manuscript, among which is especially to be noted the journal appended to Shirley's Letter to the Duke of Newcastle of October 28, 1745, and bearing the names of Pepperrell, Brigadier Waldo, Colonel Moore, and Lieutenant-Colonels Lothrop and Gridley, who attest its accuracy. Many papers have also been drawn from the Public Record Office of London.

Accounts of this affair have hitherto rested, with but slight exceptions, on English sources alone. The archives of France have furnished useful material to the foregoing narrative, notably the long report of the governor, Duchambon, to the minister of war, and the letter of the intendant, Bigot, to the same personage, within about six weeks after the surrender. But the most curious French evidence respecting the siege is the *Lettre d'un Habitant de Louisbourg contenant une Relation exacte & circonstanciée de la Prise de l'Isle-Royale par les Anglois. A Québec, chez Guillaume le Sincère, à l'Image de la Vérité,* 1745. This little work, of eighty-one printed pages, is extremely rare. I could study it only by having a *literatim* transcript made from the copy in the Bibliothèque Nationale, as it was not in the British Museum. It bears the signature B. L. N., and is dated *à . . . ce* 28 *Août,* 1745. The imprint of Québec, etc., is certainly a mask, the book having no doubt been printed in France. It severely criticises Duchambon, and makes him mainly answerable for the disaster.

For French views of the siege of Louisbourg, *see* Appendix B.

CHAPTER XXI.

1745–1747.

DUC D'ANVILLE.

THE troops and inhabitants of Louisbourg were all embarked for France, and the town was at last in full possession of the victors. The serious-minded among them — and there were few who did not bear the stamp of hereditary Puritanism — now saw a fresh proof that they were the peculiar care of an approving Providence. While they were in camp the weather had been favorable; but they were scarcely housed when a cold, persistent rain poured down in floods that would have drenched their flimsy tents and turned their huts of turf into mud-heaps, robbing the sick of every hope of recovery. Even now they got little comfort from the shattered tenements of

Louisbourg.   The siege had left the town in so filthy
a condition that the wells were infected and the water
was poisoned.

The soldiers clamored for discharge, having enlisted
to serve only till the end of the expedition; and
Shirley insisted that faith must be kept with them,
or no more would enlist.[1] Pepperrell, much to the
dissatisfaction of Warren, sent home about seven
hundred men, some of whom were on the sick list,
while the rest had families in distress and danger on
the exposed frontier.   At the same time he begged
hard for reinforcements, expecting a visit from the
French and a desperate attempt to recover Louisbourg.   He and Warren governed the place jointly,
under martial law, and they both passed half their
time in holding courts-martial; for disorder reigned
among the disgusted militia, and no less among the
crowd of hungry speculators, who flocked like vul-
tures to the conquered town to buy the cargoes of
captured ships, or seek for other prey.   The Massachusetts soldiers, whose pay was the smallest, and
who had counted on being at their homes by the end
of July, were the most turbulent; but all alike were
on the brink of mutiny.   Excited by their ring-
leaders, they one day marched in a body to the
parade and threw down their arms, but probably
soon picked them up again, as in most cases the
guns were hunting-pieces belonging to those who
carried them.   Pepperrell begged Shirley to come to

[1] *Shirley to Newcastle, 27 September, 1745.*

Louisbourg and bring the mutineers back to duty. Accordingly, on the sixteenth of August he arrived in a ship-of-war, accompanied by Mrs. Shirley and Mrs. Warren, wife of the commodore. The soldiers duly fell into line to receive him. As it was not his habit to hide his own merits, he tells the Duke of Newcastle that nobody but he could have quieted the malcontents, — which is probably true, as nobody else had power to raise their pay. He made them a speech, promised them forty shillings in Massachusetts new-tenor currency a month, instead of twenty-five, and ended with ordering for each man half a pint of rum to drink the King's health. Though potations so generous might be thought to promise effects not wholly sedative, the mutineers were brought to reason, and some even consented to remain in garrison till the next June.[1]

Small reinforcements came from New England to hold the place till the arrival of troops from Gibraltar, promised by the ministry. The two regiments raised in the colonies, and commanded by Shirley and Pepperrell were also intended to form a part of the garrison; but difficulty was found in filling the ranks, because, says Shirley, some commissions have been given to Englishmen, and men will not enlist here except under American officers.

Nothing could be more dismal than the condition of Louisbourg, as reflected in the diaries of soldiers and others who spent there the winter that followed

---

[1] *Shirley to Newcastle, 4 December,* 1745.

its capture. Among these diaries is that of the
worthy Benjamin Crafts, private in Hale's Essex
regiment, who to the entry of each day adds a pious
invocation, sincere in its way, no doubt, though
hackneyed, and sometimes in strange company.
Thus, after noting down Shirley's gift of half a pint
of rum to every man to drink the King's health, he
adds immediately: "The Lord Look upon us and
enable us to trust in him & may he prepare us for his
holy Day." On "September ye 1, being Sabath,"
we find the following record: "I am much out of
order. This forenoon heard Mr. Stephen Williams
preach from ye 18 Luke 9 verse in the afternoon from
ye 8 of Ecles: 8 verse: Blessed be the Lord that has
given us to enjoy another Sabath and opertunity to
hear his Word Dispensed." On the next day, "being
Monday," he continues, "Last night I was taken
very Bad: the Lord be pleased to strengthen my
inner man that I may put my whole Trust in him.
May we all be prepared for his holy will. Rcd part
of plunder, 9 small tooth combs." Crafts died in
the spring, of the prevailing distemper, after doing
good service in the commissary department of his
regiment.

Stephen Williams, the preacher whose sermons had
comforted Crafts in his trouble, was a son of Rev.
John Williams, captured by the Indians at Deerfield
in 1704, and was now minister of Long Meadow,
Massachusetts. He had joined the anti-papal crusade
as one of its chaplains, and passed for a man of abil-

ity, — a point on which those who read his diary will probably have doubts. The lot of the army chaplains was of the hardest. A pestilence had fallen upon Louisbourg, and turned the fortress into a hospital. "After we got into the town," says the sarcastic Dr. Douglas, whose pleasure it is to put everything in its worst light, "a sordid indolence or sloth, for want of discipline, induced putrid fevers and dysenteries, which at length in August became contagious, and the people died like rotten sheep." From fourteen to twenty-seven were buried every day in the cemetery behind the town, outside the Maurepas Gate, by the old lime-kiln on Rochefort Point; and the forgotten bones of above five hundred New England men lie there to this day under the coarse, neglected grass. The chaplain's diary is little but a dismal record of sickness, death, sermons, funerals, and prayers with the dying ten times a day. "Prayed at Hospital; — Prayed at Citadel; — Preached at Grand Batery; — Visited Capt. [illegible], very sick; — One of Capt.——'s company dy^d. — Am but poorly myself, but able to keep about." Now and then there is a momentary change of note, as when he writes: "July 29th. One of ye Captains of ye men of war caind a soldier who struck ye capt. again. A great tumult. Swords were drawn; no life lost, but great uneasiness is caused." Or when he sets down the "say" of some Briton, apparently a naval officer, "that he had tho't ye New England men were Cowards — but now he tho't yt if they had a pick axe & spade, they w'd dig ye way to Hell & storm it."[1]

Williams was sorely smitten with homesickness, but he sturdily kept his post, in spite of grievous yearnings for family and flock. The pestilence slowly abated, till at length the burying-parties that passed the Maurepas Gate counted only three or four a day. At the end of January five hundred and sixty-one men had died, eleven hundred were on the sick list, and about one thousand fit for duty.[2] The promised regiments from Gibraltar had not come. Could the French have struck then, Louisbourg might have changed hands again. The Gibraltar regiments had arrived so late upon that rude coast that they turned southward to the milder shores of Virginia, spent the winter there, and did not appear at Louisbourg till April. They brought with them a commission for Warren as governor of the fortress. He made a speech of thanks to the New England garrison, now reduced to less than nineteen hundred men, sick and well, and they sailed at last for home, Louisbourg being now thought safe from any attempt of France.

To the zealous and energetic Shirley the capture of the fortress was but a beginning of greater triumphs. Scarcely had the New England militia

[1] The autograph diary of Rev. Stephen Williams is in my possession. The handwriting is detestable.

[2] On May 10, 1746, Shirley writes to Newcastle that eight hundred and ninety men had died during the winter. The sufferings of the garrison from cold were extreme.

sailed from Boston on their desperate venture, when
he wrote to the Duke of Newcastle that should the
expedition succeed, all New England would be on
fire to attack Canada, and the other colonies would take
part with them, if ordered to do so by the ministry.[1]
And, some months later, after Louisbourg was taken,
he urged the policy of striking while the iron was
hot, and invading Canada at once. The colonists,
he said, were ready, and it would be easier to raise
ten thousand men for such an attack than one thousand to lie idle in garrison at Louisbourg or anywhere
else. France and England, he thinks, cannot live on
the same continent. If we were rid of the French,
he continues, England would soon control America,
which would make her first among the nations; and
he ventures what now seems the modest prediction
that in one or two centuries the British colonies
would rival France in population. Even now, he is
sure that they would raise twenty thousand men to
capture Canada, if the King required it of them, and
Warren would be an acceptable commander for the
naval part of the expedition; "but," concludes the
governor, "I will take no step without orders from
his Majesty."[2]

The Duke of Newcastle was now at the head of
the Government. Smollett and Horace Walpole
have made his absurdities familiar, in anecdotes
which, true or not, do no injustice to his character;

[1] *Shirley to Newcastle, 4 April*, 1745.
[2] *Ibid.*, 29 *October*, 1745.

yet he had talents that were great in their way, though their way was a mean one. They were talents, not of the statesman, but of the political manager, and their object was to win office and keep it.

Newcastle, whatever his motives, listened to the counsels of Shirley, and directed him to consult with Warren as to the proposed attack on Canada. At the same time he sent a circular letter to the governors of the provinces from New England to North Carolina, directing them, should the invasion be ordered, to call upon their assemblies for as many men as they would grant.[1] Shirley's views were cordially supported by Warren, and the levies were made accordingly, though not in proportion to the strength of the several colonies; for those south of New York felt little interest in the plan. Shirley was told to "dispose Massachusetts to do its part;" but neither he nor his province needed prompting. Taking his cue from the Roman senator, he exclaimed to his Assembly, "*Delenda est Canada;*" and the Assembly responded by voting to raise thirty-five hundred men, and offering a bounty equivalent to £4 sterling to each volunteer, besides a blanket for every one, and a bed for every two. New Hampshire contributed five hundred men, Rhode Island three hundred, Connecticut one thousand, New York sixteen hundred, New Jersey five hundred, Maryland three hundred, and Virginia one hundred. The

---

[1] *Newcastle to the Provincial Governors,* 14 *March,* 1746; *Shirley to Newcastle,* 31 *May,* 1746; *Proclamation of Shirley,* 2 *June,* 1746.

Duke of Newcastle.

Pennsylvania Assembly, controlled by Quaker non-combatants, would give no soldiers; but, by a popular movement, the province furnished four hundred men, without the help of its representatives.[1]

As usual in the English attempts against Canada, the campaign was to be a double one. The main body of troops, composed of British regulars and New England militia, was to sail up the St. Lawrence and attack Quebec, while the levies of New York and the provinces farther south, aided, it was hoped, by the warriors of the Iroquois, were to advance on Montreal by way of Lake Champlain.

Newcastle promised eight battalions of British troops under Lieutenant-General Saint-Clair. They were to meet the New England men at Louisbourg, and all were then to sail together for Quebec, under the escort of a squadron commanded by Warren. Shirley also was to go to Louisbourg, and arrange the plan of the campaign with the general and the admiral. Thus, without loss of time, the captured fortress was to be made a base of operations against its late owners.

Canada was wild with alarm at reports of English preparation. There were about fifty English prisoners in barracks at Quebec, and every device was tried to get information from them; but being chiefly rustics caught on the frontiers by Indian war-parties, they had little news to give, and often refused to give

[1] Hutchinson, ii. 381, *note.* Compare *Memoirs of the Principal Transactions of the Last War.*

even this.   One of them, who had been taken long
before and gained over by the French,[1] was used as
an agent to extract information from his countrymen,
and was called "*notre homme de confiance.*"   At the
same time the prisoners were freely supplied with
writing materials, and their letters to their friends
being then opened, it appeared that they were all in
expectation of speedy deliverance.[2]

In July a report came from Acadia that from forty
to fifty thousand men were to attack Canada; and on
the first of August a prisoner lately taken at Saratoga
declared that there were thirty-two war-ships at
Boston ready to sail against Quebec, and that thirteen thousand men were to march at once from
Albany against Montreal.   "If all these stories are
true," writes the Canadian journalist, "all the English on this continent must be in arms."

Preparations for defence were pushed with feverish
energy.   Fireships were made ready at Quebec, and
fire-rafts at Isle-aux-Coudres; provisions were gathered, and ammunition was distributed; reconnoitring
parties were sent to watch the gulf and the river;
and bands of Canadians and Indians lately sent to
Acadia were ordered to hasten back.

Thanks to the Duke of Newcastle, all these alarms
were needless.   The Massachusetts levies were ready

---

[1] "Un ancien prisonnier affidé que l'on a mis dans nos interests."

[2] *Extrait en forme de Journal de ce qui s'est passé dans la Colonie
depuis . . . le* 1 *Décembre,* 1745, *jusqu'au* 9 *Novembre,* 1746, *signé
Beauharnois et Hocquart.*

within six weeks, and Shirley, eager and impatient, waited in vain for the squadron from England and the promised eight battalions of regulars. They did not come; and in August he wrote to Newcastle that it would now be impossible to reach Quebec before October, which would be too late.[1] The eight battalions had been sent to Portsmouth for embarkation, ordered on board the transports, then ordered ashore again, and finally sent on an abortive expedition against the coast of France. There were those who thought that this had been their destination from the first, and that the proposed attack on Canada was only a pretence to deceive the enemy. It was not till the next spring that Newcastle tried to explain the miscarriage to Shirley. He wrote that the troops had been detained by head-winds till General Saint-Clair and Admiral Lestock thought it too late; to which he added that the demands of the European war made the Canadian expedition impracticable, and that Shirley was to stand on the defensive and attempt no further conquests. As for the provincial soldiers, who this time were in the pay of the Crown, he says that they were "very expensive," and orders the governor to get rid of them "as cheap as possible."[2] Thus, not for the first time, the hopes of the colonies were brought to nought by the failure of the British ministers to keep their promises.

When, in the autumn of 1746, Shirley said that for

[1] *Shirley to Newcastle*, 22 *August*, 1746.
[2] *Newcastle to Shirley*, 30 *May*, 1747.

the present Canada was to be let alone, he bethought
him of a less decisive conquest, and proposed to
employ the provincial troops for an attack on Crown
Point, which formed a halfway station between
Albany and Montreal, and was the constant rendezvous of war-parties against New York, New Hampshire, and Massachusetts, whose discords and jealousies
had prevented them from combining to attack it.
The Dutch of Albany, too, had strong commercial
reasons for not coming to blows with the Canadians.
Of late, however, Massachusetts and New York had
suffered so much from this inconvenient neighbor
that it was possible to unite them against it; and as
Clinton, governor of New York, was scarcely less
earnest to get possession of Crown Point than was
Shirley himself, a plan of operations was soon settled.
By the middle of October fifteen hundred Massachusetts troops were on their way to join the New York
levies, and then advance upon the obnoxious post.[1]

Even this modest enterprise was destined to fail.
Astounding tidings reached New England, and
startled her like a thunder-clap from dreams of conquest. It was reported that a great French fleet and
army were on their way to retake Louisbourg, recon-
quer Acadia, burn Boston, and lay waste the other
seaboard towns. The Massachusetts troops marching
for Crown Point were recalled, and the country
militia were mustered in arms. In a few days the
narrow, crooked streets of the Puritan capital were

[1] *Memoirs of the Principal Transactions of the Last War.*

crowded with more than eight thousand armed rustics from the farms and villages of Middlesex, Essex, Norfolk, and Worcester, and Connecticut promised six thousand more as soon as the hostile fleet should appear. The defences of Castle William were enlarged and strengthened, and cannon were planted on the islands at the mouth of the harbor; hulks were sunk in the channel, and a boom was laid across it under the guns of the castle.[1] The alarm was compared to that which filled England on the approach of the Spanish Armada.[2]

Canada heard the news of the coming armament with an exultation that was dashed with misgiving as weeks and months passed and the fleet did not appear. At length in September a vessel put in to an Acadian harbor with the report that she had met the ships in mid-ocean, and that they counted a hundred and fifty sail. Some weeks later the governor and intendant of Canada wrote that on the fourteenth of October they received a letter from Chibucto with "the agreeable news" that the Duc d'Anville and his fleet had arrived there about three weeks before. Had they known more, they would have rejoiced less.

That her great American fortress should have been snatched from her by a despised militia was more

---

[1] *Shirley to Newcastle*, 29 *September*, 1746. Shirley says that though the French may bombard the town, he does not think they could make a landing, as he shall have fifteen thousand good men within call to oppose them.

[2] Hutchinson, ii. 382.

than France could bear; and in the midst of a burdensome war she made a crowning effort to retrieve her honor and pay the debt with usury. It was computed that nearly half the French navy was gathered at Brest under command of the Duc d'Anville. By one account his force consisted of eleven ships-of-the-line, twenty frigates, and thirty-four transports and fireships, or sixty-five in all. Another list gives a total of sixty-six, of which ten were ships-of-the-line, twenty-two were frigates and fireships, and thirty-four were transports.[1] These last carried the regiment of Ponthieu, with other veteran troops, to the number in all of three thousand one hundred and fifty. The fleet was to be joined at Chibucto, now Halifax, by four heavy ships-of-war lately sent to the West Indies under M. de Conflans.

From Brest D'Anville sailed for some reason to Rochelle, and here the ships were kept so long by head-winds that it was the twentieth of June before they could put to sea. From the first the omens were sinister. The admiral was beset with questions as to the destination of the fleet, which was known to him alone; and when, for the sake of peace, he told it to his officers, their discontent redoubled. The Bay of Biscay was rough and boisterous, and spars, sails, and bowsprits were carried away. After they had been a week at sea, some of the ships, being

---

[1] This list is in the journal of a captured French officer called by Shirley M. Rebateau.

dull sailers, lagged behind, and the rest were forced
to shorten sail and wait for them. In the longitude
of the Azores there was a dead calm, and the whole
fleet lay idle for days. Then came a squall, with
lightning. Several ships were struck. On one of
them six men were killed, and on the seventy-gun
ship "Mars" a box of musket and cannon cartridges
blew up, killed ten men, and wounded twenty-one. A
store-ship which proved to be sinking was abandoned
and burned. Then a pestilence broke out, and in some
of the ships there were more sick than in health.

On the fourteenth of September they neared the
coast of Nova Scotia, and were in dread of the
dangerous shoals of Sable Island, the position of
which they did not exactly know. They groped
their way in fogs till a fearful storm, with thunder
and lightning, fell upon them. The journalist of
the voyage, a captain in the regiment of Ponthieu,
says, with the exaggeration common in such cases,
that the waves ran as high as the masts; and such
was their violence that a transport, dashing against
the ship "Amazone," immediately went down, with
all on board. The crew of the "Prince d'Orange,"
half blinded by wind and spray, saw the great ship
"Caribou," without bowsprit or main-topmast, driving towards them before the gale, and held their
breath in expectation of the shock as she swept close
alongside and vanished in the storm.[1] The tempest

---

[1] *Journal historique du Voyage de la Flotte commandée par M. le
Duc d'Enville.* The writer was on board the "Prince d'Orange,"

raged all night, and the fleet became so scattered
that there was no more danger of collision. In the
morning the journalist could see but five sail; but as
the day advanced the rest began to reappear, and at
three o'clock he counted thirty-one from the deck of
the "Prince d'Orange." The gale was subsiding,
but its effects were seen in hencoops, casks, and
chests floating on the surges and telling the fate of
one or more of the fleet. The "Argonaut" was
rolling helpless, without masts or rudder; the
"Caribou" had thrown overboard all the starboard
guns of her upper deck; and the vice-admiral's ship,
the "Trident," was in scarcely better condition.

On the twenty-third they were wrapped in thick
fog and lay firing guns, ringing bells, and beating
drums to prevent collisions. When the weather
cleared, they looked in vain for the admiral's ship,
the "Northumberland."[1] She was not lost, however,
but with two other ships was far ahead of the fleet
and near Chibucto, though in great perplexity, having no pilot who knew the coast. She soon after had
the good fortune to capture a small English vessel
with a man on board well acquainted with Chibucto
harbor. D'Anville offered him his liberty and a
hundred louis if he would pilot the ship in. To this
he agreed; but when he rejoined his fellow-prisoners

and describes what he saw (Archives du Séminaire de Québec;
printed in *Le Canada Français*).

[1] The "Northumberland" was an English prize captured by
Captains Serier and Conflans in 1744.

they called him a traitor to his country, on which he retracted his promise. D'Anville was sorely perplexed; but Duperrier, captain of the "Northumberland," less considerate of the prisoner's feelings, told him that unless he kept his word he should be thrown into the sea, with a pair of cannon-balls made fast to his feet. At this his scruples gave way, and before night the "Northumberland" was safe in Chibucto Bay. D'Anville had hoped to find here the four ships of Conflans, which were to have met him from the West Indies at this, the appointed rendezvous; but he saw only a solitary transport of his own fleet. Hills covered with forests stood lonely and savage round what is now the harbor of Halifax. Conflans and his four ships had arrived early in the month, and finding nobody, though it was nearly three months since D'Anville left Rochelle, he cruised among the fogs for a while, and then sailed for France a few days before the admiral's arrival.

D'Anville was ignorant of the fate of his fleet; but he knew that the two ships which had reached Chibucto with him were full of sick men, that their provisions were nearly spent, and that there was every reason to believe such of the fleet as the storm might have spared to be in no better case. An officer of the expedition describes D'Anville as a man "made to command and worthy to be loved," and says that he had borne the disasters of the voyage with the utmost fortitude and serenity.[1] Yet sus-

[1] *Journal historique du Voyage.*

pense and distress wrought fatally upon him, and at
two o'clock in the morning of the twenty-seventh he
died, — of apoplexy, by the best accounts; though it
was whispered among the crews that he had ended
his troubles by poison.[1]

At six o'clock in the afternoon of the same day
D'Estournel, the vice-admiral, with such ships as
remained with him, entered the harbor and learned
what had happened. He saw with dismay that he
was doomed to bear the burden of command over a
ruined enterprise and a shattered fleet. The long
voyage had consumed the provisions, and in some of
the ships the crews were starving. The pestilence
grew worse, and men were dying in numbers every
day. On the twenty-eighth, D'Anville was buried
without ceremony on a small island in the harbor.
The officers met in council, and the papers of the
dead commander were examined. Among them was
a letter from the King in which he urged the recapture of Louisbourg as the first object of the expedition; but this was thought impracticable, and the
council resolved to turn against Annapolis all the
force that was left. It is said that D'Estournel
opposed the attempt, insisting that it was hopeless,
and that there was no alternative but to return to
France. The debate was long and hot, and the
decision was against him.[2] The council dissolved,

---

[1] *Declaration of H. Kannan and D. Deas,* 23 *October,* 1746. *Deposition of Joseph Foster,* 24 *October,* 1746, *sworn to before Jacob Wen-
dell, J. P.* These were prisoners in the ships at Chibucto.

[2] This is said by all the writers except the author of the *Journal*

and he was seen to enter his cabin in evident distress
and agitation. An unusual sound was presently
heard, followed by groans. His door was fastened
by two bolts, put on the evening before by his order.
It was burst open, and the unfortunate commander
was found lying in a pool of blood, transfixed with
his own sword. Enraged and mortified, he had
thrown himself upon it in a fit of desperation. The
surgeon drew out the blade, but it was only on the
urgent persuasion of two Jesuits that the dying man
would permit the wound to be dressed. He then
ordered all the captains to the side of his berth, and
said, "Gentlemen, I beg pardon of God and the King
for what I have done, and I protest to the King that
my only object was to prevent my enemies from saying that I had not executed his orders;" and he
named M. de la Jonquière to command in his place.
In fact, La Jonquière's rank entitled him to do so.
He was afterwards well known as governor of Canada,
and was reputed a brave and able sea-officer.

La Jonquière remained at Chibucto till late in
October. Messengers were sent to the Acadian
settlements to ask for provisions, of which there was
desperate need; and as payment was promised in good
metal, and not in paper, the Acadians brought in a
considerable supply. The men were encamped on
shore, yet the pestilence continued its ravages. Two

historique, who merely states that the council decided to attack
Annapolis, and to detach some soldiers to the aid of Quebec. This
last vote was reconsidered.

English prisoners were told that between twenty-three and twenty-four hundred men had been buried by sea or land since the fleet left France; and another declares that eleven hundred and thirty-five burials took place while he was at Chibucto.[1]   The survivors used the clothing of the dead as gifts to the neighboring Indians, who in consequence were attacked with such virulence by the disease that of the band at Cape Sable three fourths are said to have perished. The English, meanwhile, learned something of the condition of their enemies.   Towards the end of September Captain Sylvanus Cobb, in a sloop from Boston, boldly entered Chibucto Harbor, took note of the ships lying there, and, though pursued, ran out to sea and carried the results of his observations to Louisbourg.[2]   A more thorough reconnoissance was afterwards made by a vessel from Louisbourg bringing French prisoners for exchange under a flag of truce; and it soon became evident that the British colonies had now nothing to fear.

La Jonquière still clung to the hope of a successful stroke at Annapolis, till in October an Acadian brought him the report that the garrison of that place had received a reinforcement of twelve hundred men.   The reinforcement consisted in reality of three small companies of militia sent from Boston by Shirley.   La Jonquière called a secret council, and

---

[1] Declaration of Kannan and Deas.   Deposition of Joseph Foster.
[2] Report of Captain Cobb, in Shirley to Newcastle, 13 October, 1746.

the result seems to have been adverse to any further attempt. The journalist reports that only a thousand men were left in fighting condition, and that even of these some were dying every day.

La Jonquière, however, would not yet despair. The troops were re-embarked; five hospital ships were devoted to the sick; the "Parfait," a fifty-gun ship no longer serviceable, was burned, as were several smaller vessels, and on the fourth of October what was left of the fleet sailed out of Chibucto Harbor and steered for Annapolis, piloted by Acadians. The flag of truce from Louisbourg was compelled for a time to bear them company, and Joseph Foster of Beverly, an exchanged prisoner on board of her, deposed that as the fleet held its way, he saw "a great number of dead persons" dropped into the sea every day. Ill-luck still pursued the French. A storm off Cape Sable dispersed the ships, two of which some days later made their way to Annapolis Basin in expectation of finding some of their companions there. They found instead the British fifty-gun ship "Chester" and the Massachusetts frigate "Shirley" anchored before the fort, on which the two Frenchmen retired as they had come; and so ended the last aggressive movement on the part of the great armament.

The journalist reports that on the night of the twenty-seventh there was a council of officers on board the "Northumberland," at which it was resolved that no choice was left but to return to France

with the ships that still kept together. On the
fourth of November there was another storm, and
when it subsided, the "Prince d'Orange" found
herself with but nine companions, all of which were
transports. These had on board eleven companies of
soldiers, of whom their senior officer reports that
only ninety-one were in health. The pestilence made
such ravages among the crews that four or five
corpses were thrown into the sea every day, and
there was fear that the vessels would be left helpless
in mid-ocean for want of sailors to work them.[1] At
last, on the seventh of December, after narrowly
escaping an English squadron, they reached Port
Louis in Brittany, where several ships of the fleet
had arrived before them. Among these was the
frigate "La Palme." "Yesterday," says the journalist, "I supped with M. Destrahoudal, who commands this frigate; and he told me things which
from anybody else would have been incredible. This
is his story, exactly as I had it from him." And he
goes on to the following effect.

After the storm of the fourteenth of September,
provisions being almost spent, it was thought that
there was no hope for "La Palme" and her crew but
in giving up the enterprise and making all sail at
once for home, since France now had no port of
refuge on the western continent nearer than Quebec.
Rations were reduced to three ounces of biscuit and
three of salt meat a day; and after a time half of this

1 *Journal historique.*

pittance was cut off. There was diligent hunting for rats in the hold; and when this game failed, the crew, crazed with famine, demanded of their captain that five English prisoners who were on board should be butchered to appease the frenzy of their hunger. The captain consulted his officers, and they were of opinion that if he did not give his consent, the crew would work their will without it. The ship's butcher was accordingly ordered to bind one of the prisoners, carry him to the bottom of the hold, put him to death, and distribute his flesh to the men in portions of three ounces each. The captain, walking the deck in great agitation all night, found a pretext for deferring the deed till morning, when a watchman sent aloft at daylight cried, "A sail!" The providential stranger was a Portuguese ship; and as Portugal was neutral in the war, she let the frigate approach to within hailing distance. The Portuguese captain soon came alongside in a boat, "accompanied," in the words of the narrator, "by five sheep." These were eagerly welcomed by the starving crew as agreeable substitutes for the five Englishmen; and, being forthwith slaughtered, were parcelled out among the men, who would not wait till the flesh was cooked, but devoured it raw. Provisions enough were obtained from the Portuguese to keep the frigate's company alive till they reached Port Louis.[1]

There are no sufficient means of judging how far

[1] *Relation du Voyage de Retour de M. Destrahoudal après la Tempête du 14 Septembre,* in *Journal historique.*

the disasters of D'Anville's fleet were due to a
neglect of sanitary precautions or to defieient sea-
manship. Certain it is that there were many in self-
righteous New England who would have held it
impious to doubt that God had summoned the pestilence and the storm to fight the battles of his modern
Israel.

Undaunted by disastrous failure, the French court
equipped another fleet, not equal to that of D'Anville,
yet still formidable, and placed it under La Jonquière,
for the conquest of Acadia and Louisbourg. La
Jonquière sailed from Rochelle on the tenth of May,
1747, and on the fourteenth was met by an English
fleet stronger than his own and commanded by
Admirals Anson and Warren. A fight ensued, in
which, after brave resistance, the French were totally
defeated. Six ships-of-war, including the flag-ship,
were captured, with a host of prisoners, among whom
was La Jonquière himself.[1]

[1] *Relation du Combat rendu le* 14 *Mai* (new style), *par l'Escadre du
Roy commandée par M. de la Jonquière,* in *Le Canada Français, Sup-
plément de Documents inédits,* 33. *Newcastle to Shirley,* 30 *May,*
1747

CHAPTER XXII.

1745–1747.

ACADIAN CONFLICTS.

SINCE the capture of Louisbourg, France had held
constantly in view, as an object of prime importance,
the recovery of her lost colony of Acadia. This was
one of the chief aims of D'Anville's expedition, and
of that of La Jonquière in the next year. And to
make assurance still more sure, a large body of Canadians, under M. de Ramesay, had been sent to Acadia
to co-operate with D'Anville's force; but the greater
part of them had been recalled to aid in defending
Quebec against the expected attack of the English.
They returned when the news came that D'Anville
was at Chibucto, and Ramesay, with a part of his
command, advanced upon Port Royal, or Annapolis,
in order to support the fleet in its promised attack on

that place. He encamped at a little distance from the English fort, till he heard of the disasters that had ruined the fleet,[1] and then fell back to Chignecto, on the neck of the Acadian peninsula, where he made his quarters, with a force which, including Micmac, Malicite, and Penobscot Indians, amounted, at one time, to about sixteen hundred men.

If France was bent on recovering Acadia, Shirley was no less resolved to keep it, if he could. In his belief, it was the key of the British American colonies, and again and again he urged the Duke of Newcastle to protect it. But Newcastle seems scarcely to have known where Acadia was, being ignorant of most things except the art of managing the House of Commons, and careless of all things that could not help his party and himself. Hence Shirley's hyperboles, though never without a basis of truth, were lost upon him. Once, it is true, he sent three hundred men to Annapolis; but one hundred and eighty of them died on the voyage, or lay helpless in Boston hospitals, and the rest could better have been spared, some being recruits from English jails, and others Irish Catholics, several of whom deserted to the French, with information of the state of the garrison.

The defence of Acadia was left to Shirley and his Assembly, who in time of need sent companies of militia and rangers to Annapolis, and thus on several occasions saved it from returning to France. Shirley was the most watchful and strenuous defender of

---

[1] *Journal de Beaujeu,* in *Le Canada Français, Documents,* 53.

British interests on the continent; and in the present crisis British and colonial interests were one. He held that if Acadia were lost, the peace and safety of all the other colonies would be in peril; and in spite of the immense efforts made by the French court to recover it, he felt that the chief danger of the province was not from without, but from within. "If a thousand French troops should land in Nova Scotia," he writes to Newcastle, "all the people would rise to join them, besides all the Indians."[1] So, too, thought the French officials in America. The governor and intendant of Canada wrote to the colonial minister: "The inhabitants, with few exceptions, wish to return under the French dominion, and will not hesitate to take up arms as soon as they see themselves free to do so; that is, as soon as we become masters of Port Royal, or they have powder and other munitions of war, and are backed by troops for their protection against the resentment of the English."[2] Up to this time, however, though they had aided Duvivier in his attack on Annapolis so far as was possible without seeming to do so, they had not openly taken arms, and their refusal to fight for the besiegers is one among several causes to which Mascarene ascribes the success of his defence. While the greater part remained attached to France, some leaned to the English, who bought their produce and paid them in ready coin. Money was rare

---

[1] *Shirley to Newcastle,* 29 *October,* 1745.
[2] *Beauharnois et Hocquart au Ministre,* 12 *Septembre,* **1745.**

with the Acadians, who loved it, and were so addicted
to hoarding it that the French authorities were led
to speculate as to what might be the object of these
careful savings.[1]

Though the Acadians loved France, they were not
always ready to sacrifice their interests to her.   They
would not supply Ramesay's force with provisions in
exchange for his promissory notes, but demanded
hard cash.[2]   This he had not to give, and was near
being compelled to abandon his position in consequence.   At the same time, in consideration of specie
payment, the inhabitants brought in fuel for the
English garrison at Louisbourg, and worked at
repairing the rotten *chevaux de frise* of Annapolis.[3]

Mascarene, commandant at that place, being of
French descent, was disposed at first to sympathize
with the Acadians and treat them with a lenity that
to the members of his council seemed neither fitting
nor prudent.   He wrote to Shirley: " The French
inhabitants are certainly in a very perilous situation,
those who pretend to be their friends and old masters
having let loose a parcel of banditti to plunder them;
whilst, on the other hand, they see themselves threatened with ruin if they fail in their allegiance to the
British Government."[4]

This unhappy people were in fact between two

[1] *Beauharnois et Hocquart au Ministre,* 12 *Septembre,* 1745.

[2] *Ibid.*

[3] *Admiral Knowles à* —— 1746.   Mascarene in *Le Canada Français, Documents,* 82.

[4] Mascarene, in *Le Canada Français, Documents,* 81.

fires. France claimed them on one side, and England on the other, and each demanded their adhesion,
without regard to their feelings or their welfare.
The banditti of whom Mascarene speaks were the
Micmac Indians, who were completely under the
control of their missionary, Le Loutre, and were
used by him to terrify the inhabitants into renoun-
cing their English allegiance and actively supporting
the French cause. By the Treaty of Utrecht France
had transferred Acadia to Great Britain, and the
inhabitants had afterwards taken an oath of fidelity
to King George. Thus they were British subjects;
but as their oath had been accompanied by a promise,
or at least a clear understanding, that they should
not be required to take arms against Frenchmen or
Indians, they had become known as the "Neutral
French." This name tended to perplex them, and
in their ignorance and simplicity they hardly knew
to which side they owed allegiance. Their illiteracy
was extreme. Few of them could sign their names,
and a contemporary well acquainted with them
declares that he knew but a single Acadian who
could read and write.[1] This was probably the notary,
Le Blanc, whose compositions are crude and illiter-
ate. Ignorant of books and isolated in a wild and
remote corner of the world, the Acadians knew nothing of affairs, and were totally incompetent to meet
the crisis that was soon to come upon them. In
activity and enterprise they were far behind the

[1] Moïse des Derniers, in *Le Canada Français*, i. 118.

Canadians, who looked on them as inferiors. Their pleasures were those of the humblest and simplest peasants; they were contented with their lot, and asked only to be let alone. Their intercourse was unceremonious to such a point that they never addressed each other, or, it is said, even strangers, as *monsieur*. They had the social equality which can exist only in the humblest conditions of society, and presented the phenomenon of a primitive little democracy, hatched under the wing of an absolute monarchy. Each was as good as his neighbor; they had no natural leaders, nor any to advise or guide them, except the missionary priest, who in every case was expected by his superiors to influence them in the interest of France, and who, in fact, constantly did so. While one observer represents them as living in a state of primeval innocence, another describes both men and women as extremely foul of speech; from which he draws inferences unfavorable to their domestic morals,[1] which, nevertheless, were commendable. As is usual with a well-fed and unambitious peasantry, they were very prolific, and are said to have doubled their number every sixteen years. In 1748 they counted in the peninsula of Nova Scotia between twelve and thirteen thousand souls.[2] The English rule had been of the lightest, — so light that it could scarcely be felt; and this was

---

[1] *Journal de Franquet*, Part II.

[2] *Description de l'Acadie, avec le Nom des Paroisses et le Nombre des Habitants*, 1748.

not surprising, since the only instruments for enfor-
cing it over a population wholly French were some
two hundred disorderly soldiers in the crumbling
little fort of Annapolis; and the province was left,
perforce, to take care of itself.

The appearance of D'Anville's fleet caused great
excitement among the Acadians, who thought that
they were about to pass again under the Crown of
France. Fifty of them went on board the French
ships at Chibucto to pilot them to the attack of
Annapolis, and to their dismay found that no attack
was to be made. When Ramesay, with his Canadians
and Indians, took post at Chignecto and built a fort
at Baye Verte, on the neck of the peninsula of Nova
Scotia, the English power in that part of the colony
seemed at an end. The inhabitants cut off all communication with Annapolis, and detained the officers
whom Mascarene sent for intelligence.

From the first outbreak of the war it was evident
that the French built their hopes of recovering
Acadia largely on a rising of the Acadians against
the English rule, and that they spared no efforts to
excite such a rising. Early in 1745 a violent and
cruel precaution against this danger was suggested.
William Shirreff, provincial secretary, gave it as
his opinion that the Acadians ought to be removed,
being a standing menace to the colony.[1] This is the
first proposal of such a nature that I find. Some
months later, Shirley writes that, on a false report

---

[1] *Shirreff to K. Gould, agent of Philips's Regiment, March, 1745.*

of the capture of Annapolis by the French, the Acadians sang *Te Deum*, and that every sign indicates that there will be an attempt in the spring to capture Annapolis, with their help.[1] Again, Shirley informs Newcastle that the French will get possession of Acadia unless the most dangerous of the inhabitants are removed, and English settlers put in their place.[2] He adds that there are not two hundred and twenty soldiers at Annapolis to defend the province against the whole body of Acadians and Indians, and he tells the minister that unless the expedition against Canada should end in the conquest of that country, the removal of some of the Acadians will be a necessity. He means those of Chignecto, who were kept in a threatening attitude by the presence of Ramesay and his Canadians, and who, as he thinks, had forfeited their lands by treasonable conduct. Shirley believes that families from New England might be induced to take their place, and that these, if settled under suitable regulations, would form a military frontier to the province of Nova Scotia "strong enough to keep the Canadians out," and hold the Acadians to their allegiance.[3] The Duke of Bedford thinks the plan a good one, but objects to the expense.[4] Commodore Knowles, then governor of Louisbourg, who, being threatened with consumption and convinced that the climate was killing him, vented his feelings

---

[1] *Shirley to Newcastle*, 14 *December*, 1745.

[2] *Ibid.*, 10 *May*, 1746.

[3] *Ibid.*, 8 *July*, 1747.

[4] *Bedford to Newcastle*, 11 *September*, 1747.

in strictures against everything and everybody, was of opinion that the Acadians, having broken their neutrality, ought to be expelled at once, and expresses the amiable hope that should his Majesty adopt this plan, he will charge him with executing it.[1]

Shirley's energetic nature inclined him to trenchant measures, and he had nothing of modern humanitarianism; but he was not inhuman, and he shrank from the cruelty of forcing whole communities into exile. While Knowles and others called for wholesale expatriation, he still held that it was possible to turn the greater part of the Acadians into safe subjects of the British Crown;[2] and to this end he advised the planting of a fortified town where Halifax now stands, and securing by forts and garrisons the neck of the Acadian peninsula, where the population was most numerous and most disaffected. The garrisons, he thought, would not only impose respect, but would furnish the Acadians with what they wanted most, — ready markets for their produce,

---

[1] *Knowles to Newcastle, 8 November,* 1746.

[2] Shirley says that the indiscriminate removal of the Acadians would be " unjust" and " too rigorous." Knowles had proposed to put Catholic Jacobites from the Scotch Highlands into their place. Shirley thinks this inexpedient, but believes that Protestants from Germany and Ulster might safely be trusted. The best plan of all, in his opinion, is that of " treating the Acadians as subjects, confining their punishment to the most guilty and dangerous among 'em, and keeping the rest in the country and endeavoring to make them useful members of society under his Majesty's Government." *Shirley to Newcastle,* 21 *November,* 1746. If the Newcastle Government had vigorously carried his recommendations into effect, the removal of the Acadians in 1755 would not have taken place.

— and thus bind them to the British by strong ties of interest. Newcastle thought the plan good, but wrote that its execution must be deferred to a future day. Three years later it was partly carried into effect by the foundation of Halifax; but at that time the disaffection of the Acadians had so increased, and the hope of regaining the province for France had risen so high, that this partial and tardy assertion of British authority only spurred the French agents to redoubled efforts to draw the inhabitants from the allegiance they had sworn to the Crown of England.

Shirley had also other plans in view for turning the Acadians into good British subjects. He proposed, as a measure of prime necessity, to exclude French priests from the province. The free exercise of their religion had been insured to the inhabitants by the Treaty of Utrecht, and on this point the English authorities had given no just cause of complaint. A priest had occasionally been warned, suspended, or removed; but without a single exception, so far as appears, this was in consequence of conduct which tended to excite disaffection, and which would have incurred equal or greater penalties in the case of a layman.[1] The sentence was directed, not against

[1] There was afterwards sharp correspondence between Shirley and the governor of Canada touching the Acadian priests. Thus, Shirley writes: "I can't avoid now, Sir, expressing great surprise at the other parts of your letter, whereby you take upon you to call Mr. Mascarene to account for expelling the missionary from Minas for being guilty of such treasonable practices within His

the priest, but against the political agitator. Shirley's plan of excluding French priests from the province would not have violated the provisions of the treaty, provided that the inhabitants were supplied with other priests, not French subjects, and therefore not politically dangerous; but though such a measure was several times proposed by the provincial authorities, the exasperating apathy of the Newcastle Government gave no hope that it could be accomplished.

The influences most dangerous to British rule did not proceed from love of France or sympathy of race, but from the power of religion over a simple and ignorant people, trained in profound love and awe of their Church and its ministers, who were used by the representatives of Louis XV. as agents to alienate the Acadians from England.

The most strenuous of these clerical agitators was Abbé Le Loutre, missionary to the Micmacs, and after 1753 vicar-general of Acadia. He was a fiery and enterprising zealot, inclined by temperament to methods of violence, detesting the English, and restrained neither by pity nor scruple from using threats of damnation and the Micmac tomahawk to

Majesty's government as merited a much severer Punishment." *Shirley à Galissonière, 9 Mai,* 1749.

Shirley writes to Newcastle that the Acadians "are greatly under the influence of their priests, who continually receive their directions from the Bishop of Quebec, and are the instruments by which the governor of Canada makes all his attempts for the reduction of the province to the French Crown." *Shirley to Newcastle,* 20 *October,* 1747. He proceeds to give facts in proof of his assertion. Compare " Montcalm and Wolfe," i. 110, 111, 275, *note.*

frighten the Acadians into doing his bidding. The worst charge against him, that of exciting the Indians of his mission to murder Captain Howe, an English officer, has not been proved; but it would not have been brought against him by his own countrymen if his character and past conduct had gained him their esteem.

The other Acadian priests were far from sharing Le Loutre's violence; but their influence was always directed to alienating the inhabitants from their allegiance to King George. Hence Shirley regarded the conversion of the Acadians to Protestantism as a political measure of the first importance, and proposed the establishment of schools in the province to that end. Thus far his recommendations are perfectly legitimate; but when he adds that rewards ought to be given to Acadians who renounce their faith, few will venture to defend him.

Newcastle would trouble himself with none of his schemes, and Acadia was left to drift with the tide, as before. "I shall finish my troubleing your Grace upon the affairs of Nova Scotia with this letter," writes the persevering Shirley. And he proceeds to ask, "as a proper Scheme for better securing the Subjection of the French inhabitants and Indians there," that the governor and Council at Annapolis have special authority and direction from the King to arrest and examine such Acadians as shall be "most obnoxious and dangerous to his Majesty's Government;" and if found guilty of treasonable correspondence with the enemy, to dispose of them and their estates in such manner as his Majesty shall order, at the same time promising indemnity to the rest for past offences, upon their taking or renewing the oath of allegiance.[1]

To this it does not appear that Newcastle made any answer except to direct Shirley, eight or nine months later, to tell the Acadians that, so long as they were peaceable subjects, they should be protected in property and religion.[2] Thus left to struggle unaided with a most difficult problem, entirely outside of his functions as governor of Massachusetts, Shirley did what he could. The most pressing danger, as he thought, rose from the presence of Ramesay and his Canadians at Chignecto; for that officer spared no pains to induce the Acadians to join him in another attempt against Annapolis, telling them that if they did not drive out the English, the English would drive them out. He was now at Mines, trying to raise the inhabitants in arms for France. Shirley thought it necessary to counteract him, and force him and his Canadians back to the isthmus whence they had come; but as the ministry would give no soldiers, he was compelled to draw them from New England. The defence of Acadia

---

[1] *Shirley to Newcastle*, 15 *August*, 1746.

[2] *Newcastle to Shirley*, 30 *May*, 1747. Shirley had some time before directed Mascarene to tell the Acadians that while they behave peaceably and do not correspond with the enemy, their property will be safe, but that such as turn traitors will be treated accordingly. *Shirley to Mascarene*, 16 *September*, 1746.

was the business of the home government, and not of the colonies; but as they were deeply interested in the preservation of the endangered province, Massachusetts gave five hundred men in response to Shirley's call, and Rhode Island and New Hampshire added, between them, as many more. Less than half of these levies reached Acadia. It was the stormy season. The Rhode Island vessels were wrecked near Martha's Vineyard. A New Hampshire transport sloop was intercepted by a French armed vessel, and ran back to Portsmouth. Four hundred and seventy men from Massachusetts, under Colonel Arthur Noble, were all who reached Annapolis, whence they sailed for Mines, accompanied by a few soldiers of the garrison. Storms, drifting ice, and the furious tides of the Bay of Fundy made their progress so difficult and uncertain that Noble resolved to finish the journey by land; and on the fourth of December he disembarked near the place now called French Cross, at the foot of the North Mountain, — a lofty barrier of rock and forest extending along the southern shore of the Bay of Fundy. Without a path and without guides, the party climbed the snow-encumbered heights and toiled towards their destination, each man carrying provisions for fourteen days in his haversack. After sleeping eight nights without shelter among the snowdrifts, they reached the Acadian village of Grand Pré, the chief settlement of the district of Mines. Ramesay and his Canadians were gone. On learning the approach of an English force, he had tried to persuade the Acadians that they were to be driven from their homes, and that their only hope was in joining with him to meet force by force; but they trusted Shirley's recent assurance of protection, and replied that they would not break their oath of fidelity to King George. On this, Ramesay retreated to his old station at Chignecto, and Noble and his men occupied Grand Pré without opposition.

The village consisted of small, low wooden houses, scattered at intervals for the distance of a mile and a half, and therefore ill fitted for defence. The English had the frame of a blockhouse, or, as some say, of two blockhouses, ready to be set up on their arrival; but as the ground was hard frozen, it was difficult to make a foundation, and the frames were therefore stored in outbuildings of the village, with the intention of raising them in the spring. The vessels which had brought them, together with stores, ammunition, five small cannon, and a good supply of snow-shoes, had just arrived at the landing-place, — and here, with incredible fatuity, were allowed to remain, with most of their indispensable contents still on board. The men, meanwhile, were quartered in the Acadian houses.

Noble's position was critical, but he was assured that he could not be reached from Chignecto in such a bitter season; and this he was too ready to believe, though he himself had just made a march, which, if not so long, was quite as arduous. Yet he did not neglect every precaution, but kept out scouting-parties to range the surrounding country, while the rest of his men took their ease in the Acadian houses, living on the provisions of the villagers, for which payment was afterwards made. Some of the inhabitants, who had openly favored Ramesay and his followers, fled to the woods, in fear of the consequences; but the greater part remained quietly in the village.

At the head of the Bay of Fundy its waters form a fork, consisting of Chignecto Bay on the one hand, and Mines Basin on the other. At the head of Chignecto Bay was the Acadian settlement of Chignecto, or Beaubassin, in the houses of which Ramesay had quartered his Canadians. Here the neck of the Acadian peninsula is at its narrowest, the distance across to Baye Verte, where Ramesay had built a fort, being little more than twelve miles. Thus he controlled the isthmus, — from which, however, Noble hoped to dislodge him in the spring.

In the afternoon of the eighth of January an Acadian who had been sent to Mines by the missionary Germain, came to Beaubassin with the news that two hundred and twenty English were at Grand Pré, and that more were expected.[1] Ramesay instantly formed a plan of extraordinary hardihood, and resolved, by a rapid march and a night attack, to surprise the new-comers. His party was greatly

[1] Beaujeu, *Journal de la Campagne du Détachement de Canada à l'Acadie*, in *Le Canada Français*, ii. *Documents*, 16.

Saint-Luc de la Corne.

reduced by disease, and to recruit it he wrote to La Corne, Récollet missionary at Miramichi, to join him with his Indians; writing at the same time to Maillard, former colleague of Le Loutre at the mission of Shubenacadie, and to Girard, priest of Cobequid, to muster Indians, collect provisions, and gather information concerning the English. Meanwhile his Canadians busied themselves with making snow-shoes and dog-sledges for the march.

Ramesay could not command the expedition in person, as an accident to one of his knees had disabled him from marching. This was less to be regretted, in view of the quality of his officers, for he had with him the flower of the warlike Canadian *noblesse*, — Coulon de Villiers, who, seven years later, defeated Washington at Fort Necessity; Beaujeu, the future hero of the Monongahela, in appearance a carpet knight, in reality a bold and determined warrior; the Chevalier de la Corne, a model of bodily and mental hardihood; Saint-Pierre, Lanaudière, Saint-Ours, Desligneris, Courtemanche, Repentigny, Boishébert, Gaspé, Colombière, Marin, Lusignan, — all adepts in the warfare of surprise and sudden onslaught in which the Canadians excelled.

Coulon de Villiers commanded in Ramesay's place; and on the twenty-first of January he and the other officers led their men across the isthmus from Beaubassin to Baye Verte, where they all encamped in the woods, and where they were joined by a party of Indians and some Acadians from Beaubassin and Isle

St. Jean.[1] Provisions, ammunition, and other requisites were distributed, and at noon of the twenty-third they broke up their camp, marched three leagues, and bivouacked towards evening. On the next morning they marched again at daybreak. There was sharp cold, with a storm of snow, — not the large, moist, lazy flakes that fall peacefully and harmlessly, but those small crystalline particles that drive spitefully before the wind, and prick the cheek like needles. It was the kind of snow-storm called in Canada *la poudrerie*. They had hoped to make a long day's march; but feet and faces were freezing, and they were forced to stop, at noon, under such shelter as the thick woods of pine, spruce, and fir could supply. In the morning they marched again, following the border of the sea, their dog-teams dragging provisions and baggage over the broken ice of creeks and inlets, which they sometimes avoided by hewing paths through the forest. After a day of extreme fatigue they stopped at the small bay where the town of Wallace now stands. Beaujeu says: "While we were digging out the snow to make our huts, there came two Acadians with letters from MM. Maillard and Girard." The two priests sent a mixture of good and evil news. On one hand the English were more numerous than had been reported; on the other, they had not set up the blockhouses they had brought with them. Some Acadians of the neighboring settlement joined the party at this camp, as also did a few Indians.

[1] *Mascarene to Shirley*, 8 *February*, 1746 (1747, new style).

On the next morning, January 27, the adventurers stopped at the village of Tatmagouche, where they were again joined by a number of Acadians. After mending their broken sledges they resumed their march, and at five in the afternoon reached a place called Bacouel, at the beginning of the portage that led some twenty-five miles across the country to Cobequid, now Truro, at the head of Mines Basin. Here they were met by Girard, priest of Cobequid, from whom Coulon exacted a promise to meet him again at that village in two days. Girard gave the promise unwillingly, fearing, says Beaujeu, to embroil himself with the English authorities. He reported that the force at Grand Pré counted at least four hundred and fifty, or, as some said, more than five hundred. This startling news ran through the camp; but the men were not daunted. "The more there are," they said, "the more we shall kill."

The party spent the twenty-eighth in mending their damaged sledges, and in the afternoon they were joined by more Acadians and Indians. Thus reinforced, they marched again, and towards evening reached a village on the outskirts of Cobequid. Here the missionary Maillard joined them, — to the great satisfaction of Coulon, who relied on him and his brother priest Girard to procure supplies of provisions. Maillard promised to go himself to Grand Pré with the Indians of his mission.

The party rested for a day, and set out again on the first of February, stopped at Maillard's house in

Cobequid for the provisions he had collected for them, and then pushed on towards the river Shubenacadie, which runs from the south into Cobequid Bay, the head of Mines Basin. When they reached the river they found it impassable from floating ice, which forced them to seek a passage at some distance above. Coulon was resolved, however, that at any risk a detachment should cross at once, to stop the roads to Grand Pré, and prevent the English from being warned of his approach; for though the Acadians inclined to the French, and were eager to serve them when the risk was not too great, there were some of them who, from interest or fear, were ready to make favor with the English by carrying them intelligence. Boishébert, with ten Canadians, put out from shore in a canoe, and were near perishing among the drifting ice; but they gained the farther shore at last, and guarded every path to Grand Pré. The main body filed on snow-shoes up the east bank of the Shubenacadie, where the forests were choked with snow and encumbered with fallen trees, over which the sledges were to be dragged, to their great detriment. On this day, the third, they made five leagues; on the next only two, which brought them within half a league of Le Loutre's Micmac mission. Not far from this place the river was easily passable on the ice, and they continued their march westward across the country to the river Kennetcook by ways so difficult that their Indian guide lost the path, and for a time led them astray. On the seventh,

Boishébert and his party rejoined them, and brought a reinforcement of sixteen Indians, whom the Acadians had furnished with arms. Provisions were failing, till on the eighth, as they approached the village of Pisiquid, now Windsor, the Acadians, with great zeal, brought them a supply. They told them, too, that the English at Grand Pré were perfectly secure, suspecting no danger.

On the ninth, in spite of a cold, dry storm of snow, they reached the west branch of the river Avon. It was but seven French leagues to Grand Prè, which they hoped to reach before night; but fatigue compelled them to rest till the tenth. At noon of that day, the storm still continuing, they marched again, though they could hardly see their way for the driving snow. They soon came to a small stream, along the frozen surface of which they drew up in order, and, by command of Coulon, Beaujeu divided them all into ten parties, for simultaneous attacks on as many houses occupied by the English. Then, marching slowly, lest they should arrive too soon, they reached the river Gaspereau, which enters Mines Basin at Grand Pré. They were now but half a league from their destination. Here they stopped an hour in the storm, shivering and half frozen, waiting for nightfall. When it grew dark they moved again, and soon came to a number of houses on the river-bank. Each of the ten parties took possession of one of these, making great fires to warm themselves and dry their guns.

It chanced that in the house where Coulon and his band sought shelter, a wedding-feast was going on. The guests were much startled at this sudden irruption of armed men; but to the Canadians and their chief the festival was a stroke of amazing good luck, for most of the guests were inhabitants of Grand Pré, who knew perfectly the houses occupied by the English, and could tell with precision where the officers were quartered. This was a point of extreme importance. The English were distributed among twenty-four houses, scattered, as before mentioned, for the distance of a mile and a half.[1] The assailants were too few to attack all these houses at once; but if those where the chief officers lodged could be surprised and captured with their inmates, the rest could make little resistance. Hence it was that Coulon had divided his followers into ten parties, each with one or more chosen officers; these officers were now called together at the house of the interrupted festivity, and the late guests having given full information as to the position of the English quarters and the military quality of their inmates, a special object of attack was assigned to the officer of each party, with Acadian guides to conduct him to it. The principal party, consisting of fifty, or, as another account says, of seventy-five men, was led by Coulon himself, with Beaujeu, Desligneris, Mercier, Léry, and Lusignan as his officers. This

---

[1] *Goldthwait to Shirley*, 2 *March*, 1746 (1747). Captain Benjamin Goldthwait was second in command of the English detachment.

party was to attack a stone house near the middle of
the village, where the main guard was stationed, — a
building somewhat larger than the rest, and the only
one at all suited for defence. The second party, of
forty men, commanded by La Corne, with Rigauville,
Lagny, and Villemont, was to attack a neighboring
house, the quarters of Colonel Noble, his brother,
Ensign Noble, and several other officers. The remaining parties, of twenty-five men each according
to Beaujeu, or twenty-eight according to La Corne,
were to make a dash, as nearly as possible at the
same time, at other houses which it was thought most
important to secure. All had Acadian guides, whose
services in that capacity were invaluable; though
Beaujeu complains that they were of no use in the
attack. He says that the united force was about
three hundred men, while the English Captain
Goldthwait puts it, including Acadians and Indians,
at from five to six hundred. That of the English
was a little above five hundred in all. Every arrangement being made, and his part assigned to each
officer, the whole body was drawn up in the storm,
and the chaplain pronounced a general absolution.
Then each of the ten parties, guided by one or more
Acadians, took the path for its destination, every
man on snow-shoes, with the lock of his gun well
sheltered under his capote.

The largest party, under Coulon, was, as we
have seen, to attack the stone house in the middle of
the village; but their guide went astray, and about

three in the morning they approached a small wooden
house not far from their true object. A guard was
posted here, as at all the English quarters. The
night was dark and the snow was still falling, as it
had done without ceasing for the past thirty hours.
The English sentinel descried through the darkness
and the storm what seemed the shadows of an advancing crowd of men. He cried, "Who goes there?"
and then shouted, "To arms!" A door was flung
open, and the guard appeared in the entrance. But
at that moment the moving shadows vanished from
before the eyes of the sentinel. The French, one
and all, had thrown themselves flat in the soft, light
snow, and nothing was to be seen or heard. The
English thought it a false alarm, and the house was
quiet again. Then Coulon and his men rose and
dashed forward. Again, in a loud and startled
voice, the sentinel shouted, "To arms!" A great
light, as of a blazing fire, shone through the open
doorway, and men were seen within in hurried movement. Coulon, who was in the front, said to
Beaujeu, who was close at his side, that the house
was not the one they were to attack. Beaujeu replied that it was no time to change, and Coulon
dashed forward again. Beaujeu aimed at the sentinel and shot him dead. There was the flash and
report of muskets from the house, and Coulon
dropped in the snow, severely wounded. The young
cadet, Lusignan, was hit in the shoulder; but he still
pushed on, when a second shot shattered his thigh.

"Friends," cried the gallant youth, as he fell by the side of his commander, "don't let two dead men discourage you." The Canadians, powdered from head to foot with snow, burst into the house. Within ten minutes, all resistance was overpowered. Of twenty-four Englishmen, twenty-one were killed, and three made prisoners.[1]

Meanwhile, La Corne, with his party of forty men, had attacked the house where were quartered Colonel Noble and his brother, with Captain Howe and several other officers. Noble had lately transferred the main guard to the stone house, but had not yet removed thither himself, and the guard in the house which he occupied was small. The French burst the door with axes, and rushed in. Colonel Noble, startled from sleep, sprang from his bed, receiving two musket-balls in the body as he did so. He seems to have had pistols, for he returned the fire several times. His servant, who was in the house, testified that the French called to the colonel through a window and promised him quarter if he would surrender; but that he refused, on which they fired again, and a bullet, striking his forehead, killed him instantly. His brother, Ensign Noble, was also shot down, fighting in his shirt. Lieutenants Pickering and Lechmere lay in bed dangerously ill, and were killed there. Lieutenant Jones, after, as the narrator says, "ridding himself of some of the enemy," tried to break through the rest and escape, but was run

[1] Beaujeu, *Journal.*

through the heart with a bayonet. Captain Howe was severely wounded and made prisoner.

Coulon and Lusignan, disabled by their wounds, were carried back to the houses on the Gaspereau, where the French surgeon had remained. Coulon's party, now commanded by Beaujeu, having met and joined the smaller party under Lotbinière, proceeded to the aid of others who might need their help; for while they heard a great noise of musketry from far and near, and could discern bodies of men in motion here and there, they could not see whether these were friends or foes, or discern which side fortune favored. They presently met the party of Marin, composed of twenty-five Indians, who had just been repulsed with loss from the house which they had attacked. By this time there was a gleam of daylight, and as they plodded wearily over the snowdrifts, they no longer groped in darkness. The two parties of Colombière and Boishébert soon joined them, with the agreeable news that each had captured a house; and the united force now proceeded to make a successful attack on two buildings where the English had stored the frames of their blockhouses. Here the assailants captured ten prisoners. It was now broad day, but they could not see through the falling snow whether the enterprise, as a whole, had prospered or failed. Therefore Beaujeu sent Marin to find La Corne, who, in the absence of Coulon, held the chief command. Marin was gone two hours. At length he returned, and reported that the English in the houses

which had not been attacked, together with such others as had not been killed or captured, had drawn together at the stone house in the middle of the village, that La Corne was blockading them there, and that he ordered Beaujeu and his party to join him at once. When Beaujeu reached the place he found La Corne posted at the house where Noble had been killed, and which was within easy musket-shot of the stone house occupied by the English, against whom a spattering fire was kept up by the French from the cover of neighboring buildings. Those in the stone house returned the fire; but no great harm was done on either side, till the English, now commanded by Captain Goldthwait, attempted to recapture the house where La Corne and his party were posted. Two companies made a sally; but they had among them only eighteen pairs of snow-shoes, the rest having been left on board the two vessels which had brought the stores of the detachment from Annapolis, and which now lay moored hard by, in the power of the enemy, at or near the mouth of the Gaspereau. Hence the sallying party floundered helpless among the drifts, plunging so deep in the dry snow that they could not use their guns and could scarcely move, while bullets showered upon them from La Corne's men in the house, and others hovering about them on snow-shoes. The attempt was hopeless, and after some loss the two companies fell back. The firing continued, as before, till noon, or, according to Beaujeu, till three in the afternoon, when a French officer, carrying a flag of truce, came out of La Corne's house. The occasion of the overture was this.

Captain Howe, who, as before mentioned, had been badly wounded at the capture of this house, was still there, a prisoner, without surgical aid, the French surgeon being at the houses on the Gaspereau, in charge of Coulon and other wounded men. "Though," says Beaujeu, "M. Howe was a firm man, he begged the Chevalier La Corne not to let him bleed to death for want of aid, but permit him to send for an English surgeon." To this La Corne, after consulting with his officers, consented, and Marin went to the English with a white flag and a note from Howe explaining the situation. The surgeon was sent, and Howe's wound was dressed, Marin remaining as a hostage. A suspension of arms took place till the surgeon's return; after which it was prolonged till nine o'clock of the next morning, at the instance, according to French accounts, of the English, and, according to English accounts, of the French. In either case, the truce was welcome to both sides. The English, who were in the stone house to the number of nearly three hundred and fifty, crowded to suffocation, had five small cannon, two of which were four-pounders, and three were swivels; but these were probably not in position, as it does not appear that any use was made of them. There was no ammunition except what the men had in their powder-horns and bullet-pouches, the main stock having been left, with other necessaries, on board the schooner and sloop now in the hands of the French. It was found, on examination, that they had ammunition for eight shots each, and provisions for one day. Water was only to be had by bringing it from a neighboring brook. As there were snow-shoes for only about one man in twenty, sorties were out of the question; and the house was commanded by high ground on three sides.

Though their number was still considerable, their position was growing desperate. Thus it happened that when the truce expired, Goldthwait, the English commander, with another officer, who seems to have been Captain Preble, came with a white flag to the house where La Corne was posted, and proposed terms of capitulation, Howe, who spoke French, acting as interpreter. La Corne made proposals on his side, and as neither party was anxious to continue the fray, they soon came to an understanding.

It was agreed that within forty-eight hours the English should march for Annapolis with the honors of war; that the prisoners taken by the French should remain in their hands; that the Indians, who had been the only plunderers, should keep the plunder they had taken; that the English sick and wounded should be left, till their recovery, at the neighboring settlement of Rivière-aux-Canards, protected by a French guard, and that the English engaged in the affair at Grand Pré should not bear arms during the next six months within the district about the head of the Bay of Fundy, including Chignecto, Grand Pré, and the neighboring settlements.

Captain Howe was released on parole, with the condition that he should send back in exchange one Lacroix, a French prisoner at Boston, — "which," says La Corne, "he faithfully did."

Thus ended one of the most gallant exploits in French-Canadian annals. As respects the losses on each side, the French and English accounts are irreconcilable; nor are the statements of either party consistent with themselves. Mascarene reports to Shirley that seventy English were killed, and above sixty captured; though he afterwards reduces these numbers, having, as he says, received farther information. On the French side he says that four officers and about forty men were killed, and that many wounded were carried off in carts during the fight. Beaujeu, on the other hand, sets the English loss at one hundred and thirty killed, fifteen wounded, and fifty captured; and the French loss at seven killed and fifteen wounded. As for the numbers engaged, the statements are scarcely less divergent. It seems clear, however, that when Coulon began his march from Baye Verte, his party consisted of about three hundred Canadians and Indians, without reckoning some Acadians who had joined him from Beaubassin and Isle St. Jean. Others joined him on the way to Grand Pré, counting a hundred and fifty according to Shirley, — which appears to be much too large an estimate. The English, by their own showing, numbered five hundred, or five hundred and twenty-five. Of eleven houses attacked, ten were surprised and carried, with the help of the darkness and storm and the skilful management of the assailants.

"No sooner was the capitulation signed," says Beaujeu, "than we became in appearance the best of friends." La Corne directed military honors to be rendered to the remains of the brothers Noble; and in all points the Canadians, both officers and men, treated the English with kindness and courtesy. "The English commandant," again says Beaujeu, "invited us all to dine with him and his officers, so that we might have the pleasure of making acquaintance over a bowl of punch." The repast being served after such a fashion as circumstances permitted, victors and vanquished sat down together; when, says Beaujeu, "we received on the part of our hosts many compliments on our polite manners and our skill in making war." And the compliments were well deserved.

At eight o'clock on the morning of the fourteenth of February the English filed out of the stone house, and with arms shouldered, drums beating, and colors flying, marched between two ranks of the French, and took the road for Annapolis. The English sick and wounded were sent to the settlement of Rivière-aux-Canards, where, protected by a French guard and attended by an English surgeon, they were to remain till able to reach the British fort.

La Corne called a council of war, and in view of
the scarcity of food and other reasons it was resolved
to return to Beaubassin. Many of the French had
fallen ill. Some of the sick and wounded were left
at Grand Pré, others at Cobequid, and the Acadians
were required to supply means of carrying the rest.
Coulon's party left Grand Pré on the twenty-third
of February, and on the eighth of March reached
Beaubassin.[1]

Ramesay did not fail to use the success at Grand
Pré to influence the minds of the Acadians. He sent
a circular letter to the inhabitants of the various
districts, and especially to those of Mines, in which

[1] The dates are of the new style, which the French had adopted,
while the English still clung to the old style.

By far the best account of this French victory at Mines is that
of Beaujeu, in his *Journal de la Campagne du Détachement de Canada
à l'Acadie et aux Mines en* 1746–47. It is preserved in the Archives
de la Marine et des Colonies, and is printed in the documentary
supplement of *Le Canada Français*, Vol. II. It supplies the means
of correcting many errors and much confusion in some recent accounts of the affair. The report of Chevalier de la Corne, also
printed in *Le Canada Français*, though much shorter, is necessary
to a clear understanding of the matter. Letters of Lusignan fils
to the minister Maurepas, 10 October, 1747, of Bishop Pontbriand
(to Maurepas?), 10 July, 1747, and of Lusignan père to Maurepas,
10 October, 1747, give some additional incidents. The principal
document on the English side is the report of Captain Benjamin
Goldthwait, who succeeded Noble in command. A copy of the
original, in the Public Record Office, is before me. The substance of
it is correctly given in *The Boston Post Boy* of 2 March, 1747, and
in *N. E. Hist. Gen. Reg.* x. 108. Various letters from Mascarene
and Shirley (Public Record Office) contain accounts derived from
returned officers and soldiers. The *Notice of Colonel Arthur Noble*,
by William Goold (*Collections Maine Historical Soc.*, 1881), may
also be consulted.

he told them that their country had been reconquered by the arms of the King of France, to whom he commanded them to be faithful subjects, holding no intercourse with the English under any pretence whatever, on pain of the severest punishment. "If," he concludes, "we have withdrawn our soldiers from among you, it is for reasons known to us alone, and with a view to your advantage." [1]

Unfortunately for the effect of this message, Shirley had no sooner heard of the disaster at Grand Pré than he sent a body of Massachusetts soldiers to reoccupy the place. [2] This they did in April. The Acadians thus found themselves, as usual, between two dangers; and unable to see which horn of the dilemma was the worse, they tried to avoid both by conciliating French and English alike, and assuring each of their devoted attachment. They sent a pathetic letter to Ramesay, telling him that their hearts were always French, and begging him at the same time to remember that they were a poor, helpless people, burdened with large families, and in danger of expulsion and ruin if they offended their masters, the English. [3]

[1] *Ramesay aux Députés et Habitants des Mines,* 31 *Mars,* 1747. At the end is written "A true copy, with the misspellings : signed W. Shirley."

[2] *Shirley to Newcastle,* 24 *August,* 1747.

[3] "Ainsis Monsieur nous vous prions de regarder notre bon Coeur et en meme Temps notre Impuissance pauvre Peuple chargez la plus part de familles nombreuse point de Recours sil falois evacuer a quoy nous sommes menacez tous les jours qui nous tien dans une Crainte perpetuelle en nous voyant a la proximitet de nos maitre depuis un sy grand nombre dannes " (printed *literatim*) — *Deputés des Mines à Ramesay,* 24 *Mai,* 1747.

They wrote at the same time to Mascarene at Annapolis, sending him, to explain the situation, a copy of Ramesay's threatening letter to them;[1] begging him to consider that they could not without danger dispense with answering it; at the same time they protested their entire fidelity to King George.[2]

Ramesay, not satisfied with the results of his first letter, wrote again to the Acadians, ordering them, in the name of the governor-general of New France, to take up arms against the English, and enclosing for their instruction an extract from a letter of the French governor. "These," says Ramesay, "are his words: ' We consider ourself as master of Beaubassin and Mines, since we have driven off the English. Therefore there is no difficulty in forcing the Acadians to take arms for us; to which end we declare to them that they are discharged from the oath that they formerly took to the English, by which they are bound no longer, as has been decided by the authorities of Canada and Monseigneur our Bishop.' "[3]

---

[1] This probably explains the bad spelling of the letter, the copy before me having been made from the Acadian transcript sent to Mascarene, and now in the Public Record Office.

[2] *Les Habitants à l'honorable gouverneur au for d'anapolisse royal* [sic], *Mai* (?), 1747.

On the 27th of June the inhabitants of Cobequid wrote again to Mascarene: "Monsieur nous prenons la Liberte de vous recrire celle icy pour vous assurer de nos tres humble Respect et d'un entiere Sou-mission a vos Ordres" (*literatim*).

[3] "Nous nous regardons aujourdhuy Maistre de Beaubassin et des Mines puisque nous en avons Chassé les Anglois ; ainsi il ny a aucune difficulté de forcer les Accadiens à prendre les armes pour nous, et de les y Contraindre ; leur declarons à cet effêt qu'ils sont

"In view of the above," continues Ramesay, "we order all the inhabitants of Memeramcook to come to this place [Beaubassin] as soon as they see the signal-fires lighted, or discover the approach of the enemy; and this on pain of death, confiscation of all their goods, burning of their houses, and the punishment due to rebels against the King." [1]

The position of the Acadians was deplorable. By the Treaty of Utrecht, France had transferred them to the British Crown; yet French officers denounced them as rebels and threatened them with death if they did not fight at their bidding against England; and English officers threatened them with expulsion from the country if they broke their oath of allegiance to King George. It was the duty of the British ministry to occupy the province with a force sufficient to protect the inhabitants against French terrorism, and leave no doubt that the King of England was master of Acadia in fact as well as in name. This alone could have averted the danger of Acadian revolt, and the harsh measures to which it afterwards

decharge [*sic*] du Serment prete, cy devant, à l'Anglois, auquel ils ne sont plus oblige [*sic*] comme il y a été decidé par nos puissances de Canada et de Monseigneur notre Evesque " (*literatim*).

[1] *Ramesay aux Habitants de Chignecto, etc.,* 25 *Mai,* 1747.

A few months later, the deputies of Rivière-aux-Canards wrote to Shirley, thanking him for kindness which they said was undeserved, promising to do their duty thenceforth, but begging him to excuse them from giving up persons who had acted " contraire aux Interests de leur devoire," representing the difficulty of their position, and protesting " une Soumission parfaite et en touts Respects." The letter is signed by four deputies, of whom one writes his name, and three sign with crosses.

gave rise. The ministry sent no aid, but left to Shirley and Massachusetts the task of keeping the province for King George. Shirley and Massachusetts did what they could; but they could not do all that the emergency demanded.

Shirley courageously spoke his mind to the ministry, on whose favor he was dependent. "The fluctuating state of the inhabitants of Acadia," he wrote to Newcastle, "seems, my lord, naturally to arise from their finding a want of due protection from his Majesty's Government."[1]

[1] *Shirley to Newcastle, 29 April,* 1747.
On Shirley's relations with the Acadians, *see* Appendix C.

CHAPTER XXIII.

1740–1747.

WAR AND POLITICS.

GOVERNOR AND ASSEMBLY. — SARATOGA DESTROYED. — WILLIAM JOHNSON. — BORDER RAVAGES. — UPPER ASHUELOT. — FRENCH "MILITARY MOVEMENTS." — NUMBER FOUR. — NIVERVILLE'S ATTACK. — PHINEAS STEVENS. — THE FRENCH REPULSED.

FROM the East we turn to the West, for the province of New York passed for the West at that day. Here a vital question was what would be the attitude of the Five Nations of the Iroquois towards the rival European colonies, their neighbors. The Treaty of Utrecht called them British subjects. What the word "subjects" meant, they themselves hardly knew. The English told them that it meant children; the French that it meant dogs and slaves. Events had tamed the fierce confederates; and now, though, like all savages, unstable as children, they leaned in their soberer moments to a position of neutrality between their European neighbors, watching with jealous eyes against the encroachments of both. The French would gladly have enlisted them and their tomahawks in the war; but seeing little hope of this, were generally content if they could prevent them from siding with the English, who on their part regarded them as their Indians, and were satisfied with nothing less than active alliance.

When Shirley's plan for the invasion of Canada was afoot, Clinton, governor of New York, with much ado succeeded in convening the deputies of the confederacy at Albany, and by dint of speeches and presents induced them to sing the war-song and take up the hatchet for England. The Iroquois were disgusted when the scheme came to nought, their warlike ardor cooled, and they conceived a low opinion of English prowess.

The condition of New York as respects military efficiency was deplorable. She was divided against herself, and, as usual in such cases, party passion was stronger than the demands of war. The province was in the midst of one of those disputes with the representative of the Crown, which, in one degree or another, crippled or paralyzed the military activity of nearly all the British colonies. Twenty years or more earlier, when Massachusetts was at blows with the Indians on her borders, she suffered from the same disorders; but her governor and Assembly were of one mind as to urging on the war, and quarrelled only on the questions in what way and under what command it should be waged. But in New York there was a strong party that opposed the war, being interested in the contraband trade long carried on with Canada. Clinton, the governor, had, too, an enemy in the person of the chief justice, James de

Lancey, with whom he had had an after-dinner dispute, ending in a threat on the part of De Lancey that he would make the governor's seat uncomfortable. To marked abilities, better education, and more knowledge of the world than was often found in the provinces, ready wit, and conspicuous social position, the chief justice joined a restless ambition and the arts of a demagogue.

He made good his threat, headed the opposition to the governor, and proved his most formidable antagonist. If either Clinton or Shirley had had the independent authority of a Canadian governor, the conduct of the war would have been widely different. Clinton was hampered at every turn. The Assembly held him at advantage; for it was they, and not the King, who paid his salary, and they could withhold or retrench it when he displeased them. The people sympathized with their representatives and backed them in opposition, — at least, when not under the stress of imminent danger.

A body of provincials, in the pay of the King, had been mustered at Albany for the proposed Canada expedition; and after that plan was abandoned, Clinton wished to use them for protecting the northern frontier and capturing that standing menace to the province, Crown Point. The Assembly, bent on crossing him at any price, refused to provide for transporting supplies farther than Albany. As the furnishing of provisions and transportation depended on that body, they could stop the movement of troops

and defeat the governor's military plans at their
pleasure.   In vain he told them, "If you deny me
the necessary supplies, all my endeavors must become
fruitless; I must wash my own hands, and leave at
your doors the blood of the innocent people." [1]

He urged upon them the necessity of building forts
on the two carrying-places between the Hudson and
Lakes George and Champlain, thus blocking the
path of war-parties from Canada.   They would do
nothing, insisting that the neighboring colonies, to
whom the forts would also be useful, ought to help
in building them; and when it was found that these
colonies were ready to do their part, the Assembly
still refused.   Passionate opposition to the royal governor seemed to blind them to the interests of the
province.   Nor was the fault all on their side; for
the governor, though he generally showed more self-
control and moderation than could have been expected,
sometimes lost temper and betrayed scorn for his
opponents, many of whom were but the instruments
of leaders urged by personal animosities and small
but intense ambitions.   They accused him of treating
them with contempt, and of embezzling public money;
while he retorted by charging them with encroaching
on the royal prerogative and treating the representative of the King with indecency.   Under such conditions an efficient conduct of the war was out of the
question.

[1] *Extract from the Governor's Message,* in Smith, *History of New
York,* ii. 124 (1830).

Once, when the frontier was seriously threatened, Clinton, as commander-in-chief, called out the militia to defend it; but they refused to obey, on the ground that no Act of the Assembly required them to do so.[1]

Clinton sent home bitter complaints to Newcastle and the Lords of Trade. "They [the Assembly] are selfish, jealous of the power of the Crown, and of such levelling principles that they are constantly attacking its prerogative. . . . I find that neither dissolutions nor fair means can produce from them such Effects as will tend to a publick good or their own preservation. They will neither act for themselves nor assist their neighbors. . . . Few but hirelings have a seat in the Assembly, who protract time for the sake of their wages, at a great expence to the Province, without contributing anything material for its welfare, credit, or safety." And he declares that unless Parliament takes them in hand he can do nothing for the service of the King or the good of the province,[2] for they want to usurp the whole administration, both civil and military.[3]

At Saratoga there was a small settlement of Dutch farmers, with a stockade fort for their protection.

---

[1] *Clinton to the Lords of Trade*, 10 *November*, 1747.

[2] *Ibid.*, 30 *November*, 1745.

[3] *Remarks on the Representation of the Assembly of New York, May,* 1747, in *N. Y. Col. Docs.*, vi. 365. On the disputes of the governor and Assembly see also Smith, *History of New York*, ii. (1830), and Stone, *Life and Times of Sir William Johnson*, i. *N. Y. Colonial Documents*, vi., contains many papers on the subject, chiefly on the governor's side.

This was the farthest outpost of the colony, and the only defence of Albany in the direction of Canada. It was occupied by a sergeant, a corporal, and ten soldiers, who testified before a court of inquiry that it was in such condition that in rainy weather neither they nor their ammunition could be kept dry. As neither the Assembly nor the merchants of Albany would make it tenable, the garrison was withdrawn before winter by order of the governor.[1]

Scarcely was this done when five hundred French and Indians, under the partisan Marin, surprised the settlement in the night of the twenty-eighth of November, burned fort, houses, mills, and stables, killed thirty persons, and carried off about a hundred prisoners.[2] Albany was left uncovered, and the Assembly voted £150 in provincial currency to rebuild the ruined fort. A feeble palisade work was accordingly set up, but it was neglected like its predecessor. Colonel Peter Schuyler was stationed there with his regiment in 1747, but was forced to abandon his post for want of supplies. Clinton then directed Colonel Roberts, commanding at Albany, to examine

[1] *Examinations at a Court of Inquiry at Albany*, 11 *December*, 1745, in *N. Y. Col. Docs.*, vi. 374.

[2] The best account of this affair is in the journal of a French officer in Schuyler, *Colonial New York*, ii. 115. The dates, being in new style, differ by eleven days from those of the English accounts. The Dutch hamlet of Saratoga, surprised by Marin, was near the mouth of the Fish Kill, on the west side of the Hudson. There was also a small fort on the east side, a little below the mouth of the Batten Kill.

the fort, and if he found it indefensible, to burn it,
— which he did, much to the astonishment of a
French war-party, who visited the place soon after,
and found nothing but ashes.[1]

The burning of Saratoga, first by the French and
then by its own masters, made a deep impression on
the Five Nations, and a few years later they taunted
their white neighbors with these shortcomings in no
measured terms. "You burned your own fort at
Seraghtoga and ran away from it, which was a shame
and a scandal to you."[2] Uninitiated as they were in
party politics and faction quarrels, they could see
nothing in this and other military lapses but proof of
a want of martial spirit, if not of cowardice. Hence
the difficulty of gaining their active alliance against
the French was redoubled. Fortunately for the province, the adverse influence was in some measure
counteracted by the character and conduct of one
man. Up to this time the French had far surpassed
the rival nation in the possession of men ready and
able to deal with the Indians and mould them to
their will. Eminent among such was Joncaire,
French emissary among the Senecas in western New
York, who, with admirable skill, held back that
powerful member of the Iroquois league from siding
with the English. But now, among the Mohawks of
eastern New York, Joncaire found his match in the
person of William Johnson, a vigorous and intelli-

[1] Schuyler, *Colonial New York*, ii. 121.
[2] *Report of a Council with the Indians at Albany*, 28 *June*, 1754.

gent young Irishman, nephew of Admiral Warren, and his agent in the management of his estates on the Mohawk. Johnson soon became intimate with his Indian neighbors, spoke their language, joined in their games and dances, sometimes borrowed their dress and their paint, and whooped, yelped, and stamped like one of themselves. A white man thus playing the Indian usually gains nothing in the esteem of those he imitates; but, as before in the case of the redoubtable Count Frontenac, Johnson's adoption of their ways increased their liking for him and did not diminish their respect. The Mohawks adopted him into their tribe and made him a war-chief. Clinton saw his value; and as the Albany commissioners hitherto charged with Indian affairs had proved wholly inefficient, he transferred their functions to Johnson; whence arose more heart-burnings. The favor of the governor cost the new functionary the support of the Assembly, who refused the indispensable presents to the Indians, and thus vastly increased the difficulty of his task. Yet the Five Nations promised to take up the hatchet against the French, and their orator said, in a conference at Albany, "Should any French priests now dare to come among us, we know no use for them but to roast them." [1] Johnson's present difficulties, however, sprang more from Dutch and English traders than from French priests, and he begs that an Act

---

[1] *Answer of the Six [Five] Nations to His Excellency the Governor at Albany, 23 August,* 1746.

may be passed against the selling of liquor to the
Indians, "as it is impossible to do anything with them
while there is such a plenty to be had all round the
neighborhood, being forever drunk." And he complains especially of one Clement, who sells liquor
within twenty yards of Johnson's house, and immediately gets from the Indians all the bounty money
they receive for scalps, "which leaves them as poor
as ratts," and therefore refractory and unmanageable.
Johnson says further: "There is another grand vil-
lain, George Clock, who lives by Conajoharie Castle,
and robs the Indians of all their cloaths, etc." The
chiefs complained, "upon which I wrote him twice to
give over that custom of selling liquor to the Indians;
the answer was he gave the bearer, I might hang
myself." [1] Indian affairs, it will be seen, were no
better regulated then than now.

Meanwhile the French Indians were ravaging the
frontiers and burning farmhouses to within sight of
Albany. The Assembly offered rewards for the
scalps of the marauders, but were slow in sending
money to pay them, — to the great discontent of the
Mohawks, who, however, at Johnson's instigation,
sent out various war-parties, two of which, accompanied by a few whites, made raids as far as the island
of Montreal, and somewhat checked the incursions of
the mission Indians by giving them work near home.
The check was but momentary. Heathen Indians
from the West joined the Canadian converts, and the

[1] *Johnson to Clinton, 7 May, 1747.*

frontiers of New York and New England, from the Mohawk to beyond the Kennebec, were stung through all their length by innumerable nocturnal surprises and petty attacks. The details of this murderous though ineffective partisan war would fill volumes, if they were worth recording. One or two examples will show the nature of all.

In the valley of the little river Ashuelot, a New Hampshire affluent of the Connecticut, was a rude border-settlement which later years transformed into a town noted in rural New England for kindly hospitality, culture without pretence, and good-breeding without conventionality.[1] In 1746 the place was in all the rawness and ugliness of a backwoods hamlet. The rough fields, lately won from the virgin forest, showed here and there, among the stumps, a few log-cabins, roofed with slabs of pine, spruce, or hemlock. Near by was a wooden fort, made, no doubt, after the common frontier pattern, of a stockade fence ten or twelve feet high, enclosing cabins to shelter the settlers in case of alarm, and furnished at the corners with what were called flankers, which were boxes of thick plank large enough to hold two or more men, raised above the ground on posts, and pierced with loopholes, so that each face of the stockade could be swept by a flank fire. One corner of this fort at

---

[1] Keene, originally called Upper Ashuelot. On the same stream, a few miles below, was a similar settlement, called Lower Ashuelot, — the germ of the present Swanzey. This, too, suffered greatly from Indian attacks.

Ashuelot was, however, guarded by a solid block-house, or, as it was commonly called, a "mount."

On the twenty-third of April a band of sixty, or, by another account, a hundred Indians, approached the settlement before daybreak, and hid in the neighboring thickets to cut off the men in the fort as they came out to their morning work. One of the men, Ephraim Dorman, chanced to go out earlier than the rest. The Indians did not fire on him, but, not to give an alarm, tried to capture or kill him without noise. Several of them suddenly showed themselves, on which he threw down his gun in pretended submission. One of them came up to him with hatchet raised; but the nimble and sturdy borderer suddenly struck him with his fist a blow in the head that knocked him flat, then snatched up his own gun, and, as some say, the blanket of the half-stunned savage also, sprang off, reached the fort unhurt, and gave the alarm. Some of the families of the place were living in the fort; but the bolder or more careless still remained in their farmhouses, and if nothing were done for their relief, their fate was sealed. Therefore the men sallied in a body, and a sharp fight ensued, giving the frightened settlers time to take refuge within the stockade. It was not too soon, for the work of havoc had already begun. Six houses and a barn were on fire, and twenty-three cattle had been killed. The Indians fought fiercely, killed John Bullard, and captured Nathan Blake, but at last retreated; and after they were gone, the charred remains of several of them were found among the ruins of one of the burned cabins, where they had probably been thrown to prevent their being scalped.

Before Dorman had given the alarm, an old woman, Mrs. McKenney, went from the fort to milk her cow in a neighboring barn. As she was returning, with her full milk-pail, a naked Indian was seen to spring from a clump of bushes, plunge a long knife into her back, and dart away without stopping to take the gray scalp of his victim. She tried feebly to reach the fort; but from age, corpulence, and a mortal wound she moved but slowly, and when a few steps from the gate, fell and died.

Ten days after, a party of Indians hid themselves at night by this same fort, and sent one of their number to gain admission under pretence of friendship, intending, no doubt, to rush in when the gate should be opened; but the man on guard detected the trick, and instead of opening the gate, fired through it, mortally wounding the Indian, on which his confederates made off. Again, at the same place, Deacon Josiah Foster, who had taken refuge in the fort, ventured out on a July morning to drive his cows to pasture. A gunshot was heard; and the men who went out to learn the cause, found the deacon lying in the wood-road, dead and scalped. An ambushed Indian had killed him and vanished. Such petty attacks were without number.

There is a French paper, called a record of "military movements," which gives a list of war-parties sent from Montreal against the English border between the twenty-ninth of March, 1746, and the twenty-first of June in the same year. They number thirty-five distinct bands, nearly all composed of mission Indians living in or near the settled parts of Canada, — Abenakis, Iroquois of the Lake of Two Mountains and of Sault St. Louis (Caughnawaga), Algonquins of the Ottawa, and others, in parties rarely of more than thirty, and often of no more than six, yet enough for waylaying travellers or killing women in kitchens or cow-sheds, and solitary laborers in the fields. This record is accompanied by a list of wild Western Indians who came down to Montreal in the summer of 1746 to share in these "military movements."[1]

No part of the country suffered more than the western borders of Massachusetts and New Hampshire, and here were seen too plainly the evils of the prevailing want of concert among the British colonies. Massachusetts claimed extensive tracts north of her present northern boundary, and in the belief that her claim would hold good, had built a small wooden fort, called Fort Dummer, on the Connecticut, for the protection of settlers. New Hampshire disputed the title, and the question, being referred to the Crown, was decided in her favor. On this, Massachusetts withdrew the garrison of Fort Dummer and

---

[1] *Extrait sur les différents Mouvements Militaires qui se sont faits à Montréal à l'occasion de la Guerre,* 1745, 1746. There is a translation in *N. Y. Col. Docs.*

left New Hampshire to defend her own. This the
Assembly of that province refused to do, on the
ground that the fort was fifty miles from any settlement made by New Hampshire people, and was therefore useless to them, though of great value to
Massachusetts as a cover to Northfield and other of
her settlements lower down the Connecticut, to
protect[1] which was no business of New Hampshire.
But some years before, in 1740, three brothers,
Samuel, David, and Stephen Farnsworth, natives of
Groton, Massachusetts, had begun a new settlement
on the Connecticut about forty-five miles north of
the Massachusetts line and on ground which was
soon to be assigned to New Hampshire. They were
followed by five or six others. They acted on the
belief that their settlement was within the jurisdic-
tion of Massachusetts, and that she could and would
protect them. The place was one of extreme exposure, not only from its isolation, far from help, but
because it was on the banks of a wild and lonely
river, the customary highway of war-parties on their
descent from Canada. Number Four — for so the
new settlement was called, because it was the fourth
in a range of townships recently marked out along
the Connecticut, but, with one or two exceptions,
wholly unoccupied as yet — was a rude little outpost
of civilization, buried in forests that spread unbroken
to the banks of the St. Lawrence, while its nearest

[1] *Journal of the Assembly of New Hampshire,* quoted in Saunderson, *History of Charlestown, N. H.,* 20.

English neighbor was nearly thirty miles away. As may be supposed, it grew slowly, and in 1744 it had but nine or ten families. In the preceding year, when war seemed imminent, and it was clear that neither Massachusetts nor New Hampshire would lend a helping hand, the settlers of Number Four, seeing that their only resource was in themselves, called a meeting to consider the situation and determine what should be done. The meeting was held at the house, or log-cabin, of John Spafford, Jr., and being duly called to order, the following resolutions were adopted: that a fort be built at the charge of the proprietors of the said township of Number Four; that John Hastings, John Spafford, and John Avery be a committee to direct the building; that each carpenter be allowed nine shillings, old tenor, a day, each laborer seven shillings, and each pair of oxen three shillings and sixpence; that the proprietors of the township be taxed in the sum of three hundred pounds, old tenor, for building the fort; that John Spafford, Phineas Stevens, and John Hastings be assessors to assess the same, and Samuel Farnsworth collector to collect it.[1] And to the end that their fort should be a good and creditable one, they are said to have engaged the services of John Stoddard, accounted the foremost man of western Massachusetts, Superintendent of Defence, Colonel of Militia, Judge of Probate, Chief Justice

[1] Extracts from the Town Record, in Saunderson, *History of Charlestown, N. H. (Number Four)*, 17, 18.

of the Court of Common Pleas, a reputed authority in the construction of backwoods fortifications, and the admired owner of the only gold watch in Northampton.

Timber was abundant and could be had for the asking; for the frontiersman usually regarded a tree less as a valuable possession than as a natural enemy, to be got rid of by fair means or foul. The only cost was the labor. The fort rose rapidly. It was a square enclosing about three quarters of an acre, each side measuring a hundred and eighty feet. The wall was not of palisades, as was more usual, but of squared logs laid one upon another, and interlocked at the corners after the fashion of a log-cabin. Within were several houses, which had been built close together, for mutual protection, before the fort was begun, and which belonged to Stevens, Spafford, and other settlers. Apparently they were small log-cabins; for they were valued at only from eight to thirty-five pounds each, in old tenor currency wofully attenuated by depreciation; and these sums being paid to the owners out of the three hundred pounds collected for building the fort, the cabins became public property. Either they were built in a straight line, or they were moved to form one, for when the fort was finished, they all backed against the outer wall, so that their low roofs served to fire from. The usual flankers completed the work, and the settlers of Number Four were so well pleased with it that they proudly declared their fort a better one than

Fort Dummer, its nearest neighbor, which had been built by public authority at the charge of the province.

But a fort must have a garrison, and the ten or twelve men of Number Four would hardly be a sufficient one. Sooner or later an attack was certain; for the place was a backwoods Castle Dangerous, lying in the path of war-parties from Canada, whether coming down the Connecticut from Lake Memphremagog, or up Otter Creek from Lake Champlain, then over the mountains to Black River, and so down that stream, which would bring them directly to Number Four. New Hampshire would do nothing for them, and their only hope was in Massachusetts, of which most of them were natives, and which had good reasons for helping them to hold their ground, as a cover to its own settlements below. The governor and Assembly of Massachusetts did, in fact, send small parties of armed men from time to time to defend the endangered outpost, and the succor was timely; for though, during the first year of the war, Number Four was left in peace, yet from the nineteenth of April to the nineteenth of June, 1746, it was attacked by Indians five times, with some loss of scalps, and more of cattle, horses, and hogs. On the last occasion there was a hot fight in the woods, ending in the retreat of the Indians, said to have numbered a hundred and fifty, into a swamp, leaving behind them guns, blankets, hatchets, spears, and other things, valued at forty pounds, old tenor.

— which, says the chronicle, "was reckoned a great booty for such beggarly enemies."[1]

But Massachusetts grew tired of defending lands that had been adjudged to New Hampshire, and as the season drew towards an end, Number Four was left again to its own keeping. The settlers saw no choice but to abandon a place which they were too few to defend, and accordingly withdrew to the older settlements, after burying such of their effects as would bear it, and leaving others to their fate. Six men, a dog, and a cat remained to keep the fort. Towards midwinter the human part of the garrison also withdrew, and the two uncongenial quadrupeds were left alone.

When the authorities of Massachusetts saw that a place so useful to bear the brunt of attack was left to certain destruction, they repented of their late withdrawal, and sent Captain Phineas Stevens, with thirty men, to reoccupy it. Stevens, a native of Sudbury, Massachusetts, one of the earliest settlers of Number Four, and one of its chief proprietors, was a bold, intelligent, and determined man, well fitted for the work before him. He and his band reached the fort on the twenty-seventh of March, 1747, and their arrival gave peculiar pleasure to its tenants, the dog and cat, the former of whom met them with lively demonstrations of joy. The pair

---

[1] Saunderson, *History of Charlestown, N. H.* 29. Doolittle, *Narrative of Mischief done by the Indian Enemy,* — a contemporary chronicle.

had apparently lived in harmony, and found means of subsistence, as they are reported to have been in tolerable condition.

Stevens had brought with him a number of other dogs, — animals found useful for detecting the presence of Indians and tracking them to their lurking-places. A week or more after the arrival of the party, these canine allies showed great uneasiness and barked without ceasing; on which Stevens ordered a strict watch to be kept, and great precaution to be used in opening the gate of the fort. It was time, for the surrounding forest concealed what the New England chroniclers call an "army," commanded by General Debeline. It scarcely need be said that Canada had no General Debeline, and that no such name is to be found in Canadian annals. The "army" was a large war-party of both French and Indians, and a French record shows that its commander was Boucher de Niverville, ensign in the colony troops.[1]

The behavior of the dogs was as yet the only sign of danger, when, about nine o'clock on the morning of the seventh of April, one of Stevens's men took it upon him to go out and find what was amiss. Accompanied by two or three of the dogs, he advanced, gun in hand, into the clearing, peering at every stump, lest an Indian should lurk behind it. When about twenty rods from the gate, he saw a large log,

---

[1] *Extrait en forme de Journal de ce qui s'est passé d'intéressant dans la Colonie à l'occasion des Mouvements de Guerre, etc.*, 1746, 1747 .

or trunk of a fallen tree, not far before him, and approached it cautiously, setting on the dogs, or, as Stevens whimsically phrases it, "saying *Choboy !*" to them. They ran forward barking, on which several heads appeared above the log, and several guns were fired at him. He was slightly wounded, but escaped to the fort. Then, all around, the air rang with war-whoops, and a storm of bullets flew from the tangle of bushes that edged the clearing, and rapped spitefully, but harmlessly, against the wooden wall. At a little distance on the windward side was a log-house, to which, with adjacent fences, the assailants presently set fire, in the hope that, as the wind was strong, the flames would catch the fort. When Stevens saw what they were doing, he set himself to thwart them; and while some of his men kept them at bay with their guns, the rest fell to work digging a number of short trenches under the wall, on the side towards the fire. As each trench was six or seven feet deep, a man could stand in it outside the wall, sheltered from bullets, and dash buckets of water, passed to him from within, against the scorching timbers. Eleven such trenches were dug, and eleven men were stationed in them, so that the whole exposed front of the wall was kept wet.[1] Thus,

[1] "Those who were not employed in firing at the enemy were employed in digging trenches under the bottom of the fort. We dug no less than eleven of them, so deep that a man could go and stand upright on the outside and not endanger himself; so that when these trenches were finished, we could wet all the outside of the fort, which we did, and kept it wet all night. We drew some

though clouds of smoke drifted over the fort, and
burning cinders showered upon it, no harm was done,
and the enemy was forced to other devices.   They
found a wagon, which they protected from water
and bullets by a shield of planks, — for there was a
saw-mill hard by, — and loaded it with dry fagots,
thinking to set them on fire and push the blazing
machine against a dry part of the fort wall; but the
task proved too dangerous, "for," says Stevens,
"instead of performing what they threatened and
seemed to be immediately going to undertake, they
called to us and desired a cessation of arms till sunrise the next morning, which was granted, at which
time they said they would come to a parley."   In
fact, the French commander, with about sixty of his
men, came in the morning with a flag of truce, which
he stuck in the ground at a musket-shot from the
fort, and, in the words of Stevens, "said, if we
would send three men to him, he would send as many
to us."   Stevens agreed to this, on which two Frenchmen and an Indian came to the fort, and three
soldiers went out in return.   The two Frenchmen
demanded, on the part of their commander, that the
garrison should surrender, under a promise of life,
and be carried prisoners to Quebec; and they farther
required that Stevens should give his answer to the
French officer in person.

hundreds of barrels of water; and to undergo all this hard service
there were but thirty men." — *Stevens to Colonel W. Williams,
April,* 1747.

Wisely or unwisely, Stevens went out at the gate, and was at once joined by Niverville, attended, no doubt, by an interpreter. "Upon meeting the Monsieur," says the English captain, "he did not wait for me to give him an answer," but said, in a manner sufficiently peremptory, that he had seven hundred men with him, and that if his terms were refused, he would storm the fort, "run over it," burn it to the ground, and if resistance were offered, put all in it to the sword; adding that he would have it or die, and that Stevens might fight or not as he pleased, for it was all one to him. His terms being refused, he said, as Stevens reports, "Well, go back to your fort and see if your men dare fight any more, and give me an answer quickly; for my men want to be fighting." Stevens now acted as if he had been the moderator of a town-meeting. "I went into the fort and called the men together, and informed them what the general said, and then put it to vote whether they would fight or resign; and they voted to a man to stand it out, and also declared that they would fight as long as they had life." [1]

Answer was made accordingly, but Niverville's promise to storm the fort and "run over it" was not kept. Stevens says that his enemies had not the courage to do this, or even to bring up their "fortification," meaning their fire-wagon with its shield of planks. In fact, an open assault upon a fortified place was a thing unknown in this border warfare,

[1] *Stevens to Colonel William Williams, April,* 1747.

whether waged by Indians alone, or by French and
Indians together. The assailants only raised the
war-whoop again, and fired, as before, from behind
stumps, logs, and bushes. This amusement they
kept up from two o'clock till night, when they grew
bolder, approached nearer, and shot flights of fire-
arrows into the fort, which, water being abundant, were harmless as their bullets. At daylight
they gave over this exercise, called out, "Good-
morning!" to the garrison, and asked for a suspension of arms for two hours. This being agreed
to, another flag of truce presently appeared, carried
by two Indians, who planted it in the ground within
a stone's throw of the fort, and asked that two
men should be sent out to confer with them. This
was done, and the men soon came back with a
proposal that Stevens should sell provisions to his
besiegers, under a promise on their part that they
would give him no farther trouble. He answered
that he would not sell them provisions for money,
but would exchange them for prisoners, and give five
bushels of Indian corn for every hostage placed in his
hands as security for the release of an English captive in Canada. To this their only answer was firing a few shots against the fort, after which they
all disappeared, and were seen no more. The garrison had scarcely eaten or slept for three days.
"I believe men were never known to hold out with
better resolution," writes Stevens; and "though
there were some thousands of guns shot at us, we

had but two men slightly wounded, John Brown and Joseph Ely." [1]

Niverville and his party, disappointed and hungry, now made a tour among the scattered farms and hamlets of the country below, which, incapable of resisting such an inroad, were abandoned at their approach. Thus they took an easy revenge for their rebuff at Number Four, and in a march of thirty or forty leagues, burned five small deserted forts or stockaded houses, "three meeting-houses, several fine barns, about one hundred dwellings, mostly of two stories, furnished even to chests of drawers, and killed five to six hundred sheep and hogs, and about thirty horned cattle. This devastation is well worth a few prisoners or scalps." [2] It is curious to find such exploits mentioned with complacency, as evidence of prowess.

The successful defence of the most exposed place on the frontier was welcome news throughout New England, and Commodore Charles Knowles, who was then at Boston, sent Stevens a silver-hilted sword in recognition of his conduct. The settlers of Number Four, who soon returned to their backwoods home, were so well pleased with this compliment to one of their fellows that they gave to the settlement the baptismal name of the Commodore, and the town that has succeeded the hamlet of Number Four is Charlestown to this day. [3]

[1] *Stevens to Colonel W. Williams, April,* 1747.

[2] *N. Y. Col. Docs.,* x. 97.

[3] Just after the withdrawal of the French and Indians, Stevens wrote two letters giving an account of the affair, one to Governor

Shirley, and the other to Colonel William Williams, who seems to have been his immediate military superior. At most points they are substantially the same; but that to Williams contains some passages not found in the other. The letter to Shirley is printed in Saunderson, *History of Charlestown, N. H.*, 34–37, and that to Williams in *Collections of the New Hampshire Historical Society*, iv. 109–113. Stevens also kept a diary, which was long in possession of his descendants. One of these, Mr. B. F. Stevens, kindly made a search for it, at my request, and learned that it had been unfortunately destroyed by fire, in 1856. Doolittle, in his *Narrative of Mischief*, and Hoyt, in his *Antiquarian Researches*, give other accounts. The French notices of the affair are few and short, as usual in cases of failure. For the principal one, see *N. Y. Col. Docs.*, x. 97. It is here said that Stevens asked for a parley, in order to capitulate; but all the English accounts say that the French made the first advances.

CHAPTER XXIV.

1745–1748.

FORT MASSACHUSETTS.

Frontier Defence. — Northfield and its Minister. — Military Criticisms of Rev. Benjamin Doolittle. — Rigaud de Vaudreuil: his Great War-Party; he attacks Fort Massachusetts. — Sergeant Hawks and his Garrison. — A Gallant Defence. — Capitulation. — Humanity of the French. — Ravages. — Return to Crown Point. — Peace of Aix-la-Chapelle.

Since the last war, the settlements of Massachusetts had pushed westward and begun to invade the beautiful region of mountains and valleys that now forms Berkshire. Villages, or rudiments of villages, had grown up on the Housatonic, and an establishment had been attempted at Pontoosuc, now Pittsfield, on the extreme western limits of the province. The position of these new settlements was critical, for the enemy could reach them with little difficulty by way of Lake Champlain and Wood Creek. The Massachusetts government was not unmindful of them, and when war again broke out, three wooden forts were built for their protection, forming a line of defence westward from Northfield on the northern frontier of the province. One of these forts was in

the present town of Heath, and was called Fort
Shirley; another, named Fort Pelham, was in the
present town of Rowe; while the third, Fort Massachusetts, was farther westward, in what is now the
town of Adams, then known as East Hoosac. Two
hundred men from the militia were taken into pay to
hold these posts and patrol the intervening forests.
Other defensive works were made here and there,
sometimes by the votes of town meetings, and sometimes by individuals, at their own cost. These works
consisted of a fence of palisades enclosing a farm-
house, or sometimes of a blockhouse of timber or
heavy planks. Thus, at Northfield, Deacon Ebenezer
Alexander, a veteran of sixty who had served at
Louisbourg, built a "mount," or blockhouse, on the
knoll behind his house, and carried a stockade from
it to enclose the dwelling, shed, and barn, the whole
at the cost of thirty-six pounds, one shilling, and
sixpence, in Massachusetts currency,[1] which the
town repaid him, his fortifications being of public
utility as a place of refuge for families in case of
attack. Northfield was a place notoriously dangerous, and military methods were in vogue there in
season and out of season. Thus, by a vote of the
town, the people were called to the Sunday sermon
by beat of drum, and Eleazer Holton was elected to
sound the call in consideration of one pound and ten

[1] Temple and Sheldon, *History of Northfield*, 237, give the items
from the original account. This is one of the best of the innumerable town histories of New England.

shillings a year, the drum being hired of Ensign
Field, its fortunate possessor, for the farther sum of
three shillings. This was in the earlier days of
Northfield. In 1734 the Sunday drum-beat was
stopped, and the worshippers were summoned by the
less obstreperous method of "hanging out a flagg,"
for the faithful discharge of which function Daniel
Wright received in 1744 one pound and five
shillings.[1]

The various fortifications, public and private, were
garrisoned, sometimes by the owner and his neighbors,
sometimes by men in pay of the Provincial Assembly.
As was to be expected from a legislative body under-
taking warlike operations, the work of defence was
but indifferently conducted. John Stoddard, the
village magnate of Northampton, was charged, among
the rest of his multifarious employments, with the
locating and construction of forts; Captain Ephraim
Williams was assigned to the general command on
the western frontier, with headquarters at Fort Shirley
and afterwards at Fort Massachusetts ; and Major
Israel Williams, of Hatfield, was made commissary.

At Northfield dwelt the Rev. Benjamin Doolittle,
minister, apothecary, physician, and surgeon of the
village; for he had studied medicine no less than
theology. His parishioners thought that his cure of
bodies encroached on his cure of souls, and requested
him to confine his attention to his spiritual charge;
to which he replied that he could not afford it, his

[2] Temple and Sheldon, *History of Northfield*, 218.

salary as minister being seventy-five pounds in irre-
deemable Massachusetts paper, while his medical
and surgical practice brought him full four hundred
a year. He offered to comply with the wishes of his
flock if they would add that amount to his salary, —
which they were not prepared to do, and the minister
continued his heterogeneous labors as before.

As the position of his house on the village street
seems to have been regarded as strategic, the town
voted to fortify it with a blockhouse and a stockade,
for the benefit both of the occupant and of all the
villagers. This was accordingly done, at the cost of
eighteen pounds, seven shillings, and sixpence for
the blockhouse, and a farther charge for the stockade;
and thenceforth Mr. Doolittle could write his sermons and mix his doses in peace. To his other call-
ings he added that of historiographer. When, after
a ministry of thirty-six years, the thrifty pastor was
busied one day with hammer and nails in mending
the fence of his yard, he suddenly dropped dead from
a stroke of heart-disease, — to the grief of all Northfield; and his papers being searched, a record was
found in his handwriting of the inroads of the enemy
that had happened in his time on or near the Massachusetts border. Being rightly thought worthy of
publication, it was printed at Boston in a dingy
pamphlet, now extremely rare, and much prized by
antiquarians.[1]

---

[1] *A short Narrative of Mischief done by the French and Indian
Enemy, on the Western Frontiers of the Province of the Massachusetts*

Appended to it are the remarks of the author on the conduct of the war. He complains that plans are changed so often that none of them take effect; that terms of enlistment are so short that the commissary can hardly serve out provisions to the men before their time is expired; that neither bread, meat, shoes, nor blankets are kept on hand for an emergency, so that the enemy escape while the soldiers are getting ready to pursue them; that the pay of a drafted man is so small that twice as much would not hire a laborer to take care of his farm in his absence; and that untried and unfit persons are commissioned as officers: in all of which strictures there is no doubt much truth.

Mr. Doolittle's rueful narrative treats mainly of miscellaneous murders and scalpings, interesting only to the sufferers and their friends; but he also chronicles briefly a formidable inroad that still holds a place in New England history.

It may be remembered that Shirley had devised a plan for capturing Fort Frédéric, or Crown Point,

Bay; *from the Beginning of the French War, proclaimed by the King of France, March 15th, 1743–4; and by the King of Great Britain, March 29th, 1744, to August 2nd, 1748. Drawn up by the Rev. Mr. Doolittle, of Northfield, in the County of Hampshire; and found among his Manuscripts after his Death. And at the Desire of some is now Published, with some small Additions to render it more perfect. Boston; Printed and sold by S. Kneeland, in Queen Street. MDCCL.*

The facts above given concerning Mr. Doolittle are drawn from the excellent *History of Northfield* by Temple and Sheldon, and the introduction to the *Particular History of the Five Years' French and Indian War*, by S. G. Drake.

built by the French at the narrows of Lake Champlain, and commanding ready access for war-parties to New York and New England.

The approach of D'Anville's fleet had defeated the plan; but rumors of it had reached Canada, and excited great alarm. Large bodies of men were ordered to Lake Champlain to protect the threatened fort. The two brothers De Muy were already on the lake with a numerous party of Canadians and Indians, both Christian and heathen, and Rigaud de Vaudreuil, town-major of Three Rivers, was ordered to follow with a still larger force, repel any English attack, or, if none should be made, take the offensive and strike a blow at the English frontier. On the third of August, Rigaud[1] left Montreal with a fleet of canoes carrying what he calls his army, and on the twelfth he encamped on the east side of the lake, at the mouth of Otter Creek. There was rain, thunder, and a violent wind all night; but the storm ceased at daybreak, and, embarking again, they soon saw the octagonal stone tower of Fort Frédéric.

The party set up their tents and wigwams near the fort, and on the morning of the sixteenth the elder De Muy arrived with a reinforcement of sixty Frenchmen and a band of Indians. They had just returned from an incursion towards Albany, and reported that all was quiet in those parts, and that Fort Frédéric

---

[1] French writers always call him Rigaud, to distinguish him from his brother, Pierre Rigaud de Vaudreuil-Cavagnal, afterwards governor of Canada, who is usually mentioned as Vaudreuil.

was in no danger. Now, to their great satisfaction,
Rigaud and his band saw themselves free to take the
offensive. The question was, where to strike. The
Indians held council after council, made speech after
speech, and agreed on nothing. Rigaud gave them
a wampum-belt, and told them that he meant to
attack Corlaer, — that is, Schenectady; at which they
seemed well pleased, and sang war-songs all night.
In the morning they changed their minds, and begged
him to call the whole army to a council for debating
the question. It appeared that some of them, especially the Iroquois converts of Caughnawaga, disap-
proved of attacking Schenectady, because some of
their Mohawk relatives were always making visits
there, and might be inadvertently killed by the wild
western Indians of Rigaud's party. Now all was
doubt again, for as Indians are unstable as water, it
was no easy task to hold them to any plan of action.

The Abenakis proposed a solution of the difficulty.
They knew the New England border well, for many
of them had lived upon it before the war, on terms of
friendly intercourse with the settlers. They now
drew upon the floor of the council-room a rough map
of the country, on which was seen a certain river,
and on its upper waters a fort which they recommended as a proper object of attack. The river was
that eastern tributary of the Hudson which the
French called the Kaskékouké, the Dutch the
Schaticook, and the English the Hoosac. The fort
was Fort Massachusetts, the most westerly of the

three posts lately built to guard the frontier. "My father," said the Abenaki spokesman to Rigaud, "it will be easy to take this fort, and make great havoc on the lands of the English. Deign to listen to your children and follow our advice."[1] One Cade-naret, an Abenaki chief, had been killed near Fort Massachusetts in the last spring, and his tribesmen were keen to revenge him. Seeing his Indians pleased with the proposal to march for the Hoosac, Rigaud gladly accepted it; on which whoops, yelps, and war-songs filled the air. Hardly, however, was the party on its way when the Indians changed their minds again, and wanted to attack Saratoga; but Rigaud told them that they had made their choice and must abide by it, to which they assented, and gave him no farther trouble.

On the twentieth of August they all embarked and paddled southward, passed the lonely promontory where Fort Ticonderoga was afterwards built, and held their course till the lake dwindled to a mere canal creeping through the weedy marsh then called the Drowned Lands. Here, nine summers later, passed the flotilla of Baron Dieskau, bound to defeat and ruin by the shores of Lake George. Rigaud stopped at a place known as East Bay, at the mouth of a stream that joins Wood Creek, just north of the present town of Whitehall. Here he left the younger

---

[1] *Journal de la Campagne de Rigaud de Vaudreuil en 1746 . . . présenté à Monseigneur le Comte de Maurepas, Ministre et Secrétaire d'État* (written by Rigaud).

De Muy, with thirty men, to guard the canoes. The rest of the party, guided by a brother of the slain Cadenaret, filed southward on foot along the base of Skene Mountain, that overlooks Whitehall. They counted about seven hundred men, of whom five hundred were French, and a little above two hundred were Indians.[1] Some other French reports put the whole number at eleven hundred, or even twelve hundred,[2] while several English accounts make it eight hundred or nine hundred. The Frenchmen of the party included both regulars and Canadians, with six regular officers and ten cadets, eighteen militia officers, two chaplains, — one for the whites and one for the Indians, — and a surgeon.[3]

After a march of four days, they encamped on the twenty-sixth by a stream which ran into the Hudson, and was no doubt the Batten Kill, known to the French as *la rivière de Saratogue*. Being nearly opposite Saratoga, where there was then a garrison, they changed their course, on the twenty-seventh, from south to southeast, the better to avoid scouting-parties, which might discover their trail and defeat their plan of surprise. Early on the next day they reached the Hoosac, far above its mouth; and now their march was easier, "for," says Rigaud, "we got out of the woods and followed a large road that led

---

[1] "Le 19, ayant fait passer l'armée en Revue qui se trouva de 700 hommes, scavoir 500 françois environ et 200 quelques sauvages." — *Journal de Rigaud*.

[2] See *N. Y. Col. Docs.*, x. 103, 132.

[3] *Ibid.*, x. 35.

up the river." In fact, there seem to have been two roads, one on each side of the Hoosac; for the French were formed into two brigades, one of which, under the Sieur de la Valterie, filed along the right bank of the stream, and the other, under the Sieur de Sabrevois, along the left; while the Indians marched on the front, flanks, and rear. They passed deserted houses and farms belonging to Dutch settlers from the Hudson; for the Hoosac, in this part of its course, was in the province of New York.[1] They did not stop to burn barns and houses, but they killed poultry, hogs, a cow, and a horse, to supply themselves with meat. Before night they had passed the New York line, and they made their camp in or near the valley where Williamstown and Williams College now stand. Here they were joined by the Sieurs Beaubassin and La Force, who had gone forward, with eight Indians, to reconnoitre. Beaubassin had watched Fort Massachusetts from a distance, and had seen a man go up into the watch-tower, but could discover no other sign of alarm. Apparently, the fugitive Dutch farmers had not taken pains to warn the English garrison of the coming danger, for there was a coolness between the neighbors.

Before breaking up camp in the morning, Rigaud

---

[1] These Dutch settlements on the Hoosac were made under what was called the "Hoosac Patent," granted by Governor Dongan of New York in 1688. The settlements were not begun till nearly forty years after the grant was made. For evidence on this point I am indebted to Professor A. L. Perry, of Williams College.

called the Indian chiefs together and said to them:
"My children, the time is near when we must get
other meat than fresh pork, and we will all eat it
together." "Meat," in Indian parlance, meant prisoners; and as these were valuable by reason of the
ransoms paid for them, and as the Indians had suspected that the French meant to keep them all, they
were well pleased with this figurative assurance of
Rigaud that they should have their share.[1]

The chaplain said mass, and the party marched in
a brisk rain up the Williamstown valley, till after
advancing about ten miles they encamped again.
Fort Massachusetts was only three or four miles
distant. Rigaud held a talk with the Abenaki
chiefs who had acted as guides, and it was agreed
that the party should stop in the woods near the fort,
make scaling-ladders, battering-rams to burst the
gates, and other things needful for a grand assault,
to take place before daylight; but their plan came to
nought through the impetuosity of the young Indians
and Canadians, who were so excited at the first
glimpse of the watch-tower of the fort that they
dashed forward, as Rigaud says, "like lions."
Hence one might fairly expect to see the fort assaulted
at once; but by the maxims of forest war this would
have been reprehensible rashness, and nothing of the

[1] "Mes enfans, leur dis-je, le temps approche où il faut faire
d'autre viande que le porc frais ; au reste, nous la mangerons tous
ensemble ; ce mot les flatta dans la crainte qu'ils avoient qu'après la
prise du fort nous ne nous réservâmes tous les prisonniers."— *Journal
de Rigaud*.

kind was attempted. The assailants spread to right and left, squatted behind stumps, and opened a distant and harmless fire, accompanied with unearthly yells and howlings.

Fort Massachusetts was a wooden enclosure formed, like the fort at Number Four, of beams laid one upon another, and interlocked at the angles. This wooden wall seems to have rested, not immediately upon the ground, but upon a foundation of stone, designated by Mr. Norton, the chaplain, as the "underpinning," — a name usually given in New England to foundations of the kind. At the northwest corner was a blockhouse,[1] crowned with the watchtower, the sight of which had prematurely kindled the martial fire of the Canadians and Indians. This wooden structure, at the apex of the blockhouse, served as a lookout, and also supplied means of throwing water to extinguish fire-arrows shot upon the roof. There were other buildings in the enclosure, especially a large log-house on the south side, which seems to have overlooked the outer wall, and was no doubt loop-holed for musketry. On the east side there was a well, furnished probably with one of those long well-sweeps universal in primitive New England. The garrison, when complete, consisted of fifty-one men under Captain Ephraim Williams,

[1] The term "blockhouse" was loosely used, and was even sometimes applied to an entire fort when constructed of hewn logs, and not of palisades. The true blockhouse of the New England frontier was a solid wooden structure about twenty feet high, with a pro jecting upper story and loopholes above and below.

who has left his name to Williamstown and Williams
College, of the latter of which he was the founder.
He was born at Newton, near Boston; was a man
vigorous in body and mind; better acquainted with
the world than most of his countrymen, having followed the seas in his youth, and visited England,
Spain, and Holland; frank and agreeable in manners,
well fitted for such a command, and respected and
loved by his men.[1] When the proposed invasion of
Canada was preparing, he and some of his men went
to take part in it, and had not yet returned. The
fort was left in charge of a sergeant, John Hawks,
of Deerfield, with men too few for the extent of the
works, and a supply of ammunition nearly exhausted.
Canada being then put on the defensive, the frontier forts were thought safe for a time. On the
Saturday before Rigaud's arrival, Hawks had sent
Thomas Williams, the surgeon, brother of the absent
captain, to Deerfield, with a detachment of fourteen
men, to get a supply of powder and lead. This
detachment reduced the entire force, including
Hawks himself and Norton, the chaplain, to twenty-
two men, half of whom were disabled with dysen-
tery, from which few of the rest were wholly free.[2]

[1] See the notice of Williams in *Mass. Hist. Coll.*, viii. 47. He
was killed in the bloody skirmish that preceded the Battle of Lake
George in 1755. " Montcalm and Wolfe," chap. ix.

[2] " Lord's day and Monday . . . the sickness was very distress-
ing. . . . Eleven of our men were sick, and scarcely one of us in
perfect health; almost every man was troubled with the griping
and flux." — Norton, *The Redeemed Captive.*

There were also in the fort three women and five children.[1]

The site of Fort Massachusetts is now a meadow by the banks of the Hoosac. Then it was a rough clearing, encumbered with the stumps and refuse of the primeval forest, whose living hosts stood grimly around it, and spread, untouched by the axe, up the sides of the neighboring Saddleback Mountain. The position of the fort was bad, being commanded by high ground, from which, as the chaplain tells us, "the enemy could shoot over the north side into the middle of the parade," — for which serious defect, John Stoddard, of Northampton, legist, capitalist, colonel of militia, and "Superintendent of Defence," was probably answerable. These frontier forts were, however, often placed on low ground with a view to an abundant supply of water, fire being the most dreaded enemy in Indian warfare.[2]

[1] Rigaud erroneously makes the garrison a little larger. "La garnison se trouve de 24 hommes, entre lesquels il y avoit un ministre, 3 femmes, et 5 enfans." The names and residence of all the men in the fort when the attack began are preserved. Hawks made his report to the provincial government under the title " An Account of the Company in his Majesty's Service under the command of Serg!. John Hawks . . . at Fort Massachusetts, August 20 [31, new style], 1746." The roll is attested on oath " Before William Williams, Just. Pacis." The number of men is 22, including Hawks and Norton. Each man brought his own gun. I am indebted to the kindness of Professor A. L. Perry for a copy of Hawks's report, which is addressed to " the Honble. Spencer Phipps, Esq., Lieut. Gov!. and Commander in Chief [and] the Honble his Majesty's Council and House of Representatives in General Court assembled."

[2] When I visited the place as a college student, no trace of the fort was to be seen except a hollow, which may have been the

Sergeant Hawks, the provisional commander, was, according to tradition, a tall man with sunburnt features, erect, spare, very sinewy and strong, and of a bold and resolute temper. He had need to be so, for counting every man in the fort, lay and clerical, sick and well, he was beset by more than thirty times his own number; or, counting only his effective men, by more than sixty times, — and this at the lowest report of the attacking force. As there was nothing but a log fence between him and his enemy, it was clear that they could hew or burn a way through it, or climb over it with no surprising effort of valor. Rigaud, as we have seen, had planned a general assault under cover of night, but had been thwarted by the precipitancy of the young Indians and Canadians. These now showed no inclination to depart from the cautious maxims of forest warfare. They made a terrific noise, but when they came within gunshot of the fort, it was by darting from stump to stump with a quick zigzag movement that made them more difficult to hit than birds on the wing. The best moment for a shot was when they reached a stump, and stopped for an instant to duck and hide behind it. By seizing this fleeting opportunity, Hawks himself put a bullet into the breast of an Abenaki chief from St. Francis, — "which ended

remains of a cellar, and a thriving growth of horse-radish, — a relic of the garrison garden. My friend, Dr. D. D. Slade, has given an interesting account of the spot in the *Magazine of American History* for October, 1888.

his days," says the chaplain.   In view of the nimble-
ness of the assailants, a charge of buckshot was found
more to the purpose than a bullet.   Besides the slain
Abenaki, Rigaud reports sixteen Indians and Frenchmen wounded,[1] — which, under the circumstances,
was good execution for ten farmers and a minister;
for Chaplain Norton loaded and fired with the rest.
Rigaud himself was one of the wounded, having been
hit in the arm and sent to the rear, as he stood
giving orders on the rocky hill about forty rods from
the fort.   Probably it was a chance shot, since,
though rifles were invented long before, they were
not yet in general use, and the yeoman garrison were
armed with nothing but their own smooth-bore hunting-pieces, not to be trusted at long range.   The
supply of ammunition had sunk so low that Hawks
was forced to give the discouraging order not to fire
except when necessary to keep the enemy in check,
or when the chance of hitting him should be unusually good.   Such of the sick men as were strong
enough aided the defence by casting bullets and
buckshot.

The outrageous noise lasted till towards nine in the
evening, when the assailants greeted the fort with
a general war-whoop, and repeated it three or four
times; then a line of sentinels was placed around it
to prevent messengers from carrying the alarm to
Albany or Deerfield.   The evening was dark and

---

[1] " L'Ennemi me tua un abenakis et me blessa 16 hommes, tant
Iroquois qu'Abenaquis, nipissings et françois." — *Journal de Rigaud.*

cloudy. The lights of a camp could be seen by the
river towards the southeast, and those of another
near the swamp towards the west. There was a
sound of axes, as if the enemy were making scaling-
ladders for a night assault; but it was found that
they were cutting fagots to burn the wall. Hawks
ordered every tub and bucket to be filled with water,
in preparation for the crisis. Two men, John
Aldrich and Jonathan Bridgman, had been wounded,
thus farther reducing the strength of the defenders.
The chaplain says: "Of those that were in health,
some were ordered to keep the watch, and some lay
down and endeavored to get some rest, lying down in
our clothes with our arms by us. . . . We got little
or no rest; the enemy frequently raised us by their
hideous outcries, as though they were about to attack us. The latter part of the night I kept the
watch."

Rigaud spent the night in preparing for a decisive
attack, "being resolved to open trenches two hours
before sunrise, and push them to the foot of the
palisade, so as to place fagots against it, set them on
fire, and deliver the fort a prey to the fury of the
flames."[1] It began to rain, and he determined to
wait till morning. That the commander of seven

[1] "Je passay la nuit à conduire l'ouvrage auquel j'avois destiné
le jour précédent, résolu à faire ouvrir la tranchée deux heures
avant le lever du soleil, et de la pousser jusqu'au pied de la
palissade, pour y placer les fascines, y appliquer l'artifice, et livrer
le fort en proye à la fureur du feu." — *Journal de Rigaud.* He mis-
takes in calling the log wall of the fort a palisade.

hundred French and Indians should resort to such
elaborate devices to subdue a sergeant, seven militiamen, and a minister, — for this was now the effective
strength of the besieged, — was no small compliment
to the spirit of the defence.

The firing was renewed in the morning, but there
was no attempt to open trenches by daylight. Two
men were sent up into the watch-tower, and about
eleven o'clock one of them, Thomas Knowlton, was
shot through the head. The number of effectives
was thus reduced to eight, including the chaplain.
Up to this time the French and English witnesses
are in tolerable accord; but now there is conflict of
evidence. Rigaud says that when he was about to
carry his plan of attack into execution, he saw a
white flag hung out, and sent the elder De Muy,
with Montigny and D'Auteuil, to hear what the
English commandant — whose humble rank he no-
where mentions — had to say. On the other hand,
Norton, the chaplain, says that about noon the
French "desired to parley," and that "we agreed to
it." He says farther that the sergeant, with himself
and one or two others, met Rigaud outside the gate,
and that the French commander promised "good
quarter" to the besieged if they would surrender,
with the alternative of an assault if they would not.
This account is sustained by Hawks, who says that
at twelve o'clock an Indian came forward with a flag
of truce, and that he, Hawks, with two or three
others, went to meet Rigaud, who then offered honor-

able terms of capitulation.[1] The sergeant promised
an answer within two hours; and going back to the
fort with his companions, examined their means of
defence. He found that they had left but three or
four pounds of gunpowder, and about as much lead.
Hawks called a council of his effective men. Norton
prayed for divine aid and guidance, and then they
fell to considering the situation. "Had we all been
in health, or had there been only those eight of us
that were in health, I believe every man would will-
ingly have stood it out to the last. For my part, I
should," writes the manful chaplain. But besides
the sick and wounded, there were three women and
five children, who, if the fort were taken by assault,
would no doubt be butchered by the Indians, but
who might be saved by a capitulation. Hawks therefore resolved to make the best terms he could. He
had defended his post against prodigious odds for
twenty-eight hours. Rigaud promised that all in the
fort should be treated with humanity as prisoners of
war, and exchanged at the first opportunity. He also
promised that none of them should be given to the Indians, though he had lately assured his savage allies
that they should have their share of the prisoners.

At three o'clock the principal French officers were
admitted into the fort, and the French flag was raised

---

[1] *Journal of Sergeant Hawks*, cited by William L. Stone, *Life and
Times of Sir William Johnson*, i. 227. What seems conclusive is
that the French permitted Norton to nail to a post of the fort a
short account of its capture, in which it is plainly stated that the
first advances were made by Rigaud.

over it.   The Indians and Canadians were excluded,
on which some of the Indians pulled out several of
the stones that formed the foundation of the wall,
crawled through, opened the gate, and let in the
whole crew.   They raised a yell when they saw the
blood of Thomas Knowlton trickling from the watch-
tower where he had been shot, then rushed up to
where the corpse lay, brought it down, scalped it,
and cut off the head and arms.   The fort was then
plundered, set on fire, and burned to the ground.

The prisoners were led to the French camp; and
here the chaplain was presently accosted by one
Doty, Rigaud's interpreter, who begged him to persuade some of the prisoners to go with the Indians.
Norton replied that it had been agreed that they
should all remain with the French; and that to give
up any of them to the Indians would be a breach of
the capitulation.   Doty then appealed to the men
themselves, who all insisted on being left with the
French, according to the terms stipulated.   Some of
them, however, were given to the Indians, who, after
Rigaud's promise to them, could have been pacified
in no other way.   His fault was in making a stipula-
tion that he could not keep.   Hawks and Norton,
with all the women and children, remained in the
French camp.

Hearing that men were expected from Deerfield to
take the places of the sick, Rigaud sent sixty Indians
to cut them off.   They lay in wait for the English
reinforcement, which consisted of nineteen men, gave

them a close fire, shot down fifteen of them, and captured the rest.[1] This or another party of Rigaud's Indians pushed as far as Deerfield and tried to waylay the farmers as they went to their work on a Monday morning. The Indians hid in a growth of alder-bushes along the edge of a meadow where men were making hay, accompanied by some children. One Ebenezer Hawks, shooting partridges, came so near the ambushed warriors that they could not resist the temptation of killing and scalping him. This alarmed the haymakers and the children, who ran for their lives towards a mill on a brook that entered Deerfield River, fiercely pursued by about fifty Indians, who caught and scalped a boy named Amsden. Three men, Allen, Sadler, and Gillet, got under the bank of the river and fired on the pursuers. Allen and Gillet were soon killed, but Sadler escaped unhurt to an island. Three children of Allen — Eunice, Samuel, and Caleb — were also chased by the Indians, who knocked down Eunice with a tomahawk, but were in too much haste to stop and scalp her, and she lived to a good old age. Her brother Samuel was caught and dragged off, but Caleb ran into a field of tall maize, and escaped.

The firing was heard in the village, and a few armed men, under Lieutenant Clesson, hastened to the rescue; but when they reached the spot the Indians were gone, carrying the boy Samuel Allen

[1] One French account says that the Indians failed to meet the English party. *N. Y. Col. Docs.* x. 35.

with them, and leaving two of their own number
dead. Clesson, with such men as he had, followed
their trail up Deerfield River, but could not overtake
the light-footed savages.

Meanwhile, the prisoners at Fort Massachusetts
spent the first night, well guarded, in the French
and Indian camps. In the morning, Norton, accompanied by a Frenchman and several Indians, was permitted to nail to one of the charred posts of the fort
a note to tell what had happened to him and his
companions.[1] The victors then marched back as
they had come, along the Hoosac road. They moved
slowly, encumbered as they were by the sick and
wounded. Rigaud gave the Indians presents, to
induce them to treat their prisoners with humanity.
Norton was in charge of De Muy, and after walking
four miles sat down with him to rest in Williamstown
valley. There was a yell from the Indians in the
rear. "I trembled," writes Norton, "thinking they
had murdered some of our people, but was filled
with admiration when I saw all our prisoners come
up with us, and John Aldrich carried on the back of
his Indian master." Aldrich had been shot in the
foot, and could not walk. "We set out again, and

[1] The note was as follows: "August 20 [31, new style], 1746.
These are to inform you that yesterday, about 9 of the clock, we
were besieged by, as they say, seven hundred French and Indians.
They have wounded two men and killed one Knowlton. The General de Vaudreuil desired capitulations, and we were so distressed
that we complied with his terms. We are the French's prisoners,
and have it under the general's hand that every man, woman, and
child shall be exchanged for French prisoners."

had gone but a little way before we came up with Josiah Reed." Reed was extremely ill, and could go no farther. Norton thought that the Indians would kill him, instead of which one of them carried him on his back. They were said to have killed him soon after, but there is good reason to think that he died of disease. "I saw John Perry's wife," pursues the chaplain; "she complained that she was almost ready to give out." The Indians threatened her, but Hawks spoke in her behalf to Rigaud, who remonstrated with them, and they afterwards treated her well. The wife of another soldier, John Smead, was near her time, and had lingered behind. The French showed her great kindness. "Some of them made a seat for her to sit upon, and brought her to the camp, where, about ten o'clock, she was graciously delivered of a daughter, and was remarkably well. . . . Friday: this morning I baptized John Smead's child. He called its name *Captivity*." The French made a litter of poles, spread over it a deer-skin and a bear-skin, on which they placed the mother and child, and so carried them forward. Three days after, there was a heavy rain, and the mother was completely drenched, but suffered no harm, though "Miriam, the wife of Moses Scott, hereby catched a grievous cold." John Perry was relieved of his pack, so that he might help his wife and carry her when her strength failed. Several horses were found at the farms along the way, and the sick Benjamin Simons and the wounded John

Aldrich were allowed to use two of them. Rarely,
indeed, in these dismal border-raids were prisoners
treated so humanely; and the credit seems chiefly
due to the efforts of Rigaud and his officers. The
hardships of the march were shared by the victors,
some of whom were sorely wounded; and four
Indians died within a few days.

"I divided my army between the two sides of the
Kaskékouké" (Hoosac), says Rigaud, "and ordered
them to do what I had not permitted to be done
before we reached Fort Massachusetts. Every house
was set on fire, and numbers of domestic animals of
all sorts were killed. French and Indians vied with
each other in pillage, and I made them enter the
[valleys of all the] little streams that flow into the
Kaskékouké and lay waste everything there. . . .
Wherever we went we made the same havoc, laid
waste both sides of the river, through twelve leagues
of fertile country, burned houses, barns, stables, and
even a meeting-house, — in all, above two hundred
establishments, — killed all the cattle, and ruined all
the crops. Such, Monseigneur, was the damage I
did our enemies during the eight or nine days I was
in their country."[1] As the Dutch settlers had
escaped, there was no resistance.

The French and their allies left the Hoosac at the
point where they had reached it, and retraced their
steps northward through the forest, where there was
an old Indian trail. Recrossing the Batten Kill, or

[1] *Journal de Rigaud.*

"River of Saratoga," and some branches of Wood Creek, they reached the place where they had left their canoes, and found them safe. Rigaud says: "I gave leave to the Indians, at their request, to continue their fighting and ravaging, in small parties, towards Albany, Schenectady, Deerfield, Saratoga, or wherever they pleased, and I even gave them a few officers and cadets to lead them." These small ventures were more or less successful, and produced, in due time, a good return of scalps.

The main body, now afloat again, sailed and paddled northward till they reached Crown Point. Rigaud rejoiced at finding a haven of refuge, for his wounded arm was greatly inflamed: "and it was time I should reach a place of repose." He and his men encamped by the fort and remained there for some time. An epidemic, apparently like that at Fort Massachusetts, had broken out among them, and great numbers were seriously ill.

Norton was lodged in a French house on the east side of the lake, at what is now called Chimney Point; and one day his guardian, De Muy, either thinking to impress him with the strength of the place, or with an amusing confidence in the minister's incapacity for making inconvenient military observations, invited him to visit the fort. He accepted the invitation, crossed over with the courteous officer, and reports the ramparts to have been twenty feet thick, about twenty feet high, and mounted with above twenty cannon. The octagonal tower which

overlooked the ramparts, and answered in some sort
to the donjon of a feudal castle, was a bomb-proof
structure in vaulted masonry, of the slaty black
limestone of the neighborhood, three stories in height,
and armed with nine or ten cannon, besides a great
number of patereroes, — a kind of pivot-gun much
like a swivel.[1]

In due time the prisoners reached Montreal,
whence they were sent to Quebec; and in the course
of the next year those who remained alive were exchanged and returned to New England.[2] Mrs. Smead
and her infant daughter "Captivity" died in Canada,
and, by a singular fatality, her husband had scarcely
returned home when he was waylaid and killed by
Indians. Fort Massachusetts was soon rebuilt by the
province, and held its own thenceforth till the war was
over. Sergeant Hawks became a lieutenant-colonel,
and took a creditable part in the last French war.

For two years after the incursion of Rigaud the
New England borders were scourged with partisan
warfare, bloody, monotonous, and futile, with no
event that needs recording, and no result beyond a
momentary check to the progress of settlement. At
length, in July, 1748, news came that the chief con-

[1] Kalm also describes the fort and its tower. Little trace of
either now remains. Amherst demolished them in 1759, when he
built the larger fort, of which the ruins still stand on the higher
ground behind the site of its predecessor.

[2] Of the twenty-two men in the fort when attacked, one, Knowlton, was killed by a bullet; one, Reed, died just after the surrender;
ten died in Canada, and ten returned home. *Report of Sergeant
Hawks.*

tending powers in Europe had come to terms of agreement, and in the next October the Peace of Aix-la-Chapelle was signed. Both nations were tired of the weary and barren conflict, with its enormous cost and its vast entail of debt. It was agreed that conquests should be mutually restored. The chief conquest of England was Louisbourg, with the island of Cape Breton, — won for her by the farmers and fishermen of New England. When the preliminaries of peace were under discussion, Louis XV. had demanded the restitution of the lost fortress; and George II. is said to have replied that it was not his to give, having been captured by the people of Boston.[1] But his sense of justice was forced to yield to diplomatic necessity, for Louisbourg was the indispensable price of peace. To the indignation of the northern provinces, it was restored to its former owners. "The British ministers," says Smollett, "gave up the important island of Cape Breton in exchange for a petty factory in the East Indies" (Madras), and the King deigned to send two English noblemen to the French court as security for the bargain.

Peace returned to the tormented borders; the settlements advanced again, and the colonists found a short breathing space against the great conclusive struggle of the Seven Years' War.

[1] *N. Y. Col. Docs.*, x. 147.

APPENDIX.

A.

CHAPTER XVII. ENGLAND HAS NO RIGHTFUL TITLES TO NORTH AMERICA, EXCEPT THOSE WHICH MAY BE GRANTED HER BY FRANCE.

Second Memoire concernant les limites des Colonies presenté en 1720, par Bobé prêtre de la congregation de la Mission. à Versailles. Archives Nationales.

(Extracts, printed literatim.)

" L'année Dernier 1719 je presenté un Memoire Concernant les prétensions reciproques de la grande bretagne et de la france par Raport aux Colonies des deux Nations dans L'Amerique, et au Reglement des limites des dites Colonies.

" Je ne repete pas ce que j'ay dit dans ce memoire, je prie seulement que l'on pese bien tout ce que j'y dis pour Aneantir les prétensions des Anglois, et pour les Convaincre, s'ils veullent être de bonne foy, qu'elles sont des plus mal fondées, trés Exorbitantes, et mêmes injustes, qu'ayant usurpé sur La france presque tout ce qu'ils possedent en Amerique, ils deveroient luy rendre au lieu de luy demander, et qu'ils deveroient estimer Comme un tres grand avantage pour Eux, la Compensation que j'y propose pour finir cette affaire, laqu'elle, sans cette Compensation, renai-

tra toujours jusqu'a ce qu'enfin la france soit rentrée en
paisible possession de tout ce qui luy appartient légitimement, et dont on ne L'a depoüilleé que par la force et La
malheureuse Conjoncture des tems, qui sans doute tôt ou
tard luy seront plus favorables.

"Il Est surprenant que les Anglois entendus Comme ils
sont par Raport à leurs Interests, ne fassent pas attention
qu'il Leurs est infiniment plus Avantageux de s'assurer, par
un traité raisonnable, la tranquille et perpetuelle possession
des payis ou ils etoient établis avant la paix D'utrecht, que
de vouloir profiter des Conjonctures pour oster aux françois
des payis qu'ils ne Cederont jamais de bon Coeur, et dont
ils se rempareront quand ils trouveront l'occasion favorable
pour Cela, se persuadant qu'il leur sera alors permis de
reprendre par force, ce que par force on leurs à pris, et
ce qu'ils ont été obligé de Ceder a Utrecht; et meme de
reprendre au moins une partie des payis que l'angleterre
à usurpez sur la france, qui ne les à jamais cedez par aucun
traité que je scache. . . .

"Jean Verazan par ordre de françois 1ᵉʳ fit La decouverte
de tous les payis et Costes qui sont Entre le 33ᵉ. et le 47ᵉ.
Degre de latitude, et y fit deux voyages dont le dernier fut
en 1523 et par ordre et au nom du dit Roy francois 1ᵉʳ il prit
possession de toute cette Coste et de tous ces payis, bien long
tems avant que les Anglois y Eussent Eté.

"L'an 1562 Les françois s'établirent dans La Caroline.
Champlain à La fin de la relation de ses voyages fait un
chapitre exprez Dans lequel il prouve.

"1°. Que La france a pris possession de toutes les Costes
et payis depuis la floride inclusivement jusqu'au fleuve Sᵗ
Laurent inclusivemᵗ, avant tout autre prince chrêtien.

2°. Que nos roys ont eu, dez le Commancement des
decouvertes des lieutenans generaux Dans ces payis et
Costes.

3°. Que Les françois les ont habitez avant les Anglois.

4°. Que Les prétensions des Anglois sont Mal fondées.

" La Lecture De ce chapitre fait voir que Champlain prouve invinciblement tous ces chefs, et de maniere que les Anglois n'ont rien de bon à y repondre, de sorte que s'ils veullent être de bonne foy, ils doivent Convenir que tous ces payis appartiennent Légitimement à la france qu'ils s'en sont emparez et qu'ils les Retiennent Contre toute justice. . . .

" Il Est A Remarquer que quoyque par le traité de S.^t germain l'angleterre dut restituer tout ce qu'elle Avoit occupé dans la Nouvelle france, et par Consequent toute la Coste depuis baston jusqu'a la virginie inclusivement (car alors les Anglois ne s'etoient pas encore emparez de la Caroline) laqu'elle Coste est Certainement partie de la Nouvelle france, les Anglois ne l'ont pas Cependant restituée et la gardent encore a present Contre la teneur du traité de St Germain, quoy que la france ne L'ait point Cedée a L'angleterre ni par le dit traité ni par Aucun Autre que je scache.

" Cecy Merite La plus serieuse attention de la france, et qu'elle fasse Entendre serieusement aux Anglois que par le traité de S.^t germain ils se sont obligez de luy rendre toutte cette Coste, qui incontestablement est partie de la Nouvelle france, Comme je L'ay prouvé cy devant et encore plus au long dans mon 1.^r memoire et Comme le prouvent Verazan, Champlain, Denis, et toutes les plus ancienes Cartes de l'amerique septentrionale. . . .

" Or Le Commun Consentement de toute l'Europe est de depeindre la Nouvelle france S'étendant au moins au 35.e et 36.e degrez de latitude Ainsy qu'il appert par les mappemondes imprimées en Espagne, Italie, hollande, flandres, allemagne Et Angleterre même, Sinon depuis que les Anglois se sont Emparez des Costes de la Nouvelle france, ou est

L'Acadie, Etechemains L'almouchicois, et la grande riviere de S.ᵗ l'aurens, ou ils ont imposé a leur fantaisie des Noms de nouvelle Angleterre, Ecosse, et autres, mais il est mal aisé de pouvoir Effacer une chose qui est Connué De toute la Chretienteé D'ou je Conclus,

"1°. Quavant L'Usurpation faite par les Anglois, toute Cette Coste jusqu'au 35.ᵉ Degre s'appelloit Nouvelle france, laquelle Comprenoit outre plusieurs autres provinces, l'Etechemains, L'almouchicois, et L'acadie. . . .

"Les Anglois Doivent remettre à La france le Port Royal, et La france doit insister vigoureusement sur cette restitution, et ordonner aux françois de Port Royal, Des Mines, et de Beaubassin, et autres lieux De reconaitre sa Majesté tres Chretiene pour leur Souverain, et leur deffendre d'obeir a aucun autre; de plus Commander a tous ces lieux et payis, et a toute la partie Septentrionale de la Peninsule, ainsi qu'aux payis des Almouchicois et des Etechemains [*Maine*, *New Hampshire*, *and Massachusetts*], de Reconaitre le gouverneur de l'isle Royale pour leur Gouverneur.

"Il Est même apropos De Comprendre Dans le Brevet de gouverneur de L'isle Royale tous ces payis jusqu'au Cap Cod. . . .

"Que La france ne doit point souffrir que les Anglois s'etablissent Dans les payis qu'elle n'a pas Cedez.

"Qu'elle Doit incessament s'en remettre en possession, y Envoyer quantite D'habitans, et s'y fortifier de maniere qu'on puisse Arrêter les Anglois que depuis long tems tachent de s'emparer de l'amerique francoise dont ils Conaissent L'importance, et dont ils feroient un meilleur usage que celuy que les francois en font. . . .

"Si les Anglois disent que les payis qui sont entre les rivieres de quinibequi [*Kennebec*] et de Sᵗᵉ Croix font **partie de la Nouvelle Angleterre.**

JE LEURS REPONS

" 1°. Qu'ils scavent bien le Contraire, que Ces payis ont toujours fait partie de la Nouvelle france, que Les francois les ont toujours possedez et habitez, que Mons.ʳ De S.ᵗ Castin gentilhomme francois a toujours eu, et a encore son habitation entre la Riviere de Quinibequi et celle de Pentagoet [*Penobscot*] (que même depuis les usurpations des anglois et leurs etablissements, dans leur Prétenduë Nouvelle Angleterre) les francois ont toujours prétendu que la Nouvelle france s'etend qusqu'au Cap Cod et qu'il en est fait mention dans toutes les patentes de gouverneurs francois.

" 2° Que De L'aveu même des Anglois, la Nouvelle Angleterre a une tres petite Etenduë du Costé de L'est, il est facile de le prouver par eux mêmes.

" J'ay Lu une description de la Nouvelle Angleterre et des autres Colonies Angloises, Composée par un Anglois, traduite en francois, imprimée à Paris en 1674 par Loüis Billaine, voicy les propres termes de Cet autheur Anglois, La Nouvelle Angleterre est au Septentrion de Marylande, au raport du Capitaine Smith, elle a prez de 25 Lieuës de Coste de mer.

" Ainsi selon les Anglois qui sont de Bonne foy, la Nouvelle Angleterre, qui n'a que prez de 25 lieuës de Coste de mer, ne scauroit s'etendre jusqu'e á La Riviere de Quinebequi. C'est tout au plus si elle s'etend jusqu'a deux ou trois lieuës à l'est De Baston.

" Il Semble même que les Anglois ont basti Baston, et en ont fait une ville Considerable à l'extremeté de leur pretenduë Nouvelle Angleterre.

" 1° Pour être a portée et en Etat de s'emparer sur les francois de tout ce qui est à L'est de Baston.

"2° Pour être en Etat d'Empecher les francois de s'etablir sur toute Cette Coste jusqu à La Karoline inclusivement, laquelle Coste etant de Notorieté publique de la Nouvelle france, à eté usurpez sur La france a qui elle appartenoit alors, et luy appartient Encore, ne L'ayant jamais cedeé. C'est ce que je vais prouver.

"Apres Avoir Invinciblement Convaincu les Anglois que tout ce qui est a L'est de quinibequi a Toujours appartenu et appartient encore a La france, excepté L'Acadie selon ses Ancienes limites, qu'elle a Cedée par force a L'Angleterre par La paix d'utrecht.

"Il faut Que Presentement je prouve que toute La Coste depuis la Riviere quinibequi jusqu' à La Caroline inclusivement appartient par toutes sortes de droits à La france. Sur qui les Anglois L'ont usurpeé, voicy une partie de mes preuves.

"Les françois ont decouvert tous ces payis Avant les Anglois, et en ont pris possession avant Eux. Les Roys de france ont nommé ces payis Caroline et Nouvelle france avant que les Anglois leurs eussent donné des Noms á leur mode pour faire oublier les Noms que les francois Leurs avoient imposez. Et que ces payis Appartenoient à La france.

"Les Roys de france ont Donné des lettres patentes à leurs sujets pour posseder et habiter ces payis, avant que Jacques 1ᵉ et Charles 1ᵉ Roys d'Angleterre en eussent donne à Leurs sujets.

"Pour Convaincre les Anglois de ces veritées il faut Lire avec attention ce qu'en ont Ecrit Jean verazan, Champlain, Laet, Denis.

"Les traitez faits Entre La france et L'Angleterre, et Le memoire que j'ay presenté L'anneé Dernier 1719.

"On y Trouvera tant de Choses, lesquelles il seroit trop long de Copier icy, qui prouvent que ces payis ont toujours appartenu de droit a La france, et que les Anglois s'en sont emparez par force, que La france ne les a jamais Cedez à l'angleterre par aucun traité, que je scache.

"Et Partant que La france Conserve toujours son droit sur tous ces payis, et qu'elle a droit de les redemander à l'Angleterre. Comme elle les redemande présentement, ou Bien un Equivalent.

"L'Equivalent que la france demande et dont elle veut bien se Contenter, C'est la restitution de tout ce qu'elle a Cedéé par force à L'Angleterre par Le traité D'utrecht.

"Il Est De l'honeur et de l'interest de l'angleterre d'accorder à la france cette Equivalent.

"1° Parceque n'y ayant point D'honeur à profiter des Malheurs D'un Roy pour Luy faire Ceder par force les payis qui luy appartiennent, il est de l'honeur de L'Angleterre de rendre a la france, ce qu'elle a eté Contrainte de luy ceder, et qu'elle ne possede qu'a ce mauvais tiltre.

"2° Il est aussi Contre la justice et l'honeur de l'angleterre de posseder sans aucun Tiltre, et Contre toute justice les payis qui sont depuis la Riviere de quinibequi jusqu'à la Caroline inclusivement.

"3° Il N'est pas moins de l'honeur et de l'interest de l'angleterre de profiter du moyen que la france veut bien luy presenter, pour sassurer a perpetuite toute Cette Coste, et pour la posseder justemᵗ par la Cession que la france en fera, et de tous ses droits sur ces payis moyennant L'Equivalent proposé.

"4° Parceque L'Angleterre doit Craindre que la france, dont elle ne Doit mepriser ni le Ressentiment ni la puis. sance, ne trouve une Conjoncture favorable pour faire valoir ses pretensions et ses droits, et pour Rentrer en possession de tout ce que L'Angleterre Luy a usurpée, et de tout ce qu'elle l'a obligé par force de luy Ceder.

"5° Quand on veut trop avoir, souvent on n'a Rien, et

meme on perd ce que L'on Avoit. Il est donc de la sagesse
Et de l'interest de l'Angleterre de ne pas pousser trop loin
ses demandes, et de Convenir avec La france de sorte qu'elle
puisse posseder Avec justice et tranquillement des payis que
la france Aura toujours droit de reprendre jusqu'a ce qu'elle
en ait fait une Cession libre et volontaire, et qu'il paroisse
que L'Angleterre En faveur de Cette Cession luy ait donné
un Equivalent.

" La france s'offre donc pour vivre en paix avec l'Angleterre de luy Ceder tous ses droits sur toute la Coste qui est
entre la riviere de quinibequi dans la Nouvelle france jusqu'a
la Riviere Jourdain, dans la Caroline, de sorte que ces deux
rivieres servent de limites aux francois et aux Anglois.

" La france Demande pour Equivalent de la Cession de
tant de payis, si grands, si beaux, et si a sa biensceance que
l'Angleterre luy rende Et restituë tout ce qu'elle luy à cedé
par le traité Dutrecht.

" Si La france ne peut pas engager L'Angleterre à convenir de Cet Equivalent, Elle pouroit (mais Ce ne doit être
qu'a L'extremité) Ceder Encore à l'Angleterre la Caroline
francoise, C'est a dire, ce qui est au sud de la Riviere Jourdain, Ou bien Ce qui est Entre la Riviere quinibequi, et Celle
de Pentagoet. Ou bien leur offrir une somme D'argent.

" Il Semble que L'Angleterre doive estimer Comme un
grand Avantage pour Elle, que La france veuille bien Convenir de Cet Equivalent, qui Assure Aux Anglois et leur
rend legitime La possession de Cette grande etenduë de
Costes qu'ils ont usurpez sur La france, qui ne les a jamais Cedez, qui ne les Cedera jamais, et sur lesqu'elles elle
Conservera toujours ses legitimes droit et pretensions,
jusqu'a ce qu'elle les ait Cédeés a L'angleterre moyennant
un Equivalent raisonnable tel qu'est la Restitution de tout
ce que La France luy a Cedé par force a Utrecht.

Limites.

"Suposeé L'acceptation de Cet Equivalent par L'une et l'autre Nation.

"La france toujours genereuse Consentira pour vivre en paix avec les Anglois, qu'une ligne tirée depuis l'embouchure de la Riviere de quinibequi, ou bien, depuis l'embouchure de la Riviere de Pentagoet, qui ira tout droit passer á egale distance entre Corlard [*Schenectady*] et les lacs de Champlain et du Saint Sacrement, et joindre la ligne par laqu'elle le sieur de L'isle geographe termine les terres Angloises, jusqu'a la Riviere Jourdain, ou bien jusqu'a La Caroline inclusivemͭ. La france dis-je Consentira que cette ligne serve De borne et limites aux terres des deux Nations, de sorte que tous les payis et terres qui sont entre Cette ligne et la mer appartiendront à L'Angleterre, et que tout ce qui sera au dela de cette ligne appartiendra a La france.

"Dans Le fond il est avantageux a la france de faire incessament regler les limites, tant pour Empecher les Anglois d'empieter toujours de plus en plus sous pretexte de limites Non regleés, que parcequ'il est assuré que si le droit de la france est bien soutenu le réglement lui sera Avantageux, aussi bien que l'equivalent que j'ay proposé.

"Mais il pouroit arriver que les Anglois qui ont demandé le Reglement des limites, voyant qu'il ne doit pas leur etre favorable s'il est fait selon la justice, pourroient bien eux mêmes l'eloigner, afin de pouvoir toujours empieter sur les francois sous pretexte de limites non regleés, et de se mettre toujours en possession des payis Appartenans à la france.

"En ce Cas et aussi au Cas que les Anglois ne veullent pas restituer à la france leur Nouvelle Angleterre et autres payis jusqu'a la Caroline inclusivement qu'ils luy out usur-

pez, ou bien leur rendre L'Acadie &ᶜ pour l'equivalent Dont
j'ay parlé.

"1° Il faut que la france mette incessament quantité d'habitans dans le payis qui est entre la riviere de quinibequi et
Celle de Sᵗᵉ Croix, lequel payis qui selon les Anglois N'est
point en Litige, ni partie de la pretenduë Nouvelle Ecosse,
même, selon l'etenduë imaginaire que luy á donnée leur Roy
Jacques 1ʳ qui ne la fait Commancer qu'a La riviere Sᵗᵉ
Croix, et Celle de quinibequi N'ayant jamais eté Cedé ni
par le traite D'utrecht ni par Aucun autre que je scache,
et ce payis Ayant toujours appartenu a La france, et eté
par elle possedez et habité, Mʳ de Sᵗ Castin gentilhomme
francois ayant son habitation entre la riviere de Pentagoet
et Celle de quinibequi comme je l'ay Deja dit.

"2° On peut même faire entendre a L'Angleterre que Le
Roy donnera Ce payis a la Compagnie des Indes qui scaura
bien le deffendre et le faire valoir.

"Que Le Roy donnera aussi a la Compagnie des Indes la
Caroline francoise, Comme depandance et province de la
loüisiane, a Condition qu'elle y mettera des habitans, et y
fera bâtir de bons forts, et une bonne Citadelle pour soutenir
et deffendre ce beau payis Contre les Anglois.

"Il Est Certain que si le Roy fait entendre serieusement
qu'il est resolu de donner à la Compagnie des Indes non
seulement La Caroline francoise, et le payis qui est entre
les Rivieres de quinibequi et de Sᵗᵉ Croix, mais aussi de luy
Ceder et abandonner tous ses droits sur tous les payis que
les Anglois ont usurpez sur la france.

"Il Est Certain Dis je, que les Anglois, Crainte D'Avoir
affaire avec une Compagnie si puissante, se resoudront au
Reglement des limites, tel que je l'ay proposé, et à rendre
a la france toute la Nouvelle Ecosse ou Acadie selon ses
Ancienes limites, Enfin tout ce que la france leur à Cedez a
Utrecht, moyennant une somme D'Argent, ou bien L'equivalent que j'ay Aussi proposé.

" Je finis Ce memoire en priant de faire une tres serieuse attention aux Exorbitantes prétensions des Anglois et a tout ce qu'ils ont fait Et font encore pour se rendre maitres de la pesche la Moluë, et de L'Amerique francoise.

" En Effet il est tres important que quand on traitera du reglement des limites, La france attaque les Anglois au lieu d'etre sur La defensive, C'est a dire, qu'elle doit demander aux Anglois tout ce qu'ils ont usurpez sur Elle, et le demander vigoureusement.

" C'est peut être le meilleur moyen de les mettre a la Raison, il est même apropos qu'elle les presse de finir Cette affaire, Dont sans doute La Conclusion luy sera Avantageuse, si on luy rend justice."

II.

DEMANDES DE LA FRANCE (1723).

Archives du Ministère des Affaires Etrangères.

(*Literatim.*)

" Pour tous les Raisons deduites cy devant La france demande a Langleterre.

" 1° Qu'Elle laisse jouir Tranquillement la france de Tous les pays qui sont a L'Est de la riviere Quinibequi ou de Celle de S.t Georges excepté de la seulle ville de Port Royal avec sa banlieüe et de L'accadie selon ses anciennes Limites, C'Est a dire La partie Meridionale de la Peninsule depuis le Cap fourchu jusqua Camseau Exclusivement, Que la france a cedée par la traite d'Utrecht, Tout le reste qui est a L'Est de Quinibequi [*Kennebec*], appartenant a La France en tout souveraineté depuis L'an 1524. Laquélle ne la jamais cedé ny par le Traitté d'Utrecht ny par aucun autre traitté.

" 2° Que les Anglois Laissent Vivre Tranquillement sous la domination du Roy les nations Sauvages qui sont dans Les payis a L'Est de Quinibequi et qu'ils Ninquietent point les Missionnaires qui demeureront Chés les d. Nations Ny les françois qui Iront Chés Elles.

" 3° Que Les Anglois restituent a la france ce qu'ils ont occupé a L'Est de Quinibequi et qu'ils ne Trouvent pas mauvais que les françois prennent detruisent ou gardent les forts Postes et habitations, que les Anglois ont Etablis, ou Etabliront dans tous les Pays a L'Est de Quinibiqui, ou de la Rivierre St Georges Car quand même il ne Seroist pas sure que Ces d. Paÿs appartiennent a La France, il suffit qu'ils sont Contesté pour rendre injuste et Violente L'occupation qu'En feroient les Anglois avant que la Contestation fut finie.

" 4° Que Les Anglois restituent tout ce qu'ils Occupent dans la Nouvelle france depuis Le 30e degré jusqua Quinibequi ou jusqua La Rivierre S^t georges Comme Elle y est obligeé par Le traitté de S^t germain En Laye En 1632. La france ne luy ayant jamais cedé par aucun Traitté aucune partie de toute La Nouvelle france, sinon La Ville de Port Royal avec sa Banlieüe et lacadie selon ses anciennes Limittes.

" Si les Anglois disent que la France ne s'est point opposeé aux occupations qu'ils ont fait dans la Nouvelle france

" Je Leur repons que la france sy est toujours opposeé et qu'elle s'Est Toujours Maintenuë dans la souveraineté de toute la Nouvelle france, soit en donnant tout ses Paÿs enconcession, soit en y envoyant des gouverneurs généraux, soit en Nommant Vice Roys de la Nouvelle france Les plus grands Seigneurs du Roÿaume, Tels Ont esté M. Le Comte de Soissons, M. Le Prince de Condé, M. de Montmorency, M. Le Duc de Vantadour, M. Le Cardinal de Richelieu etc.

qui des les premiers tems ont este successivement Viceroys
de la Nouvelle france et Terres Circonvoisines, par la Lecture de leurs patentes On verra que Nos Roys se sont Toujours Conservé la Souveraineté des pays qui sont Entre le
30e et Le 50e degré, et qu'ils Nont jamais Consenty que les
Anglois y fissent aucun Etablissement et que sy-ils y en ont
fait çá esté Malgré la france, que avoit trop d'affaires en
Europe pour pouvoir les Empecher, Se reservant Toujours
ses droits et la Volonté de les faire Valoir quand Elle en
Trouveroit une occasion favorable, ce qui pourroit bien arriver un jour, alors on Verroit que L'on ne s'Empare pas
Impunement et par Violence, des Domaines d'un Roy de
france et qu'il est assés puissant pour se remettre en poces-
sion Tost ou tard de ce qu'on a Usurpé sur luy, C'est a quoy
les Anglois deveroient faire attention, et ce qui devroit les
obliger de ne pas mepriser Ny maltraitter La France Comme
Ils font.

"La france s'Est encore opposeé aux Usurpations des
Anglois Les ayant obligé par le traitté de St Germain En
1632, de restituer a la france Tout ce qu'ils avoient jus-
qual'ors occupe dans la Nouvelle france, Ils Nont pas cependant Encore fait cette restitution, Mais on leur demande
présentement qu'ils la fassent incessammant N'Etant pas
juste qu'ils retiennent plus Longtems ce qui ne leur appartient pas, et qu'ils ont promis solennellement de restituer a
la france.

"Mais disent Les Anglois Nous sommes Etablis dans La
Nouvelle france depuis la Caroline Inclusivement jusqua
Quinibequi depuis 1585, jusqua presant 1723. Nous y
avons mis quantiteé d'habitans et bastis plusieurs grandes
villes. Navons Nous pas prescrit Contre La france par une
sy Longue procession."

Reponse.

" Non parce que La france sy est Toujours opposeé par
les Lettres pattentes qu'Elle a donneés aux Concésionnaires
Generaux, aux Lieutenants generaux et aux Viceroys de la
Nouvelle france.

" Non parce que La france obligea en 1632, par Le traitté
de St Germain, Langleterre de luy restituer tous les lieux
occupés dans la Nouvelle france par les Anglois, Et que le
traitté de Breda en 1667, celuy de Neutralité en 1686, et
celuy d'Utrecht en 1713, ne disent rien d'ou on puisse In-
ferer que la france ait cedé a Langleterre aucune partie
de .la Nouvelle france, sinon la province de la Cadie selon ses anciennes Limittes, et la seule ville de Port Royal
avec ses dépendances ou Banlieüe. Je dis encore que Cette
longue possession des anglois, ces Villes baties et ce grand
Nombre d'habitans mis par eux dans ces pays Nanéantissent
point le droit de la france pour les redemander. . . .

" Il y avoit Environ 150 ans que les françois avoient abandonné les postes qu'ils avoient alors sur la Coste du Bresil
les Portuguais sy Etablirent aussitost y Mirent quantité
d'habitans et y batirent de grandes Villes. Ils ne Croyoient
pas cependant que pour cela la france fut dechüe de ses
droits de proprieté et de souveraineté sur ces pays aban-
donnés par Elle depuis 150 ans, puisqua Utrecht en 1713
Le Roy de Portugal demanda au Roy qu'il luy abandonnat
ses droits sur ces pays, ce qui Le Roy fit en Consideration
du Portugal.

" Les Anglois possedoient depuis longues anneés La Ja-
maique yavoient quantité d'habitans, de forts et de riches
Villes, persuadés cependant que les droits de l'Espagne
subsisteroient Tant quelle Ny auroit pas renoncé en leur
faveur. Ils demanderent a Utrecht Cette renonciation au
Roy d'Espagne et il la leur accorda.

" Si les Anglois avoient demandé a la france une Cession
de tous ces droits sur les pays occupés par Eux dans la Nouvelle france Il y a apparance que le Roy leur auroit fait
cession a des Conditions raisonnables. Ils nont pas deman-
dés cette cession, ou sy ils lont demandeé, elle ne leur a pas
esté accordeé les droits de la france subsistent donc Toujours et Elle pretend presentement que les Anglois qui en
usent sy mal avec Elle, luy restituënt Tout ce quelle a
usurpé dans la Nouvelle france depuis le 30.ᵉ jusquau
50ᵉ degré."

" Mais disent les Anglois Commant pouvoir restituer un
sy vaste pays ou nous avons une Infinité d'habitans et un
trés grand nombre de belles et riches villes? Une Telle
restitution N'Est pas practicable."

RESPONSE.

' Javouë qu'il est bien difficile de sy resoudre même aux
personnes qui font profession d'aimer L'Equité et La
Justice.

" Mais Le Roy aime trop la nation Angloise, a trop de
Consideration pour Elle, desire trop luy faire plaisir, et est
trop généreux pour exiger d'Elle une Telle restitution Voulant luy donner Un Exemple de la moderation dont il sou-
haite que Langleterre use a son Egard.

" Il se désistera Volontiers de tous ces droits et consentira que Toute la Coste jusqua 20 Lieuës dans l'Enfonce-
ment des Terres Depuis le 32.ᵉ degré jusqua la Rivierre de
Quinibequi demeure en toute proprieté et souveraineté a
perpetuité a Langleterre a condition quelle Sobligera par
un traitté solennel et décisif de ne jamais passer ces limites.
Que la france ne sera jamais Inquieté par Langleterre dans
la Jouissance en proprieté et souveraineté de Ce qui est au

dela de ces 20 lieuës dans lenfoncement des terres et de Tous les pays qui sont a L'Est de la rivierre de Quinibequi, qui de Ce Costé la servira de Limites aux deux Nations, et que Langleterre rendra a la france Le port Royal et la Cadie avec leurs dependances, Enfin Tout ce que la france luy a Cedé par le traité d'Utrecht sans en rien Excepter.

"Cet offre du Roy doit estre agreable a Langleterre et luy faire plaisir, parceque sy elle l'accepte elle possedera a juste Titre cette grande partie de la Nouvelle france, qu'Elle possedera Toujours injustement sy Elle Naccepte pas un offre sy raisonnable que Luy fait Le Roy qui sans cette acceptation Ne renoncera jamais a ses droits de souveraineté sur une sy grande et sy belle partie de la Nouvelle France, droits que les anglois doivent Craindre qu'il Ne fasse Valoir Tost ou tard, Car si puissante que soit Langleterre, Ils ne doivent pas croire que la france ne luy cede rien en puissance ny en quoy que ce soit, et qu'on ne la meprise et maltraitte pas Impunement.

"Sy Les Anglois ont quelques autres titres et quelques autres raysons a alleguer en leur faveur, sy on me veut faire L'honneur de me les Communiquer, Je moffre d'y repondre d'une maniere a les obliger d' avouër qu'ils ont tort, sils sont de bonne foy et si ils aiment La justice et la paix.

Addition.

"On vient de me faire voire une carte de la nouvelle france presenté au Roy par les Anglois sur la quelle est tracé par une ligne tout ce qu'ils pretendent en vertu du traitté d'Utrecht.

"Ils y etendent sy loin leurs pretentions dans Les terres, qu'il y a tout lieu de Croire que cette Ligne na pas eté traceé, Ny Cette carte presenteé par ordre et au scû du Sage et judicieux ministre dangleterre, mais par quelqu'Un que donne a penser qu'il veut broüiller L'angleterre avec La france.

"Ce qui donne encore plus de lieu a avoir de luy cette penseé C'est que le traitté d'Utrecht ayant determiné les Limites des deux Nations pour la pesche, par desairs de vent, quoyque par toutes les nations les airs de vent se tracent en Ligne droite, il les a tracé en Ceintre a L'Est de Lisle de Sable, en quoy il semble avoir Intention de se mocquer de la france et de L'Irriter.

"La prise d'un vaisseau françois dans Le passage de Camceau, La Construction d'un fort a Canceau, Le nom d'albanie donné a la partye de la Nouvelle France qui est entre quinibequi et la ville de Port Royal pays qui n'a point esté Cedé par le traitté d'Utrecht, Les forts Construits, et Les Concessions donneés, Les Nations sauvages, et Les missionnaires maltraités dans ce pays appartenant a la france, ou du moins pretendu et Contesté par Elle.

"Tout cela pourroit bien Venir de quelque Anglois qui voudroit broüiller les deux Nations. C'est aux Anglois pacifiques a le punir et a la france a sopposer a de telles entreprises jusqu ce que les Limites soient regleés d'Une Maniere Equitable.

"Collationné et figuré sur une Copie de Mémoire ou notte en papier non Signeé ni dattée estant au Secrétariat du Chateau S.t Louis de Quebec ou elle est resteé Par Le Notaire Royal en la prevosté de Quebec y resident sous-signé ce jourdhuy Vingt cinq Juillet mil sept cent cinquante.

Du Laurent.

"François Bigot, Conseiller du Roy en ses Conseils, Intendant de justice, Police, finances et de la marine en la Nouvelle france.

"Certifions a tousqu'il appartiendra que M.r Dulaurent qui a signé la Collation de L'autre part Est notaire Royal en la prevosté de Quebec Et que foy doit Estre ajouteé a sa signature En la d.^e qualité; En temoin de quoy nous avons signeé et fait Contresigner ces presentes par nôtre secretaire et a Icelles fait apposer le Cachet de nos armes, fait en nôtre hotel a Quebec Le p.^{er} Aoust, mil sept cent Cinquante.

BIGOT

PAR MONSEIGNEUR

DESCHENAUX."

Endorsed. "Envoyé par Mr Bigot Intend.^t du Canada avec sa lettre au Mis de Puyzieulx du 1.er aoust 1750. No 25, 1723."

B.

CHAPTERS XIX., XX., XXI.

THE SIEGE OF LOUISBOURG AS DESCRIBED BY FRENCH WITNESSES.

Lettre d'un Habitant de Louisbourg contenant une Relation exacte et circonstanciée de la Prise de l'Isle Royale par les Anglois. À Québec, chez Guillaume le Sincère, à l'Image de la Vérité. MDCCXLV. [Extraits.]

[Literatim.]

" . . . Le mauvais succès dont cette entreprise (*against Annapolis*) a été suivie, est envisagé, avec raison, comme la cause de notre perte. Les Anglois ne nous auroient peut-être point inquietés, si nous n'eussions été les premiers à les insulter. Notre qualité d'aggresseurs nous a été funeste; je l'ai oüi conter à plus d'un ennemi, & je n'y vois que trop d'apparence. Les habitans de la nouvelle Angleterre étoient interressés à vivre en paix avec nous. Ils l'eussent sans doute fait, si nous ne nous étions point avisés mal à propos de les tirer de cette sécurité où ils etoient à notre égard. Ils comptoient que de part & d'autre, on ne prendroit aucun parti dans cette cruelle guerre qui a mis l'Europe en feu, et que nous nous tiendrions comme eux sur la seule défensive. La prudence le dictoit; mais elle n'est pas toujours la régle des actions des hommes: nous l'avons plus éprouvé que qui que ce soit. . . .

" . . . L'expedition de l'Acadie manquée, quoiqu'il y eût tout à parier qu'il reuissiroit par le peu de forces que les ennemis avoient pour nous résister, leur fit faire de serieuses réflexions sur notre crainte, ou notre faiblesse. Selon tous les apparences, ils en conclurent qu'ils devoient profiter d'une aussi favorable circonstance, puisque dès-lors ils travaillerent avec ardeur à l'armement qui leur était necessaire. Ils ne firent pas comme nous: ils se prêterent un secours mutuel: on arma dans tous leurs Ports, depuis l'Acadie jusqu'au bas de la Côte: on dépêcha en Angleterre, & on envoya, dit on, jusqu'à *la Jamaïque* afin d'en tirer tous les secours qu'il seroit possible. Cette entreprise fut concertée avec prudence, et l'on travailla tout l'hiver pour être prêt au premier beau tems.

" Les préparatifs n'en pouvaient être si secrets, qu'il n'en transpirât quelque chose. Nous en avions été informés dès les premiers instans, & assez à tems pour en pouvoir donner avis à la Cour. . . .

" Nous eumes tout l'hiver à nous, c'était plus qu'il n'en falloit pour nous mettre en état de défense; mais la terreur s'étoit emparée des esprits: on tenait des conseils, dont le résultat n'avoit rien que de bizarre et de puérile; cependant le tems s'écoulait, nous perdions de precieux momens en déliberations inutiles, & en résolutions presque aussitôt détruites que prises. Quelques ouvrages demandoient qu'on les parachevât: il en falloit renforcer quelques-uns, aug-

menter quelques autres, pourvoir à des postes, visiter tous
ceux de l'Isle, voir où la descente étoit plus facile, faire le
denombrement des personnes en état de porter les armes,
assigner à chacun son poste; enfin se donner tous les soins
et les mouvemens ordinaires en pareil cas; rien de tout cela
ne se faisoit; de sorte que nous avons été surpris, comme si
l'ennemi fût venu fondre' sur nous à l'improviste. Nous
aurions eu même assez de tems pour nous precautionner
mieux qu'on ne l'a fait, depuis le jour où nous vimes paroître les premiers Navires qui nous ont bloqués; car ils
n'y sont venues que les uns après les autres, ainsi que je
le dirai dans la suite. La négligence & la déraison avoient
conjuré la perte de notre malheureuse Isle. . . .

"Ce fut le quatorze [Mars], que nous vimes les premiers
Navires ennemis; ils n'étoient encore que deux, & nous les
primes d'abord pour des Vaisseaux François; mais nous
fumes bien tôt détrompés par leur manœuvre. Le nombre en
augmentoit de jour à autre, il en arriva jusqu'à la fin de
Mai. Ils croiserent long-tems, sans rien tenter. Le rendezvous général étoit devant notre Isle, où ils arrivoient de tous
côtez; car on avoit armé à l'Acadie, Plaisance, Baston, &
dans toute l'Amerique Anglaise. Les secours d'Europe ne
vinrent qu'en Juin. C'étoit moins une entreprise formée
par la Nation ou par le Roi, que par les seuls habitans de
la nouvelle Angleterre. Ces peuples singuliers ont des
Lois & une Police qui leur sont particulières, & leur Gouverneur tranche du Souverain. Cela est si vrai, que, quoiqu'il y eût guerre déclarée entre les deux Couronnes, il
nous la déclara lui de son chef & en son nom, comme s'il
avoit fallu qu'il eût autorisé son maître. Sa declaration
portoit, qu'il nous déclaroit la guerre pour lui, & pour tous
ses amis & alliés; il entendoit parler apparemment des
Sauvages qui leur sont soumis, qu'on appelle *Indiens*, &
que l'on distingue des Sauvages qui obéissent à la France.

On verra que l'Amiral *Warren* n'avoit rien à commander
aux troupes envoyées par le Gouverneur de Baston, & que
cet Amiral n'a été que Spectateur, quoique ce soit à lui que
nous nous soyons rendus. Il nous en avoit fait solliciter.
Ce qui marque bien l'independance qu'il y avoit entre l'armée de terre & celle de mer que l'on nous a toujours dis-
tinguées comme si elles eussent été de differentes Nations.
Quelle Monarchie s'est jamais gouvernée de la sorte?

"La plus grande partie des Bâtimens de transport étant
arrivés dans le commencement de Mai, nous les apperçûmes
le onze en ordre de bataille, au nombre de quatre-vingt seize
venant du côté de Canceaux & dirigeant leur route vers la
Pointe plate de la Baye de *Gabarus*. Nous ne doutames
plus qu'ils n'y fissent leur descente. C'est alors qu'on vit
la nécessité des precautions que nous aurions dû prendre.
On y envoya à la hâte un détachement de cent hommes, tirés
de la garnison & des Milices, sous le commandement du
sieur *Morpain*, Capitaine de Port. Mais que pouvait un
aussi faible corps, contre la multitude que les ennemis
debarquoient! Cela n'aboutit qu'à faire tuer une partie
des nôtres. Le sieur *Morpain* trouva déjà près de deux
milles hommes débarqués; il en tua quelques-uns & se retira.

"L'Ennemi s'empare de toute la campagne, & un détachement s'avance jusques auprès de la batterie Royale. Pour
le coup, la frayeur nous saisit tous; on parla dès l'instant
d'abandonner cette magnifique batterie, qui auroit été notre
plus grande défense, si l'on eût sçu en faire usage. On tint
tumultuairement divers Conseils là-dessus. Il seroit bien
difficile de dire les raisons qui portoient à un aussi étrange
procédé; si ce n'est une terreur panique, que ne nous a
plus quitté de tout le Siège. Il n'y avoit pas eu encore
un seul coup de fusil tiré sur cette batterie, que les ennemis ne pouvoient prendre qu'en faisant leurs approches
comme pour la Ville, & l'assiégeant, pour ainsi dire, dans

les régles.   On en a dit sourdement une raison sur laquelle
je ne suis point en état de décider; je l'ai pourtant entendu
assurer par une personne qui était dans la batterie; mais
mon poste étant en Ville, il y avoit long-tems que je
n'étois allé à la batterie Royale: C'est que ce qui détermina
à un abandon si criminel, est qu'il y avoit deux brêches
qui n'avoient point été réparées.   Si cela est, le crime
est encore plus grand, parce que nous avions eu plus de
loisir qu'il n'en falloit, pour mettre ordre à tout.

  " Quoiqu'il en soit, la résolution fut prise de renoncer à ce
puissant boulevard, malgré les représentations de quelques
gens sages, qui gémissoient de voir commettre une si lourde
faute.   Ils ne purent se faire écouter.   Inutilement remon-
trèrent-ils que ce seroit témoigner notre foiblesse aux ennemis, qui ne manqueroient point de profiter d'une aussi
grande étourderie, & qui tourneroient cette même batterie
contre nous; que pour faire bonne contenance & ne point
réchauffer le courage à l'ennemi, en lui donnant dès le premier jour, une si grande espérance de réussir, il falloit se
maintenir dans ce poste important le plus que l'on pourroit:
qu'il étoit évident qu'on s'y conserveroit plus de quinze
jours, & que ce délai pouvoit être employé à retirer tous
les canons dans la Ville.   On répondit que le Conseil l'avoit
résolu autrement; ainsi donc par ordre du Conseil, on aban-
donna le 13 sans avoir essuyé le moindre feu, une batterie
de trente pièces de canon, qui avoit couté au Roi des sommes
immenses.   Cet abandon se fit avec tant de précipitation,
qu'on ne se donna pas le temps d'enclouer les canons de la
manière que cela se pratique; aussi les ennemis s'en ser-
virent-ils dès le lendemain.   Cependant on se flatoit du contraire; je fus sur le point de gager qu'ils ne tarderoient
guères á nous en battre.   On étoit si peu à soi, qu'avant de
se retirer de la batterie, le feu prit à un baril de poudre, qui
pensa faire sauter plusieurs personnes, & brûla la robe

d'un Religieux Récolet. Ce n'étoit pas de ce moment que l'imprudence caracterisoit nos actions, il y avoit long-tems qu'elle s'étoit refugiée parmi nous.

"Ce que j'avois prévu arriva. Dès le quatorze les enne-mis nous saluèrent avec nos propres Canons, dont ils firent un feu épouvantable. Nous leur répondimes de dessus les murs; mais nous ne pouvions leur rendre le mal qu'ils nous faisoient, rasant nos maisons, & foudroyant tout ce qui étoit à leur portée.

"Tandis que les Anglois nous chauffoient de la batterie Royale, ils établissoient une Plate-forme de Mortiers sur la hauteur de Rabasse proche le Barachois du côté de l'Ouest, qui tirerent le seize jour où a commencé le bombardement. Ils avoient des Mortiers dans toutes les batteries qu'ils éleverent. Les bombes nous ont beaucoup incommodé. . . .

"Les ennemis paroissoient avoir envie de pousser vigou-reusement le Siège. Ils établirent une batterie auprès de la Plaine de *Brissonnet,* qui commença à tirer le dix-sept, & travaillerent encore à une autre, pour battre directement la Porte Dauphine, entre les maisons du nommé *la Roche* & *Lescenne,* Canonier. Ils ne s'en tinrent point à ces bat-teries, quoiqu'elles nous battissent en brêche; mais ils en dresserent de nouvelles pour soutenir les premières. La Plaine marécageuse du bord de la Mer à la Pointe blanche, les incommodoit fort, & empêchoit qu'ils ne poussassent leurs travaux comme ils l'auroient souhaité: pour y rémé-dier, ils pratiquerent divers boyaux, afin de couper cette Plaine; étant venus à bout de la dessécher, ils y firent deux batteries qui ne tirerent que quelques jours après. Il y en avoit une au dessus de l'habitation de *Martissance,* composée de sept pièces de canon, prises en partie de la Batterie Royale & de la Pointe plate ou s'etait fait le débarquement. On la destinoit à miner le Bastion Dau-phin; ces deux dernières batteries ont presque rasé la Porte Dauphine.

" Le dix-huit nous vîmes paroître un Navire, avec Pavillon Français, qui cherchoit à donner dans le Port. Il fut reconnu pour être effectivement de notre Nation, & afin de favoriser son entrée, nous fimes un feu continuel sur la Batterie Royale. Les Anglais ne pouvant resister à la vivacité de notre feu, qui ne discontinuoit point, ne purent empêcher ce Navire d'entrer, qu'il leur eut été facile sans cela de couler à fond. Ce petit refraichissement nous fit plaisir ; c'étoit un Navire Basque : il nous en étoit venu un autre dans le courant d'Avril.

" Nous n'eumes pas le même bonheur pour un Navire de Granville, qui se présenta aussi pour entrer, quelques jours après ; mais qui ayant été poursuivi, fut contraient de s'echouer, & se battit long-tems. Celui qui le commandoit, nomme *Daguenet*, étoit un brave homme, lequel ne se rendit qu'à la dernière extrêmité, & après avoir été accablé par le nombre. Il avoit transporté tous les Canons d'un même côté, & en fit un feu si terrible, que les ennemis n'eurent pas bon marché de lui. Il fallut armer presque toutes leurs Chaloupes pour le prendre. Nous avons sçu de ce Capitaine, qu'il avoit rencontré *le Vigilant*, & que c'étoit de ce malheureux Vaisseau, qu'il avoit apris que l'Isle Royale étoit bloquée. Cette circonstance importe au récit que je vais faire.

" Vous êtes persuadés, en France, que la prise de ce Vaisseau de guerre a occasionné la notre, cela est vraie en quelque sorte, mais nous eussions pu nous soutenir sans lui si nous n'avions pas entassé fautes sur fautes, ainsi que vous avez dû vous en apercevoir jusqu'à présent. Il est vrai que, graces à nos imprudences, lors que ce puissant secours nous arrivoit, nous commencions à être sans espérance. S'il fût entré, comme il le pouvoit, nous serions encore dans nos biens, & les Anglais eussent été forcés de se retirer.

" *Le Vigilant* parut le vingt-huit ou le vingt-neuf **de**

Mai, à environ une lieue et demie de distance de *Santarge* [*sic*]. Le vent était pour lors Nord-Est, & par conséquent bon pour entrer. Il laissoit la Flotte Anglaise à deux lieues & demi sous le vent. Rien ne pouvoit donc l'empêcher d'entrer; & c'est par la plus grande de toutes les fatalités qu'il est devenu la proye de nos Vainqueurs. Témoins de sa manœuvre, il n'étoit personne de nous qui ne donnât des malédictions à une manœuvre si mal concertée & si imprudente.

"Le Vaisseau, commandé par M. *de la Maisonfort*, au lieu de suivre sa route, ou d'envoyer sa chaloupe à terre pour prendre langue, ainsi que le requéroit la prudence, s'amusa à poursuivre un Corsaire monté en Senault qu'il rencontra malheureusement sous la terre. Ce Corsaire, que commandoit un nommé *Brousse* (Rous) manœuvre d'une autre manière que le Vaisseau Français. Il se battit toujours en retraite, forçant de voiles et attirant son ennemi vers l'Escadre Angloise; ce qui lui réussit; car le Vigilant se trouva tellement engagé, qu'il ne lui fut plus possible de se sauver, quand on eut vu le danger. Deux Frégates l'attaquerent d'abord; M. de la Maisonfort leur répondit par un feu très vif, qui en mit bien-tôt une hors de combat; elle fut démâtée de son grand mât, désemparée de toutes les manœuvres, et contrainte de se retirer. Mais il vint cinq autres Frégates qui chaufferent le Vigilant de toutes parts; le combat que nous voyons à découvert, dura depuis cinq heures du soir jusqu'à dix. Enfin il fallut céder à la force, & se rendre. Les ennemis ont beaucoup perdu dans ce combat, & le commandant Français eut quatre-vingts hommes tués ou blessés; le Vaisseau n'a été que fort peu endommagé.

"On doit dire, à la gloire de M. de la Maisonfort, qu'il a fait preuve d'une extrême valeur dans ce combat; mais il auroit mieux valu qu'il eût suivi sa destination; c'étoit

tout ce que les intérêts du Roi exigeoient. Le Ministre ne
l'envoyoit pas pour donner la chasse à aucun Vaisseau ennemi; chargé de munitions de guerre & de bouche, son
Vaisseau étoit uniquement destiné à ravitailler notre malheureuse Place, qui n'auroit jamais été en effet emportée,
si nous eussions pû recevoir un si grand secours; mais
nous étions des victimes dévouées à la colère du Ciel, qui
a voulu faire servir contre nous jusqu'à nos propres forces.
Nous avons sçu des Anglais, depuis notre reddition, qu'ils
commençoient à manquer de munitions de guerre, & que
la poudre étoit encore plus rare dans leur armée que parmi
nous. Ils avoient même tenu quelques Conseils pour lever
le Siége. La poudre trouvée dans le Vigilant fit bientôt
évanouir cette idée; nous nous apperçumes que leur feu
avoit depuis beaucoup augmenté.

"Je sçai que le Commandant de cet infortuné Vaisseau
dira, pour se justifier, qu'il étoit important pour lui d'enlever le Corsaire, afin de se régler sur les nouvelles qu'il
en auroit appris. Mais cela ne l'excuse point; il sçavoit
que Louisbourg étoit bloqué, c'en étoit assez; qu'avoit-il
besoin d'en sçavoir davantage? S'il craignoit que les
Anglais n'eussent été maîtres de la Place, il étoit aisé de
s'en instruire, en envoyant son canot ou sa chaloupe, &
sacrifiant quelques hommes pour sa sûreté; la batterie
Royale ne devoit point l'inquiéter, nous en aurions agi
comme avec le Navire Basque, dont nous facilitâmes
l'entrée par un feu excessif. La perte d'un secours si
considerable ralentit le courage de ceux qui avoient le plus
conservé de fermeté; il n'étoit pas difficile de juger que
nous serions contraints d'implorer la clémence des Anglais,
& plusieurs personnes furent d'avis qu'il falloit dès-lors demander à capituler. Nous avons cependant tenu un mois
au-delà; c'est plus qu'on n'auroit pu exiger dans l'abbate-
ment où venoit de nous jetter un si triste spectacle.

" L'Ennemi s'occupa à nous canoner & à nous bombarder
toute le reste du mois, sans faire des progrès bien sensibles,
& qui lui pussent donner de l'espoir. Comme il ne nous
attaquoit point dans les formes; qu'il n'avoit pratiqué
aucuns retranchemens pour se couvrir, il n'osoit s'aprocher
de trop près; tous nos coups portoient; au lieu que la
plûpart des siens étoient perdus: aussi ne tirons-nous que
lorsque nous le jugions nécessaire. Il tiroit, lui, plus de
cinq à six cens coups de canon par jour, contre nous vingt;
à la verité, le peu de poudre que nous avions, obligeoit à
n'en user que sobrement. La mousqueterie étoit peu
d'usage.

" J'ai oublié de dire que, dès les premiers jours du siége,
les ennemis nous avoient fait sommer de nous rendre; mais
nous répondîmes selon ce que le devoir nous prescrivoit;
l'Officier, deputé pour nous en faire la proposition, voyant
que nous rejettions ses offres, proposa de faire sortir les
Dames, avec assurance qu'elles ne seroient point insultées,
et qu'on les feroit garder dans les maisons qui subsistoient
encore en petit nombre; car l'ennemi, en débarquant, avoit
presque tout brûlé ou détruit dans la campagne. Nous re-
merçiâmes cet officier, parceque nos femmes & nos enfans
étoient sûrement dans les logemens que nous leur avions
faits. On avoit mis sur les casemates de longues piéces de
bois, placées en biais, qui, en amortissant le coup de la
bombe, la rejettent, & empêchent l'effet de son poids. C'est
là dessous que nous les avions enterrés.

" Au commencement de Juin les Assiégeans parurent reprendre une nouvelle vigueur; n'étant pas contens du peu
de succès qu'ils avoient eu jusques-là, ils s'attacherent à
d'autres entreprises, & voulurent essayer de nous attaquer
par le côté de la mer. Pour réussir, ils tenterent de nous
surprendre la batterie de l'entrée: un Détachement d'environ cinq cens hommes s'y étant transporté pendant la nuit

du six au sept, fut taillé en pièces par le sieur *Daillebout*, Capitaine de Compagnie, qui y commandoit, & qui tira sur eux à mitraille; plus de trois cens resterent sur la place, & il n'y eut de sauvés que ceux qui demandoient quartier, les blessés furent transférés dans nos hôpitaux. Nous fîmes en cette occasion cent dix-neuf prisonniers, & n'eûmes que trois hommes de tués ou blessés; mais nous perdîmes un Canonier, qui fut fort regretté. . . .

"Pour sur croit d'infortune, il arrive aux Anglois le 15 une Escadre de six Vaisseaux de guerre, venant de Londres. Ces Vaisseaux croiserent devant la Ville, avec les Frégattes sans tirer un seul coup. Mais nous avons sçu depuis que, si nous eussions tarder à capituler, tous les Vaisseaux se seroient embossés, et nous auroient fait essuyer le feu le plus vif. Leurs dispositions n'ont point eté ignorée, je rapporterai l'ordre qu'ils devoient tenir.

"Les ennemis ne s'étoient encore point avisés de tirer à boulets rouges; ils le firent le dix-huit & le dix-neuf, avec un succès qui auroit eté plus grand, sans le prompt secours qui y fut apporté. Le feu prit à trois ou quatre maisons, mais on l'eut bientôt éteint. La promptitude en ces sortes d'occasions, est la seul ressource que l'on puisse avoir.

"L'Arrivée de l'Escadre étoit, sans doute, l'objet de ce nouveau salut de la part de l'Armée de terre; son Général qui vouloit avoir l'honneur de notre conquête, étant bien aisé de nous forcer à nous soumettre avant que l'Escadre se fût mise en devoir de nous y contraindre.

"L'Amiral de son côté songeoit à se procurer l'honneur de nous reduire. Un Officier vint pour cet effet, le vingt-un, nous proposer de sa part, que si nous avions à nous rendre, il seroit plus convenable de le faire à lui, qui auroit des égards que nous ne trouverions peut être pas dans le Commandant de terre. Tout cela marquoit peu d'intelligence entre les deux Généraux, & verifie assés la remarque que j'ai ci-devant faite : on n'eût jamais dit en effet que ces troupes fussent de la même Nation & sous l'obéissance du même Prince. Les Anglais sont les seuls peuples capables de ces bizarreries, qui font cependant partie de cette précieuse liberté dont ils se montrent si jaloux.

"Nous répondîmes à l'Officier, par qui l'Amiral Warren nous avoit fait donner cet avis, que nous n'avions point de réponse à lui faire, & que quand nous en serions à cette extrémité, nous verrions le parti qu'il conviendroit d'embrasser. Cette fanfaronade eût fait rire quiconque auroit été témoin de notre embarras en particulier ; il ne pouvoit être plus grand : cet Officier dût s'en apperçevoir, malgré la bonne contenance que nous affections. Il est difficile que le visage ne décéle les mouvements du cœur. Les Conseils étoient plus frequens que jamais, mais non plus salutaires ; on s'assembloit sans trop sçavoir pourquoi, aussi ne sçavoit-on que résoudre. J'ai souvent ri de ces assemblées, où il ne se passoit rien que de ridicule, & qui n'annonçat le trouble & l'indécision. Le soin de notre défense n'étoit plus ce qui occupoit. Si les Anglois eussent sçu profiter de notre épouvante il y auroit eu longtems qu'ils nous auroient emportés, l'épée en main. Mais il faut convenir à leur louange, qu'ils avoient autant de peur que nous. Cela m'a plusieurs fois rappellé la fable du Liévre & des Grenouilles.

"Le but de nos frequens Conseils étoit de dresser des articles de capitulation. On y employa jusqu'au vingt sept, que le sieur Lopinot, Officier, sortit pour les porter au Commandant de terre. L'on se flatoit de les lui faire mieux goûter qu'à l'Amiral. Mais ils étoient si extraordinaires, que malgré l'envie que ce Général avoit de nous voir rendre à lui, il se donna à peine la patience de les écouter. Je me souviens que nous demandions par un article, cinq piéces de canon, & deux mortiers de fonte. De pareilles propositions ne quadroient guéres avec notre situation.

"Afin de réussir d'un côté ou d'autre, on envoya proposer les mêmes conditions à l'Amiral. Cette négociation avoit été confiée au sieur *Bonaventure*, Capitaine de Compagnie, qui s'intrigua beaucoup auprès de M. Warren, & qui, quoique la plûpart de nos articles fussent rejettez, en obtint pourtant d'assés honorables. On arrêta donc la Capitulation telle que les nouvelles publiques l'ont raportée. Elle nous fut annoncée par deux coups de canon tirés à bord de l'Amiral, ainsi qu'on en avoit donné l'ordre au Sieur *Bonaventure*. A cette nouvelle, nous reprimes un peu de tranquillité; car nous avions sujet d'apprehender le sort le plus triste. Nous craignons à tout moment, que les ennemis, sortant de leur aveuglement, ne se présentassent pour nous enlever d'assaut. Tout les y convioit; il y avoit deux bréches de la longueur d'environ cinquante pieds chacune, l'une à la porte Dauphine, & l'autre à l'Eperon, qui est vis-à-vis. Ils nous ont dit depuis que la resolution en avoit été prise, & l'exécution renvoyée au lendemain. Les Navires devoient les favoriser, & s'embosser de la maniere suivante.

"Quatre Vaisseaux & quatre Frégattes étoient destinés pour le bastion Dauphin: un egal nombre de Vaisseaux & de Frégattes, parmi lesquels étoit le Vigilant, devoit attaquer la piéce de la Grave: & trois autres Vaisseaux & autant de Frégattes avoient ordre de s'attacher à l'Isle de l'entree. Nous n'eussions jamais pû repondre au feu de tous ces Vaisseaux & défendre en même tems nos brêches; de façon qu'il auroit fallu succomber, quelques efforts que nous eussions pû faire, & nous voir réduits à recourir à la clémence d'un vainqueur, de la générosité duquel il y avoit à se défier. L'Armée de terre n'étoit composée que de gens ramassés, sans subordination ni discipline, qui nous auroit fait éprouver tout ce que l'insolence & la rage ont de plus furieux. La capitulation n'a point empêché qu'ils ne nous ayent bien fait du mal.

"C'est donc par une protection visible de la Providence, que nous avons prévenu une journée qui nous auroit été si funeste. Ce qui nous y a le plus déterminé, est le peu de poudre qui nous restoit: je puis assurer que nous n'en avions pas pour faire trois décharges. C'est ici le point critique & sur lequel on cherche le plus à en imposer au public mal instruit: on voudroit lui persuader qu'il nous en restoit encore vingt milliers. Fausseté insigne! Je n'ai aucune interêt à déguiser la vérité; on doit d'autant plus m'en croire, que je ne prétends pas par-là justifier entierement nos Officiers. S'ils n'ont pas capitulé trop tôt ils avoient commis assez d'autres fautes, pour ne les pas laver du blâme qu'ils ont encouru. Il est constant que nous n'avions plus que trent-sept barils de poudre, à cent livres chacun; voilà ce qui est veritable, & non pas tout ce qu'on raconte de contraire. Nous n'en trouvions même d'abord que trente-cinq; mais les recherches qu'on fit nous en procurerent deux autres, cachés apparemment par les Canoniers, qu'on sçait être partout accoutumés à ce larcin."

II.

"Lettre de Monsieur Du Chambon au Ministre, à Rochefort, le 2 Septembre, 1745.

"*Archives de la Marine.*

"Monseigneur,

"J'ai l'honneur de vous rendre compte de l'attaque et reddition de Louisbourg, ainsy que vous me l'avez ordonné par votre lettre du 20 de ce mois.

"Nous eûmes connaissance d'un battiment le quatorze mars dernier parmy les glaces qui étaient détachées du golfe; ce battiment parut à 3 ou 4 lieues devant le port et drivait vers la partie du sud-ouest, et il nous disparut l'après-midi.

" Le 19 du d. nous vîmes encore en dehors les glaces un senaux qui couroit le long de la banquise qui était etendue depuis Escartary jusques au St Esprit, plusieurs chasseurs et soldats, hivernant dans le bois, m'informèrent qu'ils avaient vu, les uns deux battiments qui avoient viré de bord à Menadou, et d'autres qu'ils avoient entendu du canon du côté du St Esprit, ce qui fit que j'ordonnai aux habitans des ports de l'isle, qui étaient à portée de la ville, de se renger aux signaux qui leur seroient faits.

" Je fis en outre rassembler les habitans de la ville et port de Louisbourg, je formai de ceux de la ville quatre compagnies, et je donnai ordre à ceux du port de se renger à la batterie Royale, et à celle de l'isle de l'entrée, au signaux que je leur fit donner.

" Le 9 avril nous aperçûmes à l'éclaircy de la brume, et parmi les glaces vers la Pointe Blanche, quatre battimens, le premier ayant tiré quelques coups de canon, l'islot lui répondit d'un coup, et le battiment l'ayant rendu sur le champ, cela nous confirma dans l'idée que c'étoient des François qui cherchoient à forcer les glaces pour entrer dans le port. D'ailleurs ils profitoient des éclaircis pour s'y enfourner vers le port, et cela nous assuroit pour ainsi dire, que ce n'étoit pas des corsaires, mais bien des François.

" Etant dans le doute si c'étoit des basttiments François ou Anglois, j'envoyai ordre à Monsieur Benoit, officier commandant au port Toulouse, de dettacher quelqu'un de confiance à Canceau, pour apprendre s'il y avoit des basttiments, et si on y travailloit, ou s'il y avoit apparance de quelque entreprise sur l'isle Royale.

" Monsieur Benoit dettacha le nommé Jacob Coste, habitant, avec un soldat de la garnison et un Sauvage, pour faire quelques prisonniers au dit lieu. Ces trois envoyés mirent pied à terre à la Grande Terre du costé de Canceau; ils eurent le bonheur de faire quatre prisonniers anglois; et revenant avec eux, les prisonniers se rendirent maitres de nos trois François, un soir qu'ils étaient endormis, et nous n'avons pu apprendre aucune nouvelle ni des envoyés ni de l'ennemy.

"Je fus informé, le 22, par deux hommes, venus par terre du port de Toulouse, qu'on entendait tirer du canon à Canceau, et qu'ils travailloient au rétablissement de cette isle, et un troisième arrivé le soir, m'assura avoir été témoin d'un grand combat sur le navire *St-Esprit*, qu'il avoit vu venir du large trois vaisseaux sur quatre qui étoient pour lors à cette coste, et que le feu ayant commencé après la Jonction de ces bastimens, il avoit duré bien avant dans la nuit, ce qui nous engageoit à nous flatter que nous avions des vaisseaux sur la coste.

"Le 30 du d. nous vîmes sept vaisseaux parmy les glaces, dont il y avoit quatre vaisseaux, deux corvettes et un brigantin, et ils se sont tenus ce jour vers les isles à Dion, sans pavillon, ni flamme.

"Ces battiments continuèrent à se faire voir pendant quelques jours, depuis la Pointe Blanche jusques à Port de Noue, sous pavillon blanc, et les glaces s'étant écartées de la coste, nous apperçûmes, le 7 mai, un navire qui faisait route pour le port; il y entra heureusement; ce navire venoit de St Jean de Luz, commandé par le Sieur Janson Dufoure; il nous apprit qu'il avoit été poursuivi la veille par trois vaisseaux, qu'une frégatte de 24 canons l'avoit joint, et qu'il s'estoit sauvé, après un combat de trois volées de canon et de mousquetterie.

"Le 8 à la pointe du jour, nous eûmes connaissance de tous les vaisseaux au vent du port dans la partie du sudouest, ce qui nous occasionna une alerte, les signaux ayant été faits, les habitans de Lorembec et de la Baleine, qui étoient les plus proches de la ville, s'y rangèrent aux postes qui leur étoient destinés, ainsi que les habitans de la ville et du port, le même jour ces vaisseaux prirent à notre vue deux caboteurs frettés par le Roy et qui venoient du port de Toulouse chargés de bois de corde pour le chauffage des troupes et des corps de garde, ils prirent aussy une chaloupe qui venoit des Isles Madame chargée de gibier.

" Comme nous doutions toujours si ces vaisseaux étoient anglois ou françois jusqu'à ce jour, les glaces empêchant l'entrée du port depuis qu'ils avoient paru ensemble, j'avois eu la précaution d'arrêter, conjointement avec monsieur Bigot, deux battiments pour les faire partir en cas de nécessité pour la France, pour porter les nouvelles à Sa Grandeur de la situation où se trouvoit la colonie, et sitôt que nous fûmes confirmés par le prise de ces caboteurs que c'étoit des vaisseaux anglois et qu'il y en avoit d'autres à Canceau, au rapport des équipages qui s'étoient sauvés, nous fîmes partir à la faveur de la brume et de la nuit obscure du 10 mai, *La Société*, capitaine Subtil, avec nos lettres pour Monseigneur, pour lui apprendre l'état de la colonie avec les circonstances de vaisseaux qui bloquèrent le port ; quand à l'autre bâtiment qui avoit été fretté, nous avons été obligé de la faire couler, après la descente faite par l'ennemy, étant impossible de la faire sortir.

" Les vaisseaux ennemis qui étoient au devant du port, se servant de la chaloupe qu'ils avoient prise chargée de gibier pour descendre et mettre pied à terre à Gabarrus, à notre vue, je fis partir, le 9, un détachement de 20 soldats sous le commandement du sieur de Lavallière pour aller par terre à Gabarrus, et un autre de 39 hommes d'habitans, sous le commandement du sieur Daccarrette dans un charroye pour s'emparer de cette chaloupe, mais ces deux détachements ne purent joindre cette chaloupe ; celui de terre y resta deux jours et ne rentra en ville que le onze du soir, et celui du

sieur Daccarrette rentra le 12 au matin, ayant été obligé
d'abandonner le charroye à fourché où il avoit été à la sortie
de Gabarrus.

"Le 11, à trois ou quatre heures du matin, nous eûmes
connoissance de dessus les remparts de la ville, d'environ
100 voiles qui parurent du côté de fourché, derrière les
isles à Dion, les vents étant de la partie de nord-ouest,
ces battiments s'approchoient à vue d'œil, je ne doute pas
que ce ne fussent des bastiments de transport, je fis tirer
les signaux qui avoient été ordonnés, plusieurs habitans et
particuliers n'ont pu s'y rendre, et entr'autres ceux des
havres éloignés, la campagne étant investie de l'ennemy,
et même plusieurs ont été faits prisonniers voulant se rendre
en ville.

"Je fis aussy commander un détachement pour s'opposer
à la descente de l'ennemy, et ce détachement au nombre de
80 hommes et 30 soldats, le surplus habitans, partit sous
le commandement de Monsieur Morpain et du Sieur Mesi-
lac, il se transporta au-dessous de la Pointe Blanche, â
l'endroit où l'ennemy avoit commencé à faire sa descente,
il le fit rembarquer dans les voitures, mais pendant le temps
qu'il étoit en cet endroit à repousser l'ennemy, celui-cy fit
faire une autre descente plus considérable de troupes de
débarquement à l'anse de la Cormorandière, entre la Pointe-
Plate et Gabarrus.

"Il s'y transporta avec ses troupes, sitôt qu'il en eût
connoissance, mais l'ennemy avoit mis pied à terre et s'étoit
emparé des lieux les plus propres qu'il jugea pour sa défense,
cela n'empêcha pas ce détachement d'aller l'attaquer, mais
l'ennemy étant beaucoup plus supérieur en nombre, il fut
contraint de se retirer dans le bois; nous avons eu à cette
occasion 4 ou 5 soldats tués ou faits prisonniers, ainsy que
4 ou 5 habitans ou particuliers du nombre desquels fut
Monsieur Laboularderie; nous eûmes encore 3 ou 4 blessés
qui rentrèrent en ville.

"Depuis la retraite de ce détachement l'ennemy acheva son débarquement au nombre de 4 à 500 hommes, ainsy que des planches et autres matériaux, au rapport de ceux du détachement qui rentrèrent les derniers en ville.

"L'ennemy ayant avancé dans la campagne, se fit voir en grand nombre, mais sans ordre, à la portée du canon de la pointe Dauphine et du bastion du Roy.

"Les montagnes qui commandent cette porte étoient couvertes de monde : à deux heures après-midi les canons, qui étoient sur la Barbette, tirèrent sur plusieurs pelotons qui paroissoient défiler du côté du fond de la baye, nous nous aperçûmes aussy qu'ils défiloient en quantité le long du bois vers la batterie royale, je fis fermer les portes et je fis pourvoir sur le champ à la sûreté de la ville et placer environ 1100 hommes qui s'y sont trouvés pour la défendre.

"Sur le soir, monsieur Thiery, capitaine de compagnie qui commandoit à la batterie royale, m'écrivit une lettre par laquelle il me marquoit le mauvois état de son poste, que cela pourroit donner de grande facilités à l'ennemy s'il s'en emparoit, qu'il croyoit pour le bien du service qu'il seroit à propos de travailler à le faire sauter après avoir encloué les canons.

"Je fis à cette occasion assembler le conseil de guerre, monsieur Verrier, ingénieur en chef, ayant aussi été appelé, fit son rapport que cette batterie avoit ses épaulements du costé de la terre démolis dès l'année dernière, que les chemins couverts n'étoient pas palissadés, et qu'il étoit hors d'état de résister à une attaque par terre de trois à quatre mille homme avec 400 hommes qu'il y avoit dedans pour la défense.

"Sur ce rapport le conseil de guerre décida unanimement qu'il convenoit pour la sûreté de la ville, manquant de monde pour la défendre, de l'abandonner après en avoir encloué les canons et enlevé le plus de munitions de guerre et de bouche qu'on pourroit.

"Je ne dois pas oublier de vous informer que le même conseil de guerre vouloit faire sauter cette batterie; mais que monsieur Verrier, s'y étant opposé fortement, on la laissa subsister.

"J'envoyai l'ordre en conséquence à monsieur Thiery pour abandonner la dite batterie, après qu'il auroit encloué les canons, et enlevé le plus de munitions de guerre et de bouche qu'il pourroit; cet officier travailla le soir à faire enclouer tous les canons; il fit transporter partie des vivres et des munitions et se retira à la ville avec sa troupe vers minuit.

"La dite batterie n'ayant pas été entiérement évacuée ce soir, je fis partir le lendemain les Sieurs St. Etienne, lieutenant, et Souvigny, enseigne, avec une vingtaine d'hommes pour parachever la dite évacuation, ce qu'ils firent à l'exception de tous les boulets de canon et bombes qui y sont restés, n'ayant pas pu les emporter.

"Ayant jugé nécessaire conjointement avec monsieur Bigot de faire couler tous les bastiments qui étoient armés dans le port, pour empêcher l'ennemy de s'en emparer, je commandai, le 12, le sieur Verger, enseigne, avec 5 soldats et des matelots pour faire couler ceux qui etoient vis-à-vis la ville, et le sieur Bellemont, enseigne, avec la même opération au fond de la baye, et retirer l'huile de la tour de la lanterne, ce qu'ils exécutèrent.

"Le 13, je fis sortir toutes les compagnies de milice avec des haches et des engins pour démolir les maisons qui étoient à la porte Dauphine jusqu'au Barruchois, et pour enlever le bois en ville pour le chauffage de la garnison, n'en ayant pas, et pour faire brûler toutes celles qu'on ne pourroit pas démolir, afin d'empêcher l'ennemy de s'y loger.

"Je fis soutenir ces travailleurs par 80 soldats François et Suisses commandé par monsieur Deganne, capitaine, et Rasser, officier Suisse.

"Comme ils finissaient et qu'ils étoient au moment de se retirer en ville, il parut au Barruchois et dans les vallons des hauteurs plusieurs pelotons de l'armée ennemie, il y eût même quelques coups de fusils de tirés par ceux qui étoient les plus près; nous n'eûmes personne de tué ni de blessé, et nos gens virent tomber deux hommes de l'ennemy.

"L'ennemy s'est emparé de la batterie Royale, le 13, et le lendemain il tira sur la ville plusieurs coups de canon de deux qu'il avoit désencloué.

"Le même jour l'ennemy commença aussi à nous tirer plusieurs bombes de 12 pouches, pesant 180 l. et de 9 pouces d'une batterie de quatre mortiers qu'ils avoient estably sur la hauteur derrière les plaines, vis-à-vis le bastion du Roy.

"Cette batterie de mortiers n'a pas cessé de tirer de distance en distance, ainsi que douze mortiers à grenades royales que l'ennemy y avoit placés, et deux autres canons qu'ils ont désencloués à la batterie royale, mais ce feu n'a fait aucun progrès jusqu'au 18, et n'a tué ni blessé personne.

"Le 16, je fis partir un exprès en chaloupe pour porter une lettre à monsieur Marin, officier de Canada, qui commandoit un détachement de Canadiens et des Sauvages à l'Acadie, avec ordre de partir pour se rendre en toute diligence à Louisbourg, avec son détachement; c'étoit une course de 20 à 25 jours au plus, s'il avoit été aux mines, ainsi que l'on m'avoit assuré; mais ce detachement étoit parti pour le port Royal lorsque l'exprès y arriva.

"Cet exprès fut obligé d'y aller: il lui remit la lettre dont il étoit chargé, il tint conseil, plusieurs de son party ne voulurent pas le suivre, mais lui s'étant mis en chemin avec ceux de bonne volonté qui voulurent le suivre, il eût toutes les peines imaginables, à ce qu'on m'a assuré, de trouver des voitures dans toute l'Acadie, propres pour son transport.

"Ils s'y embarquèrent environ 3 à 400 dans un bateau de 25 tonneaux et dans environ une centaine de canots. Comme ils étoient dans la baie à doubler une pointe, ils furent attaqués par un bateau corsaire de 14 canons et autant de pierriers; cet officier soutint l'attaque avec vigueur, et dans le temps qu'il étoit au moment d'aborder le corsaire pour l'enlever, un autre corsaire de la même force vint au secours de son camarade, ce qui obligea le dit Sieur Marin d'abandonner la partie et de faire côte.

"Cette rencontre lui a fait perdre plusieurs jours et il n'a pu se rendre sur les terres de l'Isle Royale qu'au commencement de juillet, après que Louisbourg a été rendu; si ce détachement s'étoit rendu quinze ou vingt jours avant la reddition de la ville, je suis plus que persuadé que l'ennemy auroit été contraint de lever le siège de terre, par la terreur qu'il avoit de ce détachement qu'il pensoit être au nombre de plus de 2500.

"Je dois aussi informer Sa Grandeur que ce détachement a tué et pris, comme il se retiroit du passage de Fronsac, pour aller à l'Acadie, après notre départ, treize hommes d'un corsaire anglois qui étoit à leur passage pour les empêcher de passer, ces hommes ayant été avec leurs canots pour faire de l'eau, ils sont tombés entre les mains de ceux de ce détachement.

"Le 18, messieurs les généraux anglois me sommèrent de rendre la ville, forteresses et terres en dépendant, avec l'artillerie, les armes et les munitions de guerre qui en dépendent sous l'obéissance de la Grande Bretagne, en conséquence de quoy, promettoient de traiter humainement tous les sujets du Roy mon maître qui y étoient dedans, que leurs biens leur seroient assurés, et qu'ils auraient la liberté de se transporter avec leurs effets dans quelque partie de la domination du Roy de France, en Europe, qu'ils jugeroit à propos.

"Je répondis sur le champ à cette sommation que le Roy

mon maître m'ayant confié la défense de la place, je ne
pouvois qu'après la plus rigoureuse attaque écouter une
semblable proposition, et que je n'avois d'autre réponse à
faire à cette demande que par les bouches des canons.

" L'ennemy commença à établir, le 19, une batterie de
sept pièces de canon dans les plaines et derrière un petit
étang, vis-à-vis la face du bastion du Roy, laquelle batterie
n'a pas cessé de tirer des boulets de 12, 18 et 24 depuis ce
jour jusqu'à la reddition de la place, sur le casernes, le mur
du bastion du Roy et sur la ville ; cette batterie étoit, Monseigneur, la plus dangereuse de l'ennemy pour détruire le
monde ; tous les boulets enfiloient toutes les rues jusqu'à la
porte Maurepas et au mur crénelé ; personne ne pouvoit rester
dans la ville, soit dans les maisons ou dans les rues.

" Aussy pour éteindre le feu de l'ennemy, je fis établir
deux pièces de canon de 18 sur le cavalier du dit Bastion
du Roy : on fit pour cet effet deux coffres en planches qu'on
remplit de fascines et de terres qui formoient deux embrasures par le moyen desquelles les canonniers et ceux qui
servirent ces canons étoient à l'abry du feu de l'ennemy.

" Je fis aussy percer en même temps deux embrasures au
mur du parapet de la face droite du dit bastion ; on y mit
deux autre canons de 24.

" Ces quatre canons ont été si bien servis que le feu de
l'ennemy de la dite batterie de la plaine a été éteint, puisqu'ils ne tiroient lors de la reddition de la place qu'un
canon, et qu'ils ont eu les autres démontés à la dite batterie, ainsy que ceux de nos gens qui ont été voir cette batterie, après la reddition de la place, m'en ont rendu compte.

" Le matin du 20, je fis assembler messieurs les capitaines
des compagnies pour prendre un party s'il convenoit de faire
des sorties sur l'ennemy. Il fut résolu que la ville étoit en-
tièrement dénuée de monde, qu'il étoit préjudiciable d'en faire,
qu'à peine on pourroit garder les remparts avec les 1300

hommes qu'il y avoit dans la ville y compris les deux cent
de la batterie royale.

"Je fis masquer la porte Dauphine en pierre de taille,
fascines et terre de l'épaisseur d'environ dix-huit pieds,
ainsi que les deux corps de garde qui sont joints. Sans cet
ouvrage l'ennemy auroit pu entrer en ville dés le lendemain
qu'il auroit tiré de la batterie de Francœur; cette porte
n'etoit pas plus forte que celle d'une porte cochère, les murs
de la dite porte et des corps de garde n'avoient que trois
pieds ou environ d'épaisseur. La dite porte n'étoit pas non
plus flanquée et n'avoit pour toute défense que quelques
créneaux aux corps de garde, desquels on ne pouvoit plus
se servir sitôt qu'on étoit obligé de garnir les dits corps
de garde de pierres, de terre.

"J'ordonnai qu'on fit des embrasures de gazon et de terre,
n'ayant pas le temps d'en faire de pierre, aux quatre canons
qui étoient sur la batterie du bastion Dauphin, sur le corps
de garde des soldats, joignant la porte du dit bastion, afin
d'empêcher l'ennemy en ses travaux sur les hauteurs qui
étoient devant la dite porte; lesquelles embrasures furent
faites.

"Tous les flancs des bastions de la ville furent aussy
garnis des canons des corsaires et autres qui se sont trouvés
en ville.

"L'ennemy ayant calfeutré une goelette qui étoit échouée
au fond de la baye depuis l'année dernière, il l'a remplit de
bois, goudron et autres matières combustibles, et à la faveur
d'une nuit obscure et d'un vent frais du nord-nord-est qu'il
fit le 24, il nous l'envoya en brûlot sur la ville.

"Tout le monde passoit toutes les nuits sur les remparts,
nous attendions de pied ferme l'ennemy, plustôt que des
artifices de cette nature, et ce brûlot ayant été s'échouer au
dehors de la ville vis-à-vis du terrain du Sr Ste Marie ne fit
pas l'effet que l'ennemy s'attendoit.

" L'ennemy s'étant emparé de la hauteur de Francœur qui est à la queue du glacis de la porte Dauphine, il a commencé à ouvrir des boyaux et former deux batteries malgré le feu continuel de nos canons de la barbette et du bastion Dauphin et du flanc droit du bastion du Roy et de la mousqueterie, et ces deux batteries n'ont point cessé de tirer depuis le 29 jusqu'à la reddition de la place des boulets de 18, 24, 36 et 42, pour battre en brèche la porte Dauphine et la flanc droit du bastion du Roy.

" L'ennemy, faisant plusieurs mouvements au fond de la baye et à la hauteur de la Lanterne, monsieur Vallé, lieutenant de la Compagnie des Canonniers, vint m'avertir que l'ennemy pourroit faire ces mouvements à l'occasion de plusieurs canons de dix-huit et de vingt-quatre qui avoient été mis au carénage pour servir de corps de garde depuis environ dix ans. Que parmy ces canons il y en avoit plusieurs en état de servir, qu'il avoit informé les Gouverneurs de cy-devant plusieurs fois que l'ennemy pourroit les transporter à la tour, établir une batterie pour battre l'isle de l'entree et les vaisseaux qui voudroient entrer.

" Sur un avis aussy important, et l'ennemy ayant aboré pavillon à la tour de la Lanterne, je fis faire un détachement de cinq cent jeunes gens du pays et autres de la milice et des flibustiers, sous les ordres du Sieur de Beaubassin, pour aller voir si cela étoit vrai, tâcher de suprendre l'ennemy ou empêcher de faire leurs travaux en cet endroit.

" Ce dêtachement partit en trois chaloupes le 27 may avec chacun douze jours de vivres et les munitions de guerre nécessaires qui leur furent fournies des magasins du Roy ; il mit pied à terre au grand Lorembec.

" Le lendemain, faisant son approche à la tour, il fut découvert par l'ennemy qui étoit au nombre d'environ 300.

" Ils se tirèrent quelques volées de mousqueterye, et se séparèrent, ce détachement ne voyant pas son avantage et plusieurs ayant lâché le pied, il fut contraint de se retirer dans le bois, pour brûler s'il lui étoit possible les magasins qu'il y avoit, on l'avoit assuré que cela étoit aisé, que l'ennemy dormoit avec sécurité en cet endroit.

" Koller qui étoit second du dit Sieur de Beaubassin, venant de St. Pierre par terre, quelques jours auparavant, avait été dans une des barraques du dit camp et avoit emporté une chaudière sans être découvert, ce détachement, dis-je, étoit à un demi quart de lieue à l'habitation du dit Koller, il avoit envoyé des découvreurs en attendant la nuit, mais ils eurent le malheur dêtre découverts par une douzaine d'Anglois qui se trouvèrent aux environs, ce qui fit que l'ennemy détacha un party considérable qui fut pour les attaquer. Le sieur de Beaubassin fut encore obligé de se retirer après quelques coups tirés de part et d'autre: l'ennemy, depuis lors cherchoit partout ce détachement, et plusieurs de ceux-ci ayant été obligés de jeter leurs vivres pour se sauver, ils étoient sans vivres pour passer leur douze jours, et plusieurs qui étoient des havres voisins l'avoient abandonné et s'étoient retirés chez eux; il se trouvoit par conséquent sans vivres et trop faibles pour résister à l'ennemy.

" Il fut donc obligé d'aller au petit Lorembec pour prendre des chaloupes afin de rentrer dans la ville; il se trouva en ce havre environ 40 Sauvages de la colonie qui avoient détruit, il y avoit deux ou trois jours, 18 à 20 Anglois qu'ils avoient trouvés qui pillaient ce havre.

" Comme ils étaient à même d'embarquer dans les chaloupes, il leur tomba un détachement de 2 à 300 Anglois. Les Sauvages se joignèrent à ce détachement et ces deux corps faisaient environ 120 hommes qui tinrent pied ferme à l'ennemy.

" Le feu commença de part et d'autre vers les deux heures et dura pendant plus de quatre, les Anglois avoient même été repoussés deux fois et ils auroient été défaits si dès le commencement de l'action, ceux-ci n'avoient pas envoyé avertir de leurs gens qui étoient à la batterie royale et à la tour et s'il ne leur étoit pas venu à l'entrée de la nuit un party considérable qui commença à vouloir l'entourer.

"Notre détachement voyant qu'il n'y avoit pas moyen de résister et manquant de munitions, plusieurs ayant tiré jusqu'à leur dernier coup, il se retira dans les bois, l'ennemy, supérieur comme il étoit, les poursuivit une partie de la nuit, notre detachement fut contraint de se retirer à Miré et de passer la rivière.

"Nous avons eu en cette occasion deux hommes de tués et environ 20 de blessés ou prisonniers. Monsieur de Beaubassin fut du nombre des blessés, il reçut une balle au gras de la jambre et après une heure et demie de combat, ne pouvant résister à sa blessure, il se retira. Le sieur Koller continua le combat jusqu'à la fin.

"Le dit sieur de Beaubassin, s'étant rendu en ville quelques jours après sixième dans une pirogue, m'informa de ce qui s'étoit passé à l'occasion de son détachement, que le surplus étoit refugié à Miré où il l'avait laissé sous la conduite de Koller, qu'il lui manquoit des vivres et des munitions de guerre ainsy qu'aux Sauvages.

"Sur ce rapport je fis partir une chaloupe avec 20 quarts de farine et autres vivres et des munitions, tant pour ce détachement, celui de monsieur Marin que j'attendois tous les jours, que pour les Sauvages.

"On trouva Koller avec ses gens, monsieur Marin n'y étoit pas et les Sauvages s'étoient retirés à leur village.

"Koller rentra en ville le 14 juin en chaloupe avec ceux de son détachement et les quelques autres qu'il trouva à Miré, il eût bien de la peine à passer la nuit parmy bâtiments de l'ennemy qui croisoient depuis Gabarrus jusqu'à Escatary.

"Nous avons appris depuis la reddition de la place, par des personnes de probité, que l'ennemy avoit eu au moins 150 homme de tués, et 90 de blessés au choc du petit Lorembec.

"Les canons de la porte Dauphin et ceux du flanc droit du Bastion du Roy, ne joignant pas bien la batterie que l'ennemy avoit fait sur les hauteurs de Francœur à la porte Dauphine, on perça trois embrâsures à la courtine de la grave pour battre à revers la batterie de l'ennemy de la hauteur de Francœur. Ces trois embrâsures où on avoit placé du canon de 36 furent ouvertes les 30 mai, et firent un effet merveilleux; le premier jour on leur démonta un de leurs canons, et leurs embrâsures furent toutes labourées, cela n'empêcha pas le feu continuel de l'ennemy, et quant à la batterie ce que nous défaisions le jour, ils le refaisoit la nuit.

"Le même jour, sur les trois heurs, nous eûmes connoissance d'un gros vaisseau qui donnoit chasse à un senau et ensuite qui se battoit avec le dit senau et une frégatte à environ 4 lieues du fort vers le sud-est, en même tems trois vaisseaux ennemis, qui étoient en passe vers le Cap Noir et la pointe Blanche, coururrent dessus; le gros vaisseau après s'être battu longtems prit la chasse sans doute quand il eut connoissance des trois qui courroient sur lui, et nous avons entendu tirer du canon jusque vers les 9 à 10 heures du soir, nous avons appris depuis que ce vaisseau étoit le *Vigilant*.

"J'ordonnai qu'on tirât de la poudrière du Bastion Dauphin les poudres qui y étoient et les fis transporter sous la poterne de la courtine qui est entre le Bastion du Roy et celui de la Reine.

"Comme l'ennemy avait coupé par les boulets de la batterie de Francœur, les chaines du pont levi de la porte Dauphine, j'ordonnay aussy de couper le pont de la dite porte.

"Le canon de l'ennemy de la batterie de Francœur qui

battoit le flanc droit du bastion du Roy, faisant beaucoup de progrès et entr'autres aux embrasures, je fis commencer à faire percer le mur de la face du bastion Dauphin de deux embrasures, pour y mettre deux canons, cet ouvrage malgré la mousqueterie que l'ennemy tiroit toujours, fut mis en état et notre canon a tiré et fut servi autant qu'on pouvoit désirer sur celui de l'ennemy.

" L'ennemy a aussi étably une batterie de cinq canons sur les hauteurs des Mortissans et a commencé à tirer le 2 juin des boulets de 36 et 42, en brèche sur le bastion Dauphin et sur l'éperon. La guérite a été jetée à bas, et une partie de l'angle saillant, le même jour. Cette batterie a déboulé l'épéron de la porte Dauphine en ses embrasures, lesquelles ont été racommodées plusieurs fois, autant bien qu'on pouvoit, à pierre sèche, avec des pierres de taille et des sacs de terre.

" Le même jour l'escadre ennemye s'augmenta par l'arrivée d'un vaisseaux d'environ 40 à 50 canons, et nous vismes aussy, parmy cette escadre, un vaisseau désemparé, qu'on nous a dit depuis être celui que nous avions vu se battre le 30 may.

" Le 5 l'ennemy a envoyé vers les deux heures du matin de la batterie royale, un brulot qui s'est échoué à la calle Frédéric oû il a brûlé sur une göelette, il n'a pas fait d'autre mal, quoiqu'il fut chargé de matières combustibles et de bombes qui firent leur effet; toutes les batteries de l'ennemy ne cessèrent point de tirer, pendant ce temps nos gens étoient comme de coutume tout le long des remparts et du quay, à essuyer ce feu avec intrépidité.

" La nuit du 6 au 7 nous eumes une alarme générale de l'isle de l'entrée; l'ennemy, voulant enlever cette batterie, s'embarqua au nombre de 1000 sur 35 barques, 800 autres venant derrière devoient les soutenir. La nuit étoit très obscure et faisoit une petite brume.

" Ces premiers furent mettre pied à terre, les uns à la

Pointe à Peletier, les autres vis-à-vis le corps des casernes, et le surplus au débarquement de la dite isle ; l'ennemy en debarquant commença à crier *hourrah* par trois fois ; ils attachèrent même environ 12 échelles aux embrasures afin de les escalader, mais Monsieur D'Aillebout, qui commandoit à cette batterie, les reçut à merveille ; le canon et la mousqueterie de ceux de l'isle fut servi au mieux, toutes les barques, furent toutes brisées ou coulées à fond ; le feu fut continuel depuis environ minuit jusqu'à trois heures du matin.

" Le dit S D'Ailleboust ainsy que les Srs Duchambon, son Lieutenant, et Eurry de la Perrelle, son enseigne, étoient les premiers à monter sur les embrasures et faire feu sur les ennemis pour montrer à leurs soldats l'exemple, et aux autres qui étoient avec eux à la dite batterie.

" Les soldats firent même plusieurs fois descendre leurs officiers des embrasures, leur alléguant qu'ils ne devoient point ainsi s'exposer, qu'ils n'avoient qu'à les commander et qu'ils en viendroient à bout ; à la fin l'ennemy fut contraint de demander quartier. Les huit cents qui devoient soutenir les premiers n'osèrent pas s'approcher et s'en furent : on fit 119 prisonniers, plusieurs blessés sont morts la même journée, et l'ennemy a eu plus de 250 de tués, noyés ou de blessés, ne s'étant sauvés, au rapport de nos prisonniers qui étoient à la batterie royale, que dans deux barges qui pouvoient contenir environ 30 hommes, parmy lesquels il y avoit plusieurs de blessés.

" L'ennemy pouvant attaquer la ville avec des barges par le quay, j'ordonnay une estacade de mâts qui prenoit depuis l'eperon du bastion Dauphin jusques à la pièce de grave, et cette estacade a été parachevée le 11 juin. L'ennemy qui s'étoit aperçu de cet ouvrage, n'a pas cessé de tirer des canons de ses batteries, sur les travaillants, mais inutilement.

"Les ennemis ayant toujours continué leurs travaux à la tour de la Lanterne, malgré le feu continuel de bombes et de canons de la batterie de l'isle de L'entrée, il fut décidé qu'il étoit nécessaire de blinder les casernes et la boulangerie de la dite isle, et le bois manquant pour cet ouvrage le magasin du Sieur Dacarrette fut démoli pour cela.

"Le feu continuel des batteries de l'ennemy ayant démoly les embrasures du flanc droit du bastion du Roy, où nous avions six canons de dix-huit et de vingt-quatre qui tiroient continuellement, et ces canons ne pouvant pas être servis, j'ordonnay qu'on fit aussy des contremerlons et des embrasures en bois, à quoi on y travailla avec toute la diligence possible, et ces embrasures étant parachevées le 19 juin, le canon tira toujours; mais ces mêmes embrasures n'ont pas laissé d'être démantibulées aussy par le canon de l'ennemy.

"Depuis que la batterie de martissan a été établie, elle n'a pas cessé de tirer en brèche sur la porte Dauphin et sur l'éperon. L'éperon a été tout démantibulé et racommodée plusieurs fois, ainsy que je l'ai dit ci-devant; les embrasures qui battent le long du quay ont aussy été démantelées, par cette batterie et celle de Francœur, et personne ne pouvoit rester derrière le mur du quay qui a été tout criblé, les boulets de 24, 36 et 42 le perçant d'outre en outre.

"Le 18, messieurs les généraux anglois m'envoyèrent un officier avec pavillon, portant une lettre de monsieur Warren chef de l'escadre et une autre de Monsieur de la Maisonfort, capitaine de vaisseau. Par la première ce général se plaignait des cruautés que nos François et Sauvages avoient exerceés sur ceux de sa nation, et que si, à l'avenir, pareille chose arrivoit, il ne pourroit pas empêcher ses gens d'en agir de même.

"Monsieur de la Maisonfort m'apprenoit sa prise, le 30 mai, et qu'il avoit tout lieu d'être satisfait du traitement qu'on lui faisoit, ainsy qu'à ses officiers et matelots, et de punir sévèrement, etc.

"Je répondis à celle de monsieur Warren qu'il n'y avoit point de François parmy les Sauvages qui avoient usé ainsi qu'il disoit de cruauté, comme de fait il n'y en avoit pas, qu'il devoit être persuadé que je négligeray rien pour arrêter le cours des cruautés des Sauvages autant qu'il me seroit possible de communiquer avec eux, etc.

"A celle de monsieur de la Maisonfort, que je ferai défendre aux Sauvages, lorsque je pourrai avoir communication avec eux, d'en user mieux [sic] par la suite, qu'il n'y avoit aucun des François avec eux lorsqu'ils ont usé de cruautés, etc., et l'officier porteur de ces lettres partit sur le champ.

"Le 21, la batterie que les ennemis ont établie à la tour de la Lanterne de 7 canons et un mortier a commencé à tirer sur celle de l'isle de L'entrée avec des boulets de 18 et un mortier de 12 pouces, pesant 180 l. et le feu de la dite batterie n'a pas cessé de tirer jusqu'à la reddition de la place, malgré le feu continuel de celle de l'isle.

"Les batteries de l'ennemy faisant un progrès considérable, malgré notre feu des canons du bastion du Roy, bastion Dauphin, de la pièce de la grave, et de la mousqueterie à la brèche de la porte Dauphine et aux corps de garde joignants, j'ordonnai à Monsieur Verrier, ingénieur, de faire un retranchement dans le bastion Dauphin pour défendre l'assaut que l'ennemy pourrait donner par la brèche. Cet ouvrage qui prenoit depuis le quay jusqu'au parapet de la face du bastion Dauphin, fut mis en état le 24 après bien des travaux de nuit.

"Il se fit le même jour une jonction de 4 vaisseaux, dont deux de 60, un de 50 et l'autre de 40 canons, avec ceux qui bloquoient le port. Ces vaisseaux sitôt qu'ils eurent tiré les signaux de reconnaissance s'assemblèrent et après s'être parlés, ils furent vers la baye de Gabarrus.

" Le lendemain les vaisseaux ennemis au nombre de 13 mouillèrent en ligne vers la Pointe Blanche à environ 2 lieues du port de Louisbourg. L'ennemy fit faire en même temps et le lendemain trois piles de bois pour des signaux sur les hauteurs qui sont à l'ouest du port de Louisbourg.

" Je ne puis pas m'empêcher d'informer Sa Grandeur et de lui dire avec vérité que toutes les batteries de l'ennemy soit de mortier ou de canon n'ont pas cessé de tirer depuis les jours qu'ils les ont établis, de même que la mousqueterie, sans discontinuer, de la batterie de Francœur; que toutes les maisons de la ville ont toutes été écrasées, criblées et mises hors d'état d'être logées; que le flanc du bastion du Roy a été tout démoli, ainsy que les embrasures en bois qu'on y avoit remplacées; qu'ils ont fait brèche à la porte Dauphine, le corps de garde joignant, et qu'il étoit praticable au moyen des fascines qu'ils avoient transporté pendant deux jours à la batterie de Francœur; que l'eperon joignant le corps de garde de l'officier de la porte Dauphine étoit tout demantelé, ainsi que les embrasures du quai, malgré le feu continuel de tous les canons, mortiers et mousqueterie que nous tirions de la ville et qui étoient servis avec toute la vigueur et l'activité qu'on pouvoit espérer en pareille occasion.

" La preuve en est assez évidente, Monseigneur, puisque de 67 milliers de poudre que nous avions au commencement du siège, il nous n'en restoit, le 27 juin, que 47 barils en ville, laquelle quantité m'étoit absolument nécessaire pour pouvoir capituler; nous avons aussi tiré toutes les bombes de 12 pouces que nous avions et presque toutes celles de 9 pouces.

" Je dois rendre justice à tous les officiers de la garnison, aux soldats et aux habitans qui ont défendu la place, iis ont tous en général supporté la fatigue de ce siège avec une intrépidité sans égale, pendant les 116 [?] jours qu'il a duré.

" Passant toutes les nuits au chemin couvert de la porte Dauphine, depuis que l'ennemy avoit commencé à battre en brèche cet endroit, à soutenir les travaillants qui ôtoient les décombres sur les remparts aux portes qui leur étoient destinées, sans se reposer aucune nuit et pour le jour n'ayant pas un seul endroit pour sommeiller sans courir risque d'être emporté par les canons de l'ennemy qui commandoient toute la ville.

" Aussy tout le monde étoit fatigué de travail et d'insomnie, et de 1300 que nous étions au commencement du siège, 50 ont été tués, 95 blessés hors d'état de rendre service, plusieurs étoient tombés malades par la fatigue, aussy les remparts qui n'étoient au commencement du siège garnis que de 5 à 5 pieds, se trouvoient presque tous dégarnis le 26 de juin lorsque les habitans de la ville me présentèrent leur requête tendant à ce que les forces de l'ennemy soit de terre et de mer, augmentant tous les jours, sans qu'ils nous parvint aucun secours ni apparence d'en avoir d'assez fort pour forcer l'ennemy, il me plût capituler avec les généraux afin de leur conserver le peu qu'il leur restoit.

" Cette requête, Monseigneur, me toucha jusqu'au plus vif de mon âme. D'un côté je voyois une place telle que Louisbourg et qui a coûte bien des sommes au Roi, au moment d'être enlevée par la force de l'ennemy qui avoit une brèche assez practicable pour cela et des vaisseaux en ligne qui s'installoient depuis deux jours.

" D'autre côté, il me paroissoit un nombre d'habitans, tous chargés de familles, au moment de périr, perdre par conséquent le fruit de leurs travaux depuis le commencement de l'etablissement de la colonie.

" Dans une conjoncture aussy délicate, je fis rendre compte

à monsieur Verrier, ingénieur en chef, de l'état des fortifications de la Place, et à monsieur de Ste Marie, capitaine
chargé de l'artillerie, de celui des munitions de guerre; l'un
et l'autre me firent leur rapport, je fis tenir conseil de guerre
qui décida unanimement que vu les forces de l'ennemy et
l'état de la Place il convenoit de capituler.

" J'écrivis une lettre à le sortie du Conseil à messieurs les
généraux anglois, je leur demanday une suspension d'armes,
pour le temps qu'il me seroit convenable pour leur faire
des articles de capitulation aux conditions desquelles je leur
remettrois la Place.

" Monsieur de Laperelle, fils, qui étoit porteur de cette
lettre, me rapporta le même soir leur réponse par laquelle
ils me donnoient le temps jusques au lendemain à huit
heures du matin, et que si pendant ce temps, je me déter-
minois à me rendre prisonnier de guerre, je pouvois compter
que je serois traité avec toute la générosité possible.

" Je ne m'attendois pas à une telle réponse, aussy le lendemain 27, je leur envoyai par Monsieur de Bonnaventure
les articles de capitulation avec une seconde lettre, par
laquelle je leur mandai que les conditions faites la veille
étoient trop dures, que je ne pouvois les accepter et que
c'étoit à ceux que je faisois par mes propositions que je
consentirois à leur remettre la place [sic].

" Messieurs les généraux ne voulurent pas répondre par
apostille à ces propositions, mais ils me renvoyèrent leur
réponse séparée par le dit Sieur de Bonnaventure; cette
réponse m'accordoit partie des articles que j'avois de-
mandés, mais ceux qui m'étoient le plus sensible et glorieux,
qui étoient ceux de sortir de la Place, avec les honneurs
de la guerre, avec arme et bagage, tambour battant et dra-
peaux déployés, ne s'y trouvoient pas insérés, aussy je leur
écrivis sur le champ deux lettres, l'une au chef d'escadre
et l'autre au général de terre, que je ne pouvois consentir

à laisser sortir les troupes de la place sans ces articles qui
étoient des honneurs dûs à des troupes qui avoient fait leur
devoir, que cela accordé je consentois aux articles.

" Messieurs les généraux m'écrivirent en réponse qu'ils
accordoient cet article et monsieur Warren augmenta des
conditions pour la reddition de l'Isle et de la Place.

" Les ratifications ont été signées de part et d'autre, mais
messieurs les généraux Anglois bien loin d'avoir exécuté de
leur part la dite capitulation, ainsy que j'ai fait du mien en
tout son contenu, ils ont manqué en plusieurs articles.

" Au premier article il est dit que tous les effets mobiliers
de tous les sujets du Roy de France qui étoient dans Louisbourg leur seroient laissés et qu'ils auroient la liberté de les
emporter avec eux dans tels ports d'Europe de la domination
de leur Roy qu'ils jugeront à propos.

" Tous les battiments qui étoient dans le port appartenant
aux particuliers, faisaient partie de leurs effets mobiliers,
cependant les Anglois s'en sont emparés et les ont garde
pour eux.

" Tous les particuliers généralement quelconques qui ont
passé en France n'ont pu emporter aucune armoire, chaise,
fauteuil, table, bureau, chenets et autres meubles de cette
nature, ny même aucune grosse marchandise, messieurs les
généraux n'ayant point fourni des battiments pour cela nécessaires, ils n'ont pas été pillés, mais à bien examiner la
chose, ne pouvant pas emporter le peu de meubles qu'ils
avoient faute de battiments, ils ont éte obligés de les laisser,
ce qu'ils ont laissé à Louisbourg est tout comme si on leur
avait pillé, à moins que Sa Grandeur ne fasse faire raison
par la cour d'Angleterre.

" Ils ont encore manqué à cet article, pendant le temps
que j'étois à la colonie; ils ont fait partir à mon insu 436
matelots et particuliers pour Baston; ils étoient embarqués
ainsi que les troupes sur des vaisseaux de guerre jusqu'à

leur embarquement pour la France, mais un matin le vaisseau dans lequel ils étoient eut ordre de partir pour Baston, et fit voile.

"J'en fus informé, j'en portai ma plainte, mais cela n'aboutit à autre chose sinon qu'ils n'avoient pu faire autrement faute de vivres et de battiment et qu'on les feroit repasser de Baston en France.

"Ces matelots n'ont pas été les seuls, j'ai été informé que depuis mon départ, ils ont agi de même à l'égard des familles qui n'avoient pu être placées sur les bâtiments de transport qu'ils avoient destiné pour la France, si les généraux anglois avoient voulu, les bâtiments qui ont transporté ces familles à Boston les auroient transportées pour France, ils avoient des vivres en magazin beaucoup plus que pour la traversée; mais ils n'ont agi ainsi qu'afin de disperser la colonie.

"Le 2ᵉ article regarde les battiments qui étoient dans le port et ceux qu'ils devoient fournir en cas que les premiers ne fussent pas suffisants pour faire le transport.

"J'ay fait mes remarques à ceci au précédent article, c'est un des plus considérables par rapport à la valeur des choses, y ayant quantité de battiments dans le port qui étoient coulés ou échoués, et dont l'ennemy ne pouvoit en faire sortir aucun du port ny faire aucun usage tant que nos batteries auroient existé.

"Au surplus si plusieurs particuliers de la ville n'avoient pas acheté des battiments les Anglois auroient profité de tous les effets qu'ils y ont chargés, ainsi qu'ils ont fait de ceux qui n'avoient pas le moyen d'en acheter, ces familles auroient été contraintes, ainsi que celles qui se sont embarquées en payant de gros frets, de passer à Boston.

"A l'égard du dernier article des armes, tous les habitans avoient les leurs et les ont remises en dépôt sitôt la reddition de la place; ces armes étoient partie de leurs effets, les ennemis n'ont pas voulu les rendre, je m'en suis plaint, ils m'ont fait réponse, lorsqu'ils ont envoyé les 436 matelots, qu'ils leur enverroient leurs armes, les autres habitans sont dans le même cas.

" Je crois devoir vous informer, Monseigneur, qu'ils se sont aussy emparés de tous les effets et ustensils de l'hôpital et des magasins du Roi : par la reddition de la Place ils n'ont que la ville avec les fortifications et batteries, avec toute l'artillerie armes et ustensils de guerre qui y étoient et non pas les autres effets ; cependant ils s'en sont emparés, disant que c'étoit au Roy, Monsieur Bigot leur a fait ses representations qui n'ont eu aucun fruit, il vous rendra compte à ce sujet.

" Monsieur Bigot a bien voulu se charger lorsqu'il est parti de l'isle d'Aix pour vous rendre compte de ma lettre du 15 de ce mois avec tous les originaux des papiers, concernant tout ce qui s'est passé à l'occasion du siège de Louisbourg ; je suis persuadé qu'ils les aura remis à sa grandeur et qu'a-près l'examen qu'elle en a fait, elle me rendra assez de justice que j'ay fait tout mon possible pour la défense de cette place, et que je ne l'ay rendue qu'a la dernière extrémité.

" J'oubliois d'informer monseigneur, que messieurs de la Tressillière et Souvigny, enseignes, et Lopinot, fils cadet, sont du nombre de ceux qui ont été tués pendant le siege.

" La garnison de Canceau avoit été faite prisonnière au dit lieu le 24 may de l'année dernière ; elle ne devoit pas porter les armes contre le Roy pendant l'an et jour ; monsieur Duquesnel donna la liberté à tous les officiers de cette garnison d'aller sur leur parole d'honneur à Baston et de passer au dit lieu le temps porté par leur capitulation.

" Le Sieur Jean Blastrick, officier, étoit du nombre, il a manqué à sa parole, puisqu'il les a prises au mois de mars dernier, c'étoit un des chefs de ceux qui ont brûlé Toulouse-Port et qui ont fait la descente à Gabarrus le 11 may.

"Il étoit colonel général de la milice de Baston, et il est entré en ville à la tête de cette milice, le lendemain de la reddition de la place."

<hr>

C.

CHAPTER XXII. SHIRLEY AND THE ACADIANS.

All the following correspondence is from the Public Record Office: America and West Indies.

SHIRLEY TO NEWCASTLE, 14 DEC., 1745.

(Extract.)

" . . . Having lately procur'd from Fort Major Phillips of Annapolis Royal the late Lieutenant Governour Armstrong's Original Instrument mention'd in my late State of the Province of Nova Scotia to be given by him to the French Inhabitants of that Province, by virtue of which and of another of the same tenour given 'em by him in 1730, they claim an Exemption from bearing Arms in defence of his Majesty's Government, I inclose your Grace a Copy of it. Mr. Phillips in his letter inclosing this Instrument to me observes that the 'Inhabitants of Nova Scotia at the first news of Louisbourg's being surrendred were in great Consternation and at Minas in particular they appear'd in Tears in the Publick Places, where nine months before they had assisted in singing Te Deum, on a false report that Annapolis Royal was surrendred to Monsieur Duvivier.' He goes on to say that a report was spread there that Monsieur Duvivier was arriv'd at Canada with rigging for two Men of War, and the Renommée a French thirty gun Ship with two Prizes at Quebec. And all the Nova Scotia Priests were gone to Canada for Instructions; and give out that there are 2000 Canadeans at Chignecto waiting ready for another attempt against his Majesty's Garrison. To which I would beg leave to subjoin that it seems to me far from being improbable that the French will Attempt the reduction of Nova Scotia early in the Spring, by gaining which they will have a fine provision Country to assemble 8 or 10,000 fighting men and all the tribes of Indians ready to join in an attempt against Louisbourg at a few days Warning as I observ'd to your Grace in a late Letter; But if they should not attempt Louisbourg they would irresistably break up all the Eastern Settlements of this Province and I doubt not the whole Province of New Hampshire it self, which would make 'em masters of all Mast Country and Naval Stores and of a rich Soil for Corn as well as Cattle and this would also enable 'em to make deep impressions on all the Western frontier of this Province, New York and Connecticut, and, how far they might penetrate is not Certain but so far at least as might make it very difficult to dislodge 'em and give 'em such an hold of the Continent as to make 'em think in time of pushing with the assistance of the Indians for the Mastery of it, which is richly worth contending for with all their might as it would in their hands lay the surest foundation for an Universal Monarchy by Sea and Land that ever a people had. This train of Consequences from the Enemies being Masters of Nova Scotia may seem remote, my Lord, but they are not impossible, and it may be very difficult for the French to regain Louisbourg at least without being Masters of Nova Scotia, and that seems under the present Circumstances of the Garrison where no recruits are yet Arriv'd from England and the Inhabitants of the Country Surrounding it are Enemies in their hearts no difficult acquisition and to be made with a small Train of

Artillery in three weeks at farthest. I would submit it to your Grace's consideration whether the Garrison should not be reinforc'd as soon as may be. And the Inhabitants should not be forthwith put upon a good foot of Subjection and fidelity. Thus in obedience to your Grace's Direction I have troubled you with my whole sentiments concerning the Province of Nova Scotia which as I can't think it probable that the French will sleep the next year after the blow we have given 'em at Louisbourg (which, if they don't recover it soon by retaking Cape Breton or getting Nova Scotia will prove their Death wound in North America) seems to be most likely to be attack'd by 'em of any place in these parts, and I hope your Grace will excuse my Repetition of the Danger of it.

" I am with the most Dutiful Regards

" My Lord Duke,

" Your Grace's most Obed!

" and most Devoted Servant

" W. SHIRLEY."

SHIRLEY TO NEWCASTLE, 11 FEB. 1746.

(*Extract.*)

" MY LORD DUKE.

" Since my last to your Grace I have received the Inclos'd packett from Mr. Mascarene Containing a Representation of the State of Nova Scotia from himself and his Majesty's Council of that Province with a copy of a Letter from him to me, Showing the reasons of his late Conduct towards the French Inhabitants; Your Grace will perceive that this representation is drawn up in Stronger Terms against the Inhabitants than mine; I could wish the Gentlemen had been more Explicit in what they would Recommend as the most adviseable Method of Securing his Majesty's Government within the Province and against the French Inhabitants — But as that is not done except in Short hints, And Mr. Little, to whom both Mr. Mascarene and Mr. Secretary Shirreff referr me for a Larger Account of the Sentiments of the Gentlemen of the Garrison concerning these Matters, Offers his Service to go with my dispatches to England and return directly with any Orders his Majesty may be pleased to give thereupon, I have sent him to wait upon your Grace, and it is possible that when he is upon the Spot ready to Answer any Questions, it may be of Service — Having before troubled your Grace So Largely upon this head, I will beg leave to referr to my former Letters, Mr. Little Mr. Agent Kilby and Mr. Bollan, which two last can, I believe, give Considerable Light on the affair; And shall only add that the Spring before last the Garrison was very narrowly Saved from the Enemy by the Arrival of the New England Auxiliaries, and the last Spring, by the Expedition against Cape Breton, that the preservation of it this Spring will be of the Utmost Importance to his Majesty's Service in America, and that nothing will more effectually Secure that than putting the Inhabitants upon a proper foot of Subjection, in the most Speedy Manner, to prevent their Revolt, which Cannot be done without his Majesty's Special directions for that purpose; for the procuring of which, I find Mr. Mascarene, and his whole Council have a dependance upon me; the Language of their Several Letters being that they *Commit themselves to my Care;* and will take no step without my Advice or approbation, which has been the Case for above these last two years, And I mention to your Grace in Excuse for my being So importunate in the Affairs of another Government, which the Gentlemen of the Garrison lay me Under a Necessity of being; And I am further Urg'd to this by the late Accounts, wch Mr. Mascarene and the other Gentlemen have sent me of the Appearance of four hundred Indians well Cloathed, Arm'd, and Supply'd

with Stores from Canada near St. Johns River, Seventeen
French Officers being Seen among 'em, and another Body of
French in the Neighbourhood of the Province, and Reports
that Mr. Duvivier in the Parfaite Man of Warr, and another
Ship of Force were at Qubec with Stores, and another was
seen to put into St. Johns Island; That the Priests who
went to Canada for Instructions are returned with Supplies
and large promises to the Indians (before well dispos'd and
upon the point of putting themselves under Our protection
on the taking of Louisbourg) and Encouragements for the
Inhabitants to depend upon a powerfull force against the
Fort at Annapolis Royal this Spring. These alarms indeed
have been Something Allay'd by Letters from the Deputies
of Minas and other Districts to Mr. Mascarene, which for
my own part I have no great dependance upon.

" But it seems plain upon the whole, that the French are
making the Utmost Efforts to retain the Indians of those
parts in their Interest, and gaining over the Inhabitants of
Nova Scotia, So that the Taking of Speedy measures for
Securing these last and gaining over the former which will
depend upon that, as the preservation of Nova Scotia does
upon both, is a Matter of the Highest Consequence.

" Upon this Occasion it seems necessary for me to apprise
your Grace, that Mr. Mascarene and his Council have not
So good an harmony Subsisting between them as could be
wish'd, and that all the Officers have of late differ'd in Sentiments with him particularly upon the Behaviour of the
French Inhabitants, Concerning whom he indeed has himself
alter'd his Opinion in Some measure; But I think there may
be Still danger of too much tenderness towards 'em on his
part, and perhaps rigour on theirs in carrying any Orders of
his Majesty's into Execution; So that by their Jarring, the
Execution of the Orders may possibly be Obstructed, if they
are left to themselves;

" Wherefore if their Chief Governour's Age and health, and other Circumstances would have permitted him to have been Upon the Spott, and Assisted in this Service, it would I believe have been for the Advantage of it, for him to have made 'em a short Visit at least this year, And if it could have been repeated for the two or three proceeding years it would have been still more so. . . ."

SHIRLEY TO NEWCASTLE, 10TH MAY, 1746.

(Extract.)

". . . I think it my indispensable duty to suggest again to Your Grace my Fears that the Enemy will soon find an opportunity of snatching Accadie by some Sudden Stroke from his Majesty's Government unless the danger is remov'd out of the Heart of it there by a Removal of the most dangerous of the french Inhabitants from thence, & transplanting English Families there in their room, which I think very practicable from hence, having lately found means of transplanting upwards, I believe, of an hundred Families from the Province to Louisbourg towards the Settlement of it, which yet I dont esteem of such Importance to be immediately done as the Settlement of Nova Scotia with faithful Subjects.

" In the meanwhile 'till this can be happily effected & the Indians in those parts secur'd in the English Interest, I have propos'd to Mr. Warren that a Detachment of 100 Men should be sent from Louisbourg to reinforce the garrison at Annapolis Royal, since the late Miscarriage of 182 out of 302 of the Recruits designed for Annapolis in their Passage from England to the garrison there. Ninety-six of the Remainder of 'em, which came in here, I with difficulty have got recovered in his Majesty's Castle William & at the Hospital in Boston, & sent a month ago to Annapolis where I hear they are safely arriv'd, and twenty more who are in a

fair way of being serviceable, I shall send from the Hospital
within three days; But the Garrison will still be weak as
Mr. Mascarene has dismiss'd most of the New England Auxiliaries, and they have not, I am informed, 220 effective
private Men left besides their Artificers & Workmen: I
have also recommended to Mr. Warren the frequent Sending
of a Ship of War to look into the Bason of Annapolis &
make the Garrison there a short Visit in order to prevent a
Surprise; & by his Opinion in Concurrence with Sir Willm
Pepperrell's, Mr. Mascarene's & my own a Sloop has been
hir'd & employ'd for about these last four Months to attend
upon that garrison, & carry Intelligence between Annapolis
Royal, Louisbourg & Boston concerning the State of it &
the Enemy's Motions which we conceiv'd necessary to be
done for its Security, and hope your Grace will not dis-
approve of.

" What Mr. Frontenac observed some years ago to Mr Pont-
chartrain concerning the french King's recovering of Accadie
& making himself absolute Master of the great Bank [of
Newfoundland] as in the inclos'd Extract of his Letter,
seems so seasonable to be consider'd at this time, that I would
beg leave to observe to your Grace upon it, that his Maj$^{ty's}$
holding the Possession of Annapolis Royal & Newfoundland
(already conceded to his Crown by the Treaty of Utrecht)
with his late Acquisition of Cape Breton, will put the whole
Cod Fishery more in his Power than Mr Frontenac's Scheme
could have put it into the French Kings, and that besides
what Mr Frontenac calls a Commerce more advantageous than
the Conquest of the Indies, and computes the Returns of at
twenty Millions (I suppose french Livres) per annum, it
would furnish his Majesty with as good a Nursery of Seamen
for the Royal Navy as the Colliery in England does, not to
mention the great consumption of British Manufactures
which must be occasioned in carrying the Fishery on; — that

the holding of Annapolis Royal in particular will be establishing to his Majesty the Mastery of the Northern Part of this Continent against the French, Secure to him inexhaustible Nurseries of Masts, Yards, Bowsprits & other Stores for his Navy, & Timber for Ship building within his Northern Colonies independent of any foreign State to be purchased with British Manufactures & transported in British Vessels — that the Inhabitants of the Northern Colonies would in time make such an Addition of Subjects to the Crown of Great Britain as would make their number Superior to that of any Prince's upon the Continent of Europe; and in the meanwhile the Vent of Woolen & other British Manufactures, & all Kinds of European Commodities imported into the Colonies from Great Britain must increase in proportion to the Increase of their Inhabitants : by all which means the main Sources of Wealth, & a larger Extent of Power by Sea & Land than any State in Christendom at present enjoys, seems capable of being secur'd to his Maj$^{ty's}$ Dominions; But which will in the End otherwise be in all human Probability the Lot of the french Dominions; And I would in particular observe to your Grace the most practicable Step the Enemy can attempt making towards their obtaining that seems clearly to be their rendring themselves Masters of Nova Scotia, the Consequences of wch would give 'em so strong an hold upon this Continent as would make it difficult to dislodge 'em & put it very much in their Power to harrass & annoy his Maj^{tys} Colonies both by Land & Sea, in such manner as to weaken 'em extremely, if not by degrees finally subdue 'em.

" I am with the most dutiful Regards,
" My Lord Duke,
" Your Grace's most devoted
" and obedient Servant
" W. SHIRLEY."

SHIRLEY TO NEWCASTLE, 31 MAY, 1746.

(*Extract.*)

" . . . I would beg Leave to observe to your Grace, y^t the Danger to his Majesty's garrison arises chiefly from within the heart of the government itself, the Inhabitants & neighboring Indians whose Numbers are sufficient of themselves with a small assistance from Canada & the help of a proper Train of Artillery, slipt up the Bay in small Vessells (wch would give 'em great Encouragement to take up Arms ag^t the garrison) to reduce it. However while the Attempt against Canada is depending, that will certainly go far towards holding the Inhabitants of Nova Scotia in suspense, till the success of it is known; & I hope by next Spring they may either be put upon a better foot of Subjection, or the most dangerous among 'em removed. . . ."

SHIRLEY TO NEWCASTLE, 18 JUNE, 1746.

(*Extract.*)

" . . . I may assure your Grace y^t one of the principal motives I had to desire I might succeed General Phillips in his Command, was the hopes I have of it's putting it in my power to promote his Majesty's Service in his Province of Acadie, or Nova Scotia by securing the fidelity & Allegiance of the Inhabitants there to his Majesty's Government in the best manner, and thereby preventing the French from making themselves masters of it, the Acquisition of wch to them with the help of the Indians would likewise endanger the Loss of the Province of New Hampshire & the Mast Country to his Majesty with the Fishery of the Acadie or Cape Sable's Shoar, including that of Canso, to his Subjects here in present, & should not Canada be reduc'd, would enable the enemy to harrass & Diminish all his Majesty's Colonies & on the Continent, & have an inevitable Tendency to make themselves masters of the whole of it in time; not to mention the Continual Danger, wch their possession of Nova Scotia would at the same time expose Cape Breton & even Newfoundland to.

"The Considerations have induc'd me to take the Liberty of submitting it to your Grace, whether it might not be for his Majesty's Service, that before the six Regiments to be employ'd ag^t Canada return to England, orders may be sent that such part of 'em as shall be thought necessary to assist in removing the most obnoxious of the French Inhabitants of Nova Scotia from thence, should be employ'd in that Service, wch would not take up much time; I am not certain whether a sufficient Strength might not be spar'd from the Garrison at Louisbourg a short time for this purpose, wch if it could, would make the Assistance of any other Troops needless.

"And I would particularly submit it to your Grace's Consideration, whether in case of any Disappoinment in the present Attempt for the reduction of Canada, the immediate removal of some at least of the French Inhabitants of Nova Scotia, & securing the province in the best manner would not be . . . adviseable and even necessary.

"If your Grace should think this deserves so much of your Attention there will be time enough for transmitting his Majesty's Commands to me upon it before the present Expedition is over.

  "I am with the most Dutifull Regard
   "My Lord Duke
    "Your Grace's most Devoted
     "& most obedient Servant
       "W. SHIRLEY."

(*Extract.*)

" I must acknowledge I should rather apprehend the french Fleet (if it is design'd for North America) is order'd to Canada; or else to Annapolis Royal, where the Enemy may depend that upon the Apperance of such an Armament the french Inhabitants of Nova Scotia (to the Amount of between 5 & 6000 fighting men) and a considerable Number of Indians & some Canadeans, would immediately join 'em, and they would have a most convenient Country to rendezvous in within a very few days sail of Chappeaurouge Bay at Cape Breton, and be not far from Canada, than that they should attempt to enter Louisbourg Harbour with their Ships; and I am the more inclin'd to this Opinion from the Accounts I have receiv'd lately from Mr Mascarene, and the Officers of the Garrison at Annapolis Royal which inform me that the french Inhabitants at Menis & Schiegneto (in Nova Scotia) have cut off all communication with the garrison for these last five Weeks, and have stop'd the Messengers sent from thence by Mr Mascarene for Intelligence; being in Expectation of an Armament from France; And indeed it seems probable that this will for ever be the Case; and that the Province of Nova Scotia will never be out of Danger, whilst the french Inhabitants are suffer'd to remain in Nova Scotia upon their present Foot of Subjection."

SHIRLEY TO NEWCASTLE, 15 AUG. 1746.

(*Extract.*)

" I shall finish my troubleing your Grace upon the Affairs of Nova Scotia with this Letter after having once more

Submitted it to your Grace's Consideration as a proper
Scheme for better securing the Subjection of the French
Inhabitants and Indians there; that the Governour &
Council or such other Person or Persons as his Majesty
shall think fitt to join with 'em, should have a special
authority and directions from his Majesty, forthwith to
Apprehend & Examine a convenient number of such of
the Inhabitants, as shall be by them judg'd to be most
obnoxious & Dangerous to his Majesty's Government, &
upon finding 'em guilty of holding any treasonable Correspondence with the Enemy &c to dispose of them & their
Estates in such manner, as his Majesty shall order by his
Commissions and to promise his Majesty's Gracious Pardon
& a general Indemnity to the Rest for what is past upon
their taking the Oaths of Allegiance to his Majesty; And
to Cause either two strong Blockhouses (or small Forts)
capable of holding 100 Men each to be Built, one in Menis
& the other in Schiegnecto, which may be Garrison'd out
of Phillip's Regiment when Compleated, or else that at
least one Blockhouse (or small Fort) should be Built at
Menis capable of holding 150 men; and a trading house
be kept at the Fort at Menis or some other part of the
Province well Stock'd with all proper Supplies for the
Indians to be sold or barter'd to 'em for Furrs &c at
the most reasonable Rates, and some presents annually
distributed to 'em: by which means and removing the
Romish Priests out of the Province, & introducing Protestant English Schools, and French Protestant Ministers,
and due encouragement given to such of the Inhabitants,
as shall Conform to the Protestant Religion, and send their
Children to the English Schools, the present Inhabitants
might probably at least be kept in Subjection to his
Majesty's Government, and from treasonable correspond-
encies with the Canadians; and the next Generation in a

great measure become true Protestant Subjects; and the Indians there soon Reclaim'd to an entire dependance upon & subjection to his Majesty; which might also have an happy Influence upon some of the Tribes now in the French Interest.

"Your Grace will be pleas'd to Excuse all
"Incorrectness in this rough Sketch.
"I am with the most Dutifull Regard,
"My Lord Duke,
"Your Grace's most Devoted &
"Most Obedient Servant
"W. SHIRLEY."

SHIRLEY TO MASCARENE, BOSTON, SEPT^R 16, 1746.

"SIR,

"Having been inform'd that the french Inhabitants of Nova Scotia entertain some Jealousy of a Design in the English Government to remove them with their Families from their Settlements, & transport them to France or elsewhere; I desire (if you think it may be for his Majesty's Service) that you would be pleas'd to signify to 'em, that it is probable if his Majesty had declar'd such Intention I might have heard of the same, but that I am perfectly unaquainted with any such Design, and am perswaded there is no just Ground for this Jealousy; And be pleas'd to assure 'em that I shall use my best Endeavours by a proper Representation of their Case to be laid before his Majesty, to obtain the Continuance of his Royal Favour & Protection to such of them, as shall behave dutifully, & refuse to hold any Correspondence with his Enemies; and I doubt not but that all such of 'em will be protected by his Majesty in the Possession of their Estates & Settlements in Nova Scotia.

" And I desire you would also be pleas'd to inform them that it is expected from his Maj^{tys} french Subjects in that Province, who have for so long time enjoyed the same Privileges with his natural born Subjects there, & have been under a much easier Government than any of the french King's Subjects are in the neighbouring Province of Canada & other Parts of the french King's Dominions, that their Interest as well as their Duty and Gratitude should bind them to a strict Fidelity & Obedience to his Majesty and His Government; But on the contrary if any of the Inhabitants of the said Province shall join with the Enemy (especially those that have been sent from Canada to seduce them from their Duty to his Majesty & Attachment to the English Interest) they must expect to be treated in the same manner as his Majesty's English Subjects would be under the like Provocations.

" I am with great regard
" Sir,
" Your most obedient
" humble servant
" W. SHIRLEY."

SHIRLEY TO NEWCASTLE, BOSTON, SEPTEMBER 19, 1746.

" MY LORD DUKE,

" I express'd some hopes in my last but one to your Grace, that I should not be oblig'd to add to my former Accounts of the imminent danger, his Majesty's Province of Nova Scotia was in of being surpriz'd by the Enemy; But find my self under a Necessity of doing it from the Advices which I have since receiv'd from Mr Mascarene, and the Intelligence contain'd in three Declarations upon Oath, Copies of all which are inclos'd.

" Upon the Receipt of Mr Mascarene's Letter, the Contents of which are confirm'd to me by other authentick Accounts, it appear'd to me that there was no room to doubt but that a considerable Body of French and Indians from Canada was assembled in Nova Scotia, with Expectations of a Reinforcement from France; and if they fail'd of that this Year a Design of at least wintering in Minas or some other Part of the Country, by which means they would have an Opportunity of fortifying themselves in it, transporting their great artillery (which there was then the utmost reason to believe they had landed either at Bay Verte or Chebucto Harbour) to Annapolis, and work upon the French Inhabitants already ripe for a Revolt to join 'em in attacking his Majesty's Garrison there so early in the Spring that it would be extremely difficult if not impracticable to relieve it by any Succours either from Louisbourg or the Colonies on the Continent. Whereupon I immediately sent Mr Mascarene an Assurance that I would send him as soon as possible 300 of the new Levies from this Province, 200 of 'em (which seems to be as many as the Garrison can hold at present besides the Troops already there) for the Reinforcement of it, and 100 of 'em to be employ'd in two Sloops up the Bay in the manner Mr Mascarene proposes in his Letter to me, and that I would do the utmost in my Power to make the number up 2000 soon afterwards, in order to dislodge the Enemy, & prevent 'em from wintering in the Province; And in the mean time upon my advising with Rear Admiral Warren (who is still here) he immediately sent his Majesty's Ship Chester a 50 Gun Ship to Annapolis Royal for the further Countenance & Protection of the Garrison there.

"Some Days after this I receiv'd Information that a Fleet of upwards of 30 Sail were discover'd about 15 Leagues to the Westward of Chibucto Harbour, which lies upon the Cape Sable Shoar (the Coast of Accadie or Nova

Scotia) about 150 Leagues to the Eastward of Boston, and about 60 Leagues Westward of Louisbourg, & about 80 distant from Annapolis Royal according to Champions inclos'd Deposition, which was confirm'd by another of the same Tenour made by one Thornton sent me from Piscataqua, upon which I dispatched an arm'd Brigantine with orders to look into Chibucto Harbour, & if the Master should discover any thing to proceed directly to Louisbourg, & give Vice Admiral Townsend & Govern.ʳ Knowles Intelligence of it, & to send me Advice of it Express by some fishing Vessel taken up at Sea; But the Brigantine return'd in less than 24 hours with one Stanwood a Fisherman on board, whose Vessel fell in with the Fleet on the 9ᵗʰ day of Sept.ʳ about 10 Leagues to the Westward of Chibucto, the particulars of which are contain'd in his inclos'd Deposition; and the day after Stanwood's falling in with this Fleet, Haskell another Master of a fishing Vessel discover'd it standing a right course for Chibucto about 8 Leagues to the Westwᵈ of it, & was chas'd by one of 'em according to the inclos'd Deposition; which Series of Intelligence, as no Vessel has arriv'd here yet from this Fleet (which must in all probability have happen'd had it come from England) compar'd with the Accounts in the English News Papers of the Brest Fleet's sailing, & the Intelligence gain'd from a french Prize lately taken by one of Mʳ Townsend's Squadron near the Mouth of Sᵗ Lawrence, that she came out with the Brest Squadron & sail'd in Company with it eight days; the Account we had of two large french Ships being seen to go into Chibucto Harbour about two Months ago; the behavior of the French in Nova Scotia, & their declar'd Expectations of a large French Armament about this time, seems to make it very probable that these Ships may be part of the Brest Squadron, & that they have an immediate design upon Nova Scotia at least. — Hereupon

I sent an Express Boat to Louisbourg to apprize Admiral Townsend & Mr Knowles of it, & another to Annapolis Royal to give Mr Mascarene Advice of it, & to let him know that I was embarking 300 Men for the Reinforcement of the Garrison under his Command (which is done & part of 'em sail'd) with a Promise of farther Succours, and to apprize him that from the publick Accounts in the English Prints we had reason to depend upon the speedy Arrival of Lieut.^t General St Clair with the British Troops under his Command, & a Squadron of his Majesty's Ships with 'em at Louisbourg; And as I have reason to think that an Apprehension generally prevails among the french Inhabitants of Nova Scotia, that they shall all of 'em soon be remov'd from their Settlements there without Distinction, which may have a bad Influence upon 'em in favour of the Enemy at this critical Time. I have wrote Mr Mascarene a Letter (a copy of which I inclose to your Grace) which is translated into French, & printed, in order to be dispers'd among the french inhabitants, if Mr Mascarene (to whose Discretion I have submitted it either to make Use of or suppress the printed Copies) shall be of Opinion that the Publication of it among 'em may be for his Majesty's Service.

"If the Fleet discover'd on the Cape Sable Coast should be Part of that from Brest, doubtless their visit to Nova Scotia has been encourag'd by the general Disposition of the Inhabitants, & the strength they will add to 'em for the Reduction of that Province, & afterwards for an Attempt upon Louisbourg (if they should think it adviseable to make one) as also for the defence of Canada. Should they succeed in an immediate Attempt upon Nova Scotia (which I should not be surpriz'd at) & General St Clair with the Squadron expected from England should arrive in time for that purpose, I should propose attempting the immediate recovery of it out of the Enemy's hands this Year; For their holding that Province till they can fortify it and farther strengthen themselves there must be attended with very bad Consequences to his Majesty's Service, worse than may be immediately apprehended, & create no inconsiderable Perplexities; at least it seems a clear point to me, that if the French should hold the Possession of Nova Scotia in Addition to Canada, the fate of Affairs in his Majesty's Northern Colonies will be suddenly alter'd in a surprizing manner & it will then soon be discern'd that the Mastery of the Northern Parts of this Continent, together with the Sources of Wealth & Power depending upon it, will be in a very fair way of being finally transfer'd to the Enemy.

" Upwards of two Months ago upon receiving Intelligence of the Appearance of two large French Ships being seen to go into Chibucto Harbour, Mr Warren & I sent Mr Townsend notice of it; But as we had not learn'd whether any Vessell had been sent from Louisbourg to look into that Harbour, I sent an arm'd Brigantine to make Discoveries there, which was hinder'd from proceeding thither as is before mention'd; & I have now sent a Schooner thither with a Person who has undertaken to go into it in a Whale boat high enough to make an exact discovery of the Enemy's strength (if any of their Ships are there) & to carry the Account to Louisbourg; But it seems possible if any of 'em have been there, that after landing some Troops and Stores at Chibucto, & getting what Intelligence they can from the Nova Scotians, their Ships may be gone to Canada; for which Place we have been inform'd that sixteen french Vessels, some of 'em Ships of War, had some time ago pass'd up the River of St Laurence; & since that six other Vessels with Stores; so that it is very probable that Quebec is much better prepar'd to receive a Visit from his Majesty's Land & Sea Forces now than it was a little time ago. "

(Extract.)

" It is agreed by all the Prisoners that the French have
not fortify'd at Chebucto, nor sent any Troops from thence
by Land to join the Canadeans; as also that Mr Destonnel
the chief D'escadre & Commandant upon the Death of the
Duke D'Anville, who was of Opinion, to return to France
after the Admiral's Death without attempting any thing,
upon being over rul'd in a Council of War & having his
Flagg struck, fell upon his Sword, & dy'd of his Wound
as all of 'em say, except Sanders.

" It seems very observable from Sander's Declaration
how ready a Disposition the Nova Scotians show'd to afford
Refreshm.^{ts} & Pilots to the Enemy, & that they had signified to the french Ministry their readiness to join with any
force they should send for the Reduction of his Majes$^{ty's}$
Garrison at Annapolis Royal. Also from the number of
Engineers the French had with 'em that their Scheme was
to hold & fortify Annapolis, for wch Purpose it seems to be
that the 50 brass Cannon were brought, rather than for
raising Batteries against the Fort: and that from the Number of their small Arms, which they had with 'em to arm
the Nova Scotians (doubtless) as well as the Indians, they
had a dependance upon being join'd by them. Likewise
the Apprehensions which prevail among the Nova Scotians
that they are at present rather Neutrals than Subjects to
the Crown of Great Britain. And I think it is not to be
doubted now but that the principal Part of the french
Scheme was the Reduction of Nova Scotia in the first
Place.

" Upon the whole the sickly State of the French Fleet,
w^c. is extremely ill mann'd, the hurry & Uneasiness they

discover'd upon seeing the Contents of the Packets which fell into their hands, & precipitate departure from Chebucto, with their detaining the Flag of Truce & English Prisoners 'till they were got 30 Leagues from Chebucto, & then dismissing 'em with a Notion that their Fleet was going up the Bay of Fundy to Annapolis (instead of carrying 'em up there with 'em to prevent that's being known to us) makes it seem probable that the Enemy is making the best of their way to France or the West Indies, & was afraid of even M̄ᵣ Townsend's following 'em.

"I am with the most dutiful Regard
"My Lord Duke,
"Your Grace's most Devoted
"and most Obedient Servant
"W. SHIRLEY."

SHIRLEY TO NEWCASTLE, BOSTON, 21 Nov. 1746.

(*Extracts.*)

"MY LORD DUKE,

"I am afraid your Grace will think, from my incessant Representations of the State of Nova Scotia, that I imagine that Province should be the sole Object of your Attention: Nothing could induce me to be so importunate with your Grace upon this Subject, but the fullest perswasion of the very great Importance of that Place to the Crown, & the British Subject, of the immediate bad Consequences of the Loss of it to his majesty's Service, & the imminent danger of its being lost, unless something is forthwith done for the effectual Security of it.

"The inclos'd Extract from M̄ᵣ Mascarene's Letter & Copy of Lieut̄ Colonel Gorham's will disclose in a great Measure to your Grace their Apprehensions, & the Condition of the Province: The number of the Enemy, are increas'd at Menis; they have again stop't all Communication between the Inhabitants & the Garrison, & are likely to keep footing there this Winter; and particularly from Col? Gorham's Letter your Grace will perceive what Pains the Canadeans and Malcontents among the Inhabitants take to prevent my Letter lately dispers'd among 'em, in order to setle the Minds of the Inhabitants, (a Copy of which I have before sent your Grace) from having its proper Influence; & how the Nova Scotians are alarm'd at the Rumour of a design to remove 'em from their Settlements; And it appears to me by what I farther learn from Captain Fotheringham to whom M.ʳ Mascarene refers me in his Letter, that unless something vigorous, as that Letter intimates, is done by the Middle of April at farthest, the greatest Part of the Province at least will be in the hands of the Canadeans, and it will be too late then to attempt to reclaim the Inhabitants.

. . . .

" For the securing Nova Scotia from its present dangers I would further humbly propose it as my Opinion to be consider'd by your Grace, that if his Majesty should be pleas'd as soon as possibly might be after the Receipt of this, to cause it to be signified to the Inhabitants of Nova Scotia, that the Assurances lately given 'em by me of his Royal Protection to such of 'em as should behave dutifully and avoid all traiterous Correspondence with the Enemy at this Juncture (or to that Effect) were approv'd of by him, and should be made good to 'em, it would have a great Tendency to remove their present Apprehensions of being sent off with their Families from their Settlements in Nova Scotia, which seems to distress & perplex 'em; & effectually to prevent 'em from being drawn over to take up Arms against his Majesty, unless it should be some of the most obnoxious of 'em; which if his Majesty would be pleas'd to send over at the same time his special directions to apprehend, and proceed against, such a Proceeding against the Delinquents and gracious Declaration towards the others, would, I dare say, have a proper Effect for securing the general Fidelity of the Inhabitants, at least so far as to keep 'em from joining with the Enemy; And least the Succours now sent to Annapolis should not be a sufficient force to dislodge the Enemy this Winter, I would farther humbly propose it for your Graces' Consideration, that his Majesty's Orders should be forthwith sent to myself and the other three Governments of New England, that in case the Canadeans should not be withdrawn out of Nova Scotia, they should immediately cause the Soldiers rais'd in their respective Colonies & Provinces for his Majesty's Service in the Expedition against Canada to be transported to Annapolis Royal, as their Place of Rendezvous istead of Louisbourg, & to be employed in driving the Canadeans out of Nova Scotia, and be farther subjected to such Orders as his Majesty shall be pleas'd to signify in those Directions; and if this Order was to extend to the Governour of New York, it might not be an unnecessary Caution. I am apprehensive if such Orders are not sent, that the Attention of the several Governm.ts to the Reduction of Crown Point might very much interfere with the Preservation of Nova Scotia, which is of infinitely more Consequence.

" These are the things which occur to me at present, & which I would submit to your Grace's Consideration, as what seems to require more immediate Dispatch; As to the danger of the french Fleet's early Return from the West Indies to Nova Scotia and what Strength of Ships may be necessary to protect that Province, Cape Breton, and the other Colonies against that Fleet, or any other french Armament which may be sent from Europe in the Spring to visit these Parts, I leave to Admiral Warren, who now

goes to England in the Chester, and with whom, pursuant
to the Directions of your Grace's two Letters to me in
March & April last, I have acted in Concert upon all such
Occasions as requir'd my consulting him with the greatest
Satisfaction and Harmony, having had the Pleasure to find
my own Sentiments agreable to his in all Matters of Consequence, and a most hearty Disposition in him for his
Majesty's Service, and to whom I have often talk'd over
the Affairs of Nova Scotia.

. . . .

" I will avoid repeating what I have particularly mention'd to your Grace in late Letters concerning fortifying
of Chebucto Harbour and building a Blockhouse or small
Fort for 150 Men at Menis, with a Trading House there
for the Indians, and a Blockhouse only at Canso for 100
Men, instead of new building and enlarging that at Annapolis Royal, and erecting a larger Fortification at Canso;
which in my humble Opinion would greatly strengthen
that Province, and together with the introducing of french
Protestant Ministers, and English Schools, & some small
Encouragement by Privileges to such as should conform to
the Prtestant Religion, or send their Children to the
English Schools, and Presents to the Indians with Supplies of all necessaries for 'em at the most reasonable Rates,
in Exchange for their Furrs &c. ; the Disallowance of the
publick Exercise of the Roman Catholic Religion, at least
after a short Term of Years, & forbidding Romish Priests
under severe Penalties to come into the Country either
among the Inhabitants or Indians; and if it might be consistent with his Majesty's Pleasure, a Civil Government
to be in due time introduc'd among the Inhabitants; These
things, I say, my Lord together with making Examples
of the most obnoxious among the Inhabitants, and his
Majesty's extending his Clemency and the Continuance of

his Protection to the rest upon taking the proper Oath of Allegiance, seem to me to have the most promising Aspect for making good Subjects of the present Generation of Inhabitants, at least better than they are now and good Protestants of the next Generation of 'em; especially if there was to be a Mixture of English or other Protestants introduc'd among 'em, which the Invitation of a Civil Government to be set up among 'em would bid fair for doing: and the Trading House would create in the Indians a firm Dependance upon, and Attachment to his Majesty's Government, especially if a proper Protestant Missionary or two was supported to live among 'em at their head Quarters, as is the Method of the french Priests; by wch means they gain so great an Ascendency over them.

" Just as I had finished the last Paragraph a Letter from Governor Knowles to Admiral Warren & myself, dated the 10th Instant, was deliver'd to me, in which he informs me that ' he has given his Opinion in his Letters to your Grace, that it will be necessary to drive *all the French* (I suppose he means *Inhabitants*) out of Accadie (Nova Scotia) in the ' Spring, and that he hopes he shall have Orders to assist ' in doing it, if Admiral Warren does not go upon the ' Expedition to Quebeck, which he apprehends is rendred ' more difficult than it was, by such a Number of Ships be- ' ing got safe up to Quebeck this Year, as no doubt they ' have carried all manner of warlike Stores.' And in his Letter to me of the 24th of October he says 'if his Majesty ' should be pleas'd to transport the Rebels who are Objects ' of his Mercy, & encourage other Highland Families to ' come over, he thinks the Colony of Nova Scotia would ' soon be repeopled; ' which it is possible he may have also propos'd to your Grace as in his Opinion the best Method for peopling that Colony, after the present french Inhabitants are drove off.

"As the Sentiments, which I have taken the Liberty to offer to your Grace upon this Subject, happen to be something different from M.ʳ Knowles's, I think it may not only be proper but my Duty to mention the Reasons of my preferring the Scheme for attempting to make the present french Inhabitants good Subjects to his Majesty, and keeping 'em in the Country, to that of driving 'em off & introducing some of the Rebels and other Highlanders in their Room.

"It seems very difficult to drive all the Inhabitants of Accadie out of so large a Province as that is, and which consists chiefly of Woods; It is most probable that many of the hardiest Men would retire (for some time at least) with their Cattle into the Woods, & form Parties with the Indians; and the remainder would doubtless retreat with their Families to Canada: Those, who are acquainted with the Indian Manner of Life & making War know that one hundred of 'em under Cover of the Woods can confine a very large Frontier within their Garrisons, even tho' they have Companies continually scouting between one Garrison and another: this is at present the Case of this Province & the other Colonies of New England & New York, tho' the People there are us'd to the Woods, & the Skulking of the Indians behind the Bushes & in Ditches with their other Wiles, & have large numbers of the Militia constantly upon Guard for their Protection; their Cattle is continually destroy'd; if any of 'em venture out into their Fields, they are frequently kill'd & scalp'd; and sometimes not only single Families or Garrisons are surpriz'd and cut off, as has happen'd lately in this Province, but even whole Villages, as was the Case of Sarahtoga in New York a few Months ago; so that those of the french Inhabitants, who should mix with the Indians in the Woods, would have it in their Power to put his Majesty's Garrison under such

Circumstances as that it could not possibly subsist longer in the Country than they could do it without fresh Provisions, Wood & other Materials & Supplies from thence; from all which they would be wholly cut off, when the Inhabitants were drove away; And as to such of the Inhabitants, who should go with their Families to Canada, it must be expected that a very large Body of the Men would return arm'd next Spring with some Canadeans to join the Indians; from all which it seems justly to be apprehended that an Attempt to drive all the french Inhabitants from their Settlements, should it succeed, would in Effect be driving 5 or 6000 Men to take up Arms against his Majesty's Government there every Year during the War; make the reclaiming of the Indians of Nova Scotia impracticable, & render it impossible for his Majesty's Garrison there to subsist long in the Country in time of War even with the Indians only; Besides, the Addition of about 6000 fighting Men with their Families to Canada, which would greatly strengthen the French upon this Continent, and would entail upon the Posterity of those who are thus expell'd (for several Generations at least) a Desire of recovering their former Possessions in Nova Scotia, seems to be no inconsiderable Matter, but what next to the Loss of the Country itself should be avoided on the Part of his Majesty, & is I dare say an Event, which the French next to their Acquisition of this Colony would desire: It is indeed now to be wish'd that General Nicholson had upon the first Reduction of the Colony to the Obedience to the Crown of Great Britain, remov'd the french Inhabitants, when they were but a few, out of the Country, as was done at Louisbourg; and that during the Interval of Peace the Colony had been planted with Protestant Subjects; But after their having remain'd so long in the Country upon the foot of British Subjects under the Sanction of the treaty of Utrecht, and making Improvements on their Lands for one or two Generations, and being grown up into such a Number of Families, to drive 'em all off their Settlements without farther Inquiry seems to be liable to many Objections. Among others it may be doubted whether under the Circumstances of these Inhabitants it would clearly appear to be a just Usage of 'em; it is true that the Notion of their Neutrality (which seems to have been entertain'd for some time by the English as well as themselves) is ill-grounded, and does not comport with the Terms of their Allegiance to his Majesty, to which such of 'em as chose to remain in the Province are bound by the treaty of Utrecht; whereby the french King yielded up the Inhabitants as well as the Soil of Accadie, and together with their Persons transferred their Allegiance to the Crown of Great Britain; But if it is consider'd that this Notion was founded upon an Act of the late Lieut^t Governour Armstrong then the residing Commander in Chief of the Province, whereby he took upon himself to grant 'em by a Writing under his Hand an Exemption from bearing Arms upon any Account whatever, on their consenting to take an Oath of Allegiance to his present Majesty, which, whether it was done by him with, or without Authority, appear'd at least to them to be authentick; it may perhaps be deem'd too rigorous a Punishment for their behavior grounded on such a Mistake, to involve the innocent with the Guilty in the Loss of their Estates, and the Expulsion of their Families out of the Country; it is not improbable but that there may be many among 'em who would even prefer his Majesty's Governm^t to a french one, & have done nothing to deserve such a Forfeiture; Some Allowances may likewise be made for their bad Situation between the Canadeans, Indians & English, the Ravages of all which they have felt by Turns in the Course of the War; during which they

seem to have been continually plac'd between two fires, the
force and Menaces of the Canadeans & Indians plundering
'em of whatever they wanted, & deterring 'em in the
strongest manner from having any Communication with his
Majesty's Garrison, on the one hand; and the Resentm[ts]
of the Garrison for their withholding their Intelligence &
Supplies on the other, tho' at the same time it was not in
a Condition to protect 'em from the Enemy; Wherefore
it seems a Matter worthy of your Grace's Consideration,
whether under such doubtful Circumstances the driving
all the French Inhabitants of Nova Scotia off their Settlements, and thereby very greatly strengthening the Enemy
upon this Continent, not only against the Garrison in
present, but finally against all the British Colonies there,
and depopulating one of his Majesty's Provinces for some
time (how long may be uncertain) is more eligible than
treating 'em as Subjects, confining their Punishm[t] to the
most guilty & dangerous among 'em, & keeping the rest in
the Country, and endeavouring to make them & their Posterity useful Members of Society under his Majesty's Government: I can't omit likewise observing to your Grace,
that it would be exceeding difficult to fill up the Chasm
which driving off the Inhabitants would make in the Country; During the Rupture with France it would certainly
be impracticable, and I doubt whether it would not be so
when Peace shall be made with France, if the Indians
should continue at War with us; For what Number of
Families can be propos'd to begin a Settlem[t] in the Country, after the Expulsion of the French Inhabitants, with
safety against the Indians, & which would be continually
expos'd to be destroyed by 'em, whilst they were carrying
on their Settlements; They must expect no Protection
against the Indians from within the Garrison, out of the
Reach of their great Guns; the Company of Rangers, which

live without the Walls of the Fort, would afford more of that than a thousand Garrison Soldiers would do: Whereas if the Stock of french Inhabitants was continued in the Country, an Accommodation with the Indians would be more easily brought about and preserv'd, they would be a Cover for any Number of Families that might be introduc'd among 'em whilst they were carrying on Settlements; & secure to the Garrison its necessary Supplies of fresh Provisions, Fuel, Materials for repairing the Works, & Stores of Sorts that the Country affords.

" As to repeopling the Province with some of the late Rebels and other Highland Families, it seems much to be doubted whether it might not be too hazardous to fill that Colony, wch should be the Barrier of all his Majesty's Colonies upon this Continent, with a Set of poor, ignorant, deluded Wretches just come out of a most unnatural Rebellion; that from their Neighbourhood to Canada would be continually expos'd to the Artifices and Attempts of french Romish Priests upon 'em who it is reasonable to think would not fail to instill the same Notions into 'em in America, which seduc'd 'em from their Allegiance in Great Britain, with a Promise of more effectual Support & Protection from the French here, than they had in the Highlands; Indeed, my Lord, this seems to be a dangerous experiment, and what might produce the worst of Consequences.

" I beg leave to submit it to your Grace's Consideration, whether the most staunch Protestants, & Families the most zealously affected to his Majesty's Government, a Number at least of such, should not rather, if possible, be transplanted there as soon as may be; I could wish four or five hundred of 'em could be induc'd to go from some Part of New England; I think from the Experience I had of the Inhabitants of this Province at least upon the late Alarm

given by the french Fleet, I might safely venture to be
answerable to his Majesty, that if I had suggested in my
late Orders for assembling a Body of 'em under Arms in
Boston from all Parts of this Province to oppose any
Attempt of the Enemy, that there was a design of landing
a Son of the Pretender's here, it would not have been possible to have kept any one Man, who was capable of marching hither, from appearing under Arms with the most
determin'd Resolution of hazarding his Life to the utmost
in defence of his Majesty's Governmᵗ ; And as the late
Appearances of a fondness for removing from hence to Cape
Breton seem to be quite vanished at present, I should not
be without hopes of some families removing from these
Parts to Nova Scotia upon due Encouragement; Protestants
likewise from among the Swiss Cantons, & other Northern
Parts in Germany, who are generally bred up in the Exercise of arms, and make sober and industrious Settlers, might
be safely trusted in Accadie; Great Numbers of 'em yearly
flock into Pensilvania, whereby the Inhabitants of that
Province are almost incredibly increas'd within these
twenty Years; And from the behavior of the Irish coming
out of the Northern Parts of Ireland hither, a Number of
which is setled in the Eastern Parts of this Province, I
should think they too might be safely trusted in Nova
Scotia; and it is certain that these poor unhappy Highlanders (I mean such of 'em as may be design'd to be transported into the Plantations) would be more safely dispos'd
of among the four Governmᵗˢ of New England, or in New
York & the Jerseys, where they would not be in danger
either of corrupting the Inhabitants, or being again seduc'd
themselves, but might make useful Subjects to his Majesty.

" I hope, my Lord, I shall be excus'd if I have gone
beyond my Line in submitting these Observations to your
Grace, at a time when the fate of one of his Majesty's

Northern Colonies, the most important of 'em all to the Crown in many respects, as I apprehend, and which will be in the hands of the french the Key to all the other British Colonies upon this Continent, & even to Cape Breton, And in his Majesty's Possession the Barrier of em against the Enemy seems to come to a Crisis."

SHIRLEY TO NEWCASTLE, BOSTON, NEW ENGLAND, 27 FEBRUARY, 1747.

" MY LORD DUKE,

" I am sorry that I am now to Acquaint your Grace with the Advices I receiv'd last night by Express from Nova Scotia giving me an Account that the Detachment of Troops under the Command of Lieut. Colonel Noble, which I Inform'd your Grace in my last of the 21.st instant had taken possession of Minas, and had kept it near two months, was for want of a proper Security for the Men and Intelligence from the Inhabitants surpriz'd on the 31.st of January last at three o'Clock in the morning by between 5 & 600 Canadeans & Indians in which Lieut. Col? Noble with four Officers more and about 80 men were killed, and three Officers and about 60 Men were wounded and taken prisoners before it was light enough for our people to get together; they however obliged the Enemy, upwards of 20 of whom were kill'd, and about 15 wounded, to allow 'em an honourable Capitulation, a Copy of which I inclose to your Grace together with the Account given of this Affair by the Officer who was Commandant of the Detachment at the time of the Capitulation, & Extracts from Lieut. Governour Mascarene's Letter to me upon this Subject, from whence I choose your Grace should receive the Acco.t in the same light it has been Conveyed to me in, and which upon the best Inquiry I can make, seems to be a just one. I also Inclose to your Grace an Extract from Col. Noble's Letter to me dated two days before his death, giving me an Account of the Situation of Affairs then at Minas; from whence your Grace wi!l perceive that even then he was in Expectation of being Join'd by the Rhode Island Forces & the Company from this Province, which had the Misfortune to be Shipreck'd; and that, had they arriv'd at Annapolis, and the New Hampshire Companies had not return'd home without acting, the Enemy would in all probability have been drove out of Nova Scotia, and every good purpose, which I had propos'd, been answer'd before this time. As it is I shall use my best Endeavours forthwith to fit out a sufficient force by Sea to destroy Mr Ramsay's Vessels at Schiegnecto, and recover our own by Spring, & to send Mr Mascarene such a Reinforcement of Troops as may still drive the Enemy out of Nova Scotia by the same time and prevent any bad Consequences from the late Accident there, which seems necessary to be done (if possible) and I shall hope to succeed in, if the neighbouring Governments of New England will assist in, which I shall urge 'em to do.

"I likewise inclose the Answer of the Inhabitants of Minas to the French Letter which I some time ago Inform'd your Grace I sent Mr Mascarene last Fall, and a Paragraph out of one of his Letters to me upon the same matter; whereby your Grace will perceive that that Letter seems to have had an happy Effect upon the Inhabitants at a most critical Conjuncture.

"The late Secresy of the Inhabitants of Minas with regard to the Enemys Motions, and the very certain Intelligence which the Enemy gain'd of the particular Quarters of the English Officers, notwithstanding their Supplying the King's Troops with Provisions, and the Curtesy of their Behavior to 'em before this Surprize, and their professions of being sorry for it afterwards seems to shew the necessity of his Majesty's Keeping a strong Blockhouse there with a Garrison of 150 men; And the constant ill behavior of the Inhabitants of Schiegnecto seems to make another Blockhouse with a like Garrison there equally necessary, as I at first propos'd to your Grace from Louisbourg; and these two with a Fort and Garrison at Chebucto of 300 Men at least, and the continuance of a Garrison of 300 at Annapolis Royal as it is at present, with a strong Blockhouse at Canso garrison'd with 100 Men would through the constant Correspondence that might be kept up between the several Garrisons be an effectual Security to the Province against the Enemy, and oblige the Inhabitants in a little time to contribute towards the protection & Expence of the Government, and for ever frustrate any hopes the French could Entertain of making themselves Masters of it, by their constant Endeavours to Seduce the Inhabitants from their Allegiance; all which would make Nova Scotia really His Majesty's which it seems scarcely to have been yet: And I would Submit it to your Grace's Consideration whether a Company of Rangers consisting of 100 Indians, or rather two Companies, consisting of 50 each, one to be posted at the Blockhouse at Minas, and the other in Schiegnecto would not be of the greatest Service, in Scouting thro' every part of the Province and in the Woods upon all Emergencies (for which the Regular Troops are by no means fit) and particularly in preventing the French from Introducing Men from Canada into the Province by the Bay Vert; I think the great Service which Lieu^t Colonel Gorham's Company of Rangers has been of to the Garrison at Annapolis Royal, is a demonstration of the Usefulness of such a Corps, besides that it may be a means of bringing Indians out of the French Interest into his Majesty's Service, and go far towards reclaiming 'em in general; especially if (as I have before propos'd for your Grace's Consideration) two Trading or Truck Houses were to be maintain'd one at Minas, and the other at Chiegnecto, for supplying the Indians with all necessaries in Exchange for furrs, and proper presents were made to 'em in the manner which the French use to Keep 'em in their Interest.

" And if your Grace would allow me the Freedom to offer my Sentiments concerning what appears to me to be farther necessary for putting this important Province of Nova Scotia (I think I may justly call it the most important to the Crown of any upon this Continent) in Security, I sho'd propose one of His Majesty's Arm'd Sloops (or Snows) with a Tender to be constantly employ'd in the Bay of Fundy for visiting all parts of it upon every occasion, as well as the several Harbours on the Cape Sable Coast; and one of his Majesty's Frigates to be employ'd for the protection of the Fishery at Canso (as was always usual in time of peace) which together with a Tender would also be of great Service in duly attending the Bay Verte, upon every Occasion, and likewise visiting the Coast of Accadie (or Cape Sables) besides protecting the Fishery.

" Since writing the last Paragraph I have heard of some other particular circumstances, which make it very suspicious that several of the Inhabitants at least of Minas knew of the Enemy's Motions, & I find that it is the general Opinion of the Officers that they did.

" I am with the most dutiful Regard,

" My Lord Duke,

" Your Grace's most devoted,

" & most humble Servant

" W. Shirley "

Shirley to Newcastle, Boston, April 29th, 1747.

(*Extract.*)

" My Lord Duke,

" Since finishing Governour Knowles's, & my joint Letter to your Grace, I have learn'd from one of the English Pris-

oners just Arriv'd from Schiegnecto in Exchange for one
of the French Prisoners sent by me from Boston, and who
was carry'd Captive from Minas, where he was taken by the
Enemy in the late Surprize, that when the Canadeans went
from Minas to Schiegnecto they march'd out of the Grand
Prè about 500, but were reduc'd to about 350 before they
reach'd Schiegnecto, by several of their party's leaving 'em
at every great Village in Minas, thro' which they pass'd
which makes it Evident that 150 of the Inhabitants of that
District had Join'd the Canadeans in their late Attack upon
the English at Grand Prè, and may Serve farther to shew
your Grace the imminent Danger of all the Inhabitants of
Minas's still Joining the Enemy, unless speedy measures are
taken for driving the Canadeans out of the Country, and Securing the fidelity of the Inhabitants in some better manner
than it is at present; and how opportunely the forces sent
last Winter from hence to Annapolis, and the Assurances I
took the liberty of sending the Nova Scotians that those, who
behav'd as good Subjects, sho'd have His Majesty's protection in their Estates, arriv'd there for saving the whole District of Minas from an open Revolt.

"This fluctuating State of the Inhabitants of Accadie
seems, my Lord, naturally to arise from their finding a
want of due protection from His Majesty's Government;
and their Apprehensions that the French will soon be
Masters of the Province, which their repeated Attempts
every year for the Reduction of His Majesty's Fort at
Annapolis Royal, and the Appearance of the late Duke
D'Anville's Squadron from France upon their Coast with
that View strongly Impress upon 'em, as does also the
Residence of the Enemy in the Province, and the Sollici-
tations of their own Priests; and to this, I believe, may be
added some Jealousy, which the Enemy and Priests are for
ever instilling into 'em, that the English want only a safe

Opportunity of driving all the French Inhabitants off their Settlements; which tho' M.ʳ Mascarene assures me that his communicating to 'em my printed Letter promising 'em His Majesty's protection, had so far allay'd as together with the Arrival of the late Detachment of Soldiers sent from hence in the Winter for the Defence & protection of the Province, to disappoint M.ʳ de Ramsay's Attempt upon the Inhabitants of Minas for bringing 'em to an open Revolt, and to make him retire from Minas to Schiegnecto, yet as the hopes my Letter may have made 'em entertain have not been yet Confirm'd by Assurances of His Majesty's Royal protection directly from England I cant but think, there is a most apparant danger of Nova Scotia's being soon lost, if the Expedition against Canada should not proceed this year, nor any Measures be taken, or particular Orders be sent by His Majesty for Securing the Province against the Enemy & strengthening his Government among the Inhabitants, For I perceive that the General Assembly of this Province, from whence only the Succours & Support which His Majesty's Garrison at Annapolis Royal has hitherto received for the Protection & Defence of Nova Scotia, have been sent, are tir'd of having 'em drawn wholly from their own people, and despair of its being effectual without His Majesty's more immediate Interposition for the protection of that province; And I look upon it as a very happy Incident, that I had it in my power to send M.ʳ Mascarene the Support, I did the last Winter, and beginning of the Spring, out of the Levies rais'd for the Expedition against Canada, which I insisted upon doing as they were in His Majesty's Pay (tho' rais'd for another Service) but should not have been able to do it (I believe) had it depended wholly upon the Consent of the Assembly, tho' generally well dispos'd for His Majesty's Service."

Newcastle to Shirley, 30 May, 1747.

(*Extract.*)

" As you and Mr Warren have represented, That an Opinion prevailed amongst the Inhabitants of Nova Scotia, That It was intended to remove Them from their Settlements and Habitations in that Province; And as that Report may probably have been artfully spread amongst Them in order to induce Them to withdraw Themselves from their Allegiance to His Majesty, and to take Part with the Enemy; His Majesty thinks it necessary, That proper measures should be taken, to remove any such ill-grounded Suggestions; and, for that Purpose, It is the King's Pleasure, That you should declare in some publick and authentick manner to His Majesty's Subjects, Inhabitants of that Province, That there is not the least Foundation for any Apprehension of that nature; But That, on the contrary, It is His Majesty's Resolution to protect, and maintain, all such of Them as shall continue in their Duty, and Allegiance to His Majesty, in the quiet & peaceable Possession of their respective Habitations, and Settlements And That They shall continue to enjoy the free Exercise of their Religion.

" His Majesty did propose to have signed a Proclamation to the purport above mentioned and to have transmitted it to you, to have been published in Nova Scotia; But as the Advices, that have been received here, of a Body of the New England Troops, which were advanced to Menis having been surprised by a Party of the French Canadeans and their Indians, and having been either cut off, or taken Prisoners; And the great Probability there is, That this Misfortune could not have happened to that Body of Troops, without the Assistance or, at least, Connivance of the Inhabitants of Nova Scotia; make it very difficult to fix the Terms of the intended Proclamation; His Majesty thinks it more advisable to leave it to you to make such a Declaration in His Name, as you shall be of Opinion, the present Circumstances of the Province may require."

SHIRLEY TO NEWCASTLE, 8 JUNE, 1747.

(Extract.)

"I have nothing to add to my Letters, which I have lately transmitted to your Grace, except that Mr de Ramsay is still at Chiegnecto with his party in Expectation of a Reinforcement from Canada, and the Arrival of an Armament from France, and that he has not thought fit to venture again to Manis [*Mines*], but insists in his Messages to the Inhabitants there that they should look upon themselves as Subjects to the French King since the New England Troops were oblig'd to retire out of their District by Capitulation, but that this has had no Effect upon the Inhabitants, the Reinforcement, which I sent there afterwards, having taken repossession of Manis, and hoisted the King's Flagg there, and the Deputies of Manis having thereupon renew'd their Oaths of Fidelity to His Majesty at Annapolis Royal; I continue the last Reinforcement at the Garrison still for the Security of that and Manis; But it is not strong enough to drive the French from Schiegnecto, it being suspected that the Inhabitants of that District, who were ever refractory to His Majesty's Government, would not scruple to Join the Enemy in case of an attack upon 'em; And I could not think it adviseable for me to send all the Forces, which I had rais'd for the Expedition against Canada within this Government upon another Service (as I must have done to have been strong enough to force the Enemy out of Schiegnecto after the Action at Minas) when I was in daily Expectation of receiving His

Majesty's Commands concerning the prosecution of the intended expedition, and besides, the Assembly, which has been at a great Expence for the raising of the men for the service of the Expedition only, strongly insisted upon my reserving 1500 of 'em to go against Crown Point, as your Grace will perceive by the inclos'd Copy of their Answer to my Message; However the several Reinforcements, which I did send to Annapolis, have preserv'd the Garrison and province from falling into the Enemys hands the last year, and not only made the Enemy quit Manis, but still Confine 'em to Schiegnecto; and had the Rhode Island & New Hampshire Troops Join'd the Massachusetts Forces at Manis, as was propos'd, and both those Governments promis'd me they should, and one of the Massachusetts Companies had not been lost in their passage, we should have been strong enough (I am perswaded) to have drove the Enemy the last Winter quite out of the Province of Nova Scotia: As it is, I doubt not, if no Armament arrives from France, we shall be able to keep 'em out of Annapolis and Manis till I receive His Majesty's Commands, which I am in daily Expectation of, and will, I hope, Enable me to take effectual Measures for getting rid of the Enemy and Securing the Province against their Attempts for the future."

SHIRLEY TO NEWCASTLE, BOSTON, 25 JUNE, 1747.

(*Extract.*)

"MY LORD DUKE,

"Since my last to your Grace, I have Accounts from Nova Scotia, that the French have rais'd a Battery of Nine Guns on the back of Schiegnecto to oppose the landing of Forces from Bay Verte, that they were also building a Fort & had landed Cannon & Mortars there, which they were

now hawling by Land, and may use either for Fortifying
that District, or transport from thence to Annapolis Royal
for the Reduction of his Majesty's Garrison; There has
been likewise further Accounts from thence that the Inhabitants were in Expectation of 1000 Men from Canada,
which together with the Indians & People of Schiegnecto,
& some of Manis, it is said, would make up M.ʳ De
Ramsay's Party 5000, who were then to proceed against
Annapolis; and that three large French Ships of Force had
been seen in Bay Verte, viz.ᵗ two from Canada & one from
France and landed Troops & Stores.   These Accounts gain
Credit the more easily as it seems not to be doubted, but
that the French have the Reduction of Nova Scotia extremely at heart, and will be continually making some
Attempt or other against it, whilst the Warr lasts; and I
am sorry to find by a Message lately sent me from the
Assembly desiring I would recall the Soldiers, I last sent
to Annapolis, that they seem out of heart about the effectual Preservation of it from the Enemy.   Should the
French gain it by any sudden Stroke, I am perswaded, they
would be so strong there by the Addition of all the Inhabitants to their other Forces, as well as the Numbers they
would draw from Canada, & by immediate Fortifications of
it, that it would require a very considerable Armament &
Number of Troops to recover it from 'em; which makes me
think it my Indispensable Duty to trouble your Grace with
so frequent a Repetition of my Apprehensions concerning
it.   The enemy may indeed be now look'd upon as Masters
of Scheignecto which Place it is evident they are busy in
fortifying; & would have been so likewise of Manis by this
time, had they not been oblig'd to withdraw their Troops
from thence last Fall by the Arrival of the Detachments, I
sent there."

SHIRLEY TO NEWCASTLE, 8 JULY, 1747.

(*Extract.*)

" I shall now take the Liberty to submit to your Grace's
Consideration the most practicable Scheme, that occurs to
me at present for effectually driving & keeping the Canadeans out of Nova Scotia; viz. if Mr Knowles when the
Season is too far advanc'd for the French to make an
Attempt from France against Louisbourg, should detach
1000 Men out of that Garrison to be join'd by 2000 from
New England at Annapolis Royal, and from thence to proceed to Schiegnecto; that Force would, I apprehend, drive
the Enemy off, and easily make us Masters of all the Inhabitants of that District, who seem to have ever been so
deeply engaged on the Side of the Enemy as to make 'em
forfeit all pretence of right to hold their Possessions; and
if the 2000 New England Men were to share among 'em
that District upon Condition of their setling there with
their Families in such a defensible manner as they should
be directed to do, and the french Inhabitants of that District were to be transplanted into New England, and
distributed among the four Governments there; That I
apprehend might be a Settlement of the District of Schiegnecto strong enough to keep the Canadeans out, and to
defend themselves against the Indians; and the Inhabitants
of the two other Districts of Nova Scotia, viz. Menis &
Annapolis, being thus lock'd up between the Settlement
in Schiegnecto at one End, and his Majesty's Garrison at
the other, and aw'd by the removal of the french Inhabitants of Schiegnecto from off their Lands, would be constantly held to their good behaviour, and by Intermarriages
& the spreading of the English Settlement from Schiegnecto, the whole Province, or at least the greatest part of
it, might in two or three Generations become English

Protestants — I would add that such an Exchange of the present Inhabitants of Schiegnecto for New England Men, would make up to the four Colonies of New England the Loss of the Families propos'd to be remov'd from thence to Nova Scotia upon this Occasion, hinder Canada's being strengthened by the Expulsion of the French from their Possessions, & prevent the English Settlement at Schiegnecto from being harrass'd by their continual Attempts to recover their former Lands; And the Encouragement given to the New England Men by the propos'd Distribution of the Lands among 'em would besides make the raising of 2000 Men for this Service much more practicable, & less expensive to the Crown.

"Upon the whole, my Lord, if the War continues, unless some measures are very suddenly taken for the better Security of Nova Scotia, there seems to be great danger that that Province will not long remain his Majesty's.

"I am with the most dutiful regard,
"My Lord Duke,
"Your Grace's most devoted and
"most Obedient Servant
"W Shirley."

SHIRLEY TO NEWCASTLE, 24 AUGUST, 1747.

"My Lord Duke,

"The French Declaration, of which the inclos'd is a Copy, did not come to my hands till I had finished the letter, wch. accompanies it: And I send it your Grace, as it may serve to shew the Views of the French with respect to Accadie, the Dependance they have upon the Dispositions of the Inhabitants, what advantage they propos'd to themselves from the New England Levies under the Command of the late Lieuten: Col. Noble's quitting Menis by Capitulation, and the necessity there was of my sending the last Detachment of soldiers to M: Mascarene to take repossession of Menis, and make the Inhabitants of it renew their oath of fidelity to his Majesty; which had its desir'd Effect.

" I am with the most Dutifull regard
" My Lord Duke,
" Your Grace's Most Devoted,
" and Most Obedient Humble Servant
" W SHIRLEY."

SHIRLEY TO NEWCASTLE, 20 OCT. 1747.

(*Extract.*)

" The general Inclination which, the french Inhabitants of Nova Scotia have to the french Interest, proceeds from their Ties of Consanguinity to the French of Canada, but more especially from those of their Religion, which last seems to put 'em greatly under the Influence of their Priests, who continually receive their Directions from the Bishop of Quebeck, & are the Instruments, by which the Governour of Canada makes all his Attempts for the Reduction of the Province to the french Crown, & Keeps the Indians of Nova Scotia (commonly called the Cape Sable Indians) in their Dependence upon him; particular Instances of which may be given in the first Body of French & Indians, which attack'd the King's Garrison soon after the Declaration of the present War's being headed by a Priest of Nova Scotia; and the principal Part in giving Intelligence to the Enemy, maintaining the Correspondence between Canada and Nova Scotia, assembling Cape Sable Indians, & influencing such of the Inhabitants as had joined

with or assisted the Enemy, has been manag'd by another
Priest of that Province; Other Instances of this Kind
might be given, as particularly the Attempt to bring the
Inhabitants into Revolt soon after the late Surprize at
Menis by endeavouring to influence 'em with the Authority
of the Bishop of Quebeck pronouncing 'em to be free from
their Oath of Allegiance to his Majesty. But I shall content myself with observing to your Grace only one piece of
Policy made use of by the french Priests in Nova Scotia
for preserving the whole Body of the People intirely
french, and Roman Catholick's, viz: forbidding all Inter-
marriages with the English under Pain of Excommunication, (of which I am informed there has been one or two
late Instances in actual Excommunication upon this Occasion) & which has had so general an Effect as to prevent
the Settlement of any one English Family within the
Province, from the first Reduction of it to the present
time, tho' some have attempted to setle in the Country;
& to Keep out Inter-marriages between the French & his
Majesty's English Subjects, as that I never heard of any
one Instance besides the before mentioned ones; And I
would humbly submit it to your Grace's Consideration if
the free Exercise of the Roman Catholick Religion and
an unlimited Toleration of Roman Priests in Nova Scotia
should continue to have the same Effect in that Colony for
the next succeeding forty years, as it has had within these
last forty; the Inhabitants there are suffer'd to remain a
distinct Body of French in the Neighbourhood of Canada,
with the Ties of Consanguinity & Religion between *them*
& the Canadeans still growing stronger, untill they double
or perhaps treble their Number (the French of Canada likewise at the same time increasing their Strength & Numbers) whether it may not prove in the End cherishing a
Colony of Inhabitants for the subversion of the King's

Government in it, & the strengthening of the french Interest upon the Continent.

"The Treaty of Utrecht, my Lord, by which the cession of Accadie (or Nova Scotia) with its Inhabitants was made to the Crown of Great Britain does not seem to lay his Majesty under an Obligation to allow the french Inhabitants the Exercise of the Roman Catholick Religion; and as his Majesty is as yet under no Promise to do it, I should hope that Methods might be found for weakening the Ties of Consanguinity & Religion between even the present Generation of the french inhabitants of Nova Scotia & those of Canada, by beginning new ones between his Majesty's English & french subjects there, and at the same time controuling the pernicious Power of the Romish Priests over the french Inhabitants & the Indians of that Province, which may possibly be cut off or at least obstructed by his Majesty's making a Promise to continue the french Inhabitants in the free Exercise of their Religion.

"Wherefore as his Majesty has been pleas'd to refer it to my Opinion to fix the Terms of the Declaration, which he has commanded me to make in his Name to the Inhabitants of Nova Scotia; whereby it became my Duty to avoid every thing in it, which appear'd to me to have a Tendency to disserve his Government within that Province, I have taken the Liberty to suspend promissing 'em the free Exercise of the Romish Religion, tho' it is mention'd in your Grace's Letter to have been part of what was at first propos'd to have been included in his Majesty's intended Proclamation, till I could transmit my Sentiments to your Grace, and I should have his Majesty's farther Directions upon it; & have in the mean time made a Declaration of such Points, as seem'd necessary to be ascertained to the Inhabitants for quieting their Minds, & would not admit of Delay.

"I might mention to your Grace some local Reasons for

my Omitting in the Declaration what I have done, but shall not presume to trouble you with any but what I thought it my indispensable Duty to lay before your Grace.

 " I am with the most dutiful Regard
  " My Lord Duke,
   " Your Grace's most Devoted
    " and most Obedient Servant
      " W SHIRLEY."

INDEX.

INDEX.

Carheil, the Jesuit, on the ruins of Michilimackinac, i. 17 ; aversion of Cadillac for, i. 19 ; his quarrels with Cadillac, i. 20, 30.

" Caribou," the, ii. 62, 159, 160.

Carignan, regiment of, ii. 8.

Carolina, i. 148 ; French settlement in, ii. 258 ; ii. 259, 262, 263, 264, 265, 266, 269.

Carolina traders, the, i. 321, 323.

Carter, Ebenezer, released from Indian captivity, i. 87.

Carter, Marah, murdered by the French and Indians, i. 65.

Carthagena expedition, the, ii. 72.

Cartier, Jacques, at Hochelaga, i. 18, 279.

Casco, i. 36, 39 ; attacked by the French and Indians, i. 99.

Casco Bay, i. 129 ; the Boston treaty ratified at, i. 255.

Casco, the treaty of, i. 39.

Casgrain, Abbé, i. 196, 211.

Castine, town of, i. 38, 122.

Castle William, ii. 157, 317.

Catholicism, bound up with the old political order, i. 192.

Catholic Jacobites, ii. 177.

Catlin, George, the painter, among the Mandans, ii. 20.

Catlin, John, killed by the French and Indians, i. 64.

Catlin, Mrs. John, shows wonderful generosity to a wounded French officer, i. 64 ; death of, i. 65.

Catlin, Joseph, attacked by the French and Indians, i. 63.

Caughnawaga, ii. 236 ; see also Sault St. Louis.

Caughnawaga, the Iroquois mission of, i. 13 ; the converted Iroquois settle at, i. 14 ; Eunice Williams at, i. 80 ; i. 217, 234.

Caughnawagas, the, i. 13 ; carry

VOL. II. — 24

on a contraband trade between New York and Canada, i. 15 ; i. 36 ; join the expedition against New England, i. 56 ; draw out of an expedition against New England, i. 96 ; promise Schuyler not to attack New England, i. 100 ; in the conquest of Canada, i. 139.

Caulfield, deputy-governor at Annapolis, i. 196, 205, 206.

Chacornacle, Lieutenant, joins Cadillac, i. 28.

Chamberlain, John, tradition of his meeting with Paugus, i. 268.

Chambly, death of, i. 98.

Chambly, settlement of, i. 75, 77, 140, 141, 142 ; stone fort built by the French at, ii. 55.

Champigny, the intendant, opposes Cadillac's plan of a settlement at Detroit, i. 26, 28 ; i. 348.

Champlain, Lake, i. 15, 77, 135, 139, 140, 165, 177, 252 ; ii. 48, 55, 153, 208, 221, 230, 235, 265.

Champlain, Samuel de, in the Onondaga country, i. 18, 279 ; ii. 259, 262.

" Chapeau Rouge " Bay, see Gabarus Bay.

Chardon, the missionary, urges the extermination of the Outagamies, i. 337.

Charles I., ii. 262.

Charles II., of England, i. 133, 273.

Charlestown, named after Commodore Charles Knowles, ii. 228. See also Number Four.

Charlestown Neck, ii. 90.

Charlevoix, the Jesuit historian, on the French responsibility for Queen Anne's War, i. 46 ; on the essential purpose of Queen Anne's War, i. 47 ; on Ramesay's expedition against Nichol·

Denis, ii. 259, 262.

Denonville, Marquis de, recognizes the importance of possessing Detroit, i. 22 ; ii. 53.

Denys, M. de la Ronde, i. 157 ; sent to treat with the "Bastonnais," i. 159 ; taken prisoner, i. 160 ; on the losses of the English expedition against Canada, i. 181 ; sent to Annapolis, i. 194 ; in the Acadian settlements, i. 196.

"Deptford," the, i. 125.

Derniers, Moïse des, on the illiteracy of the Acadians, ii. 173.

Deruisseau, i. 141.

Des Chaillons, Saint-Ours, commands an expedition against New England, i. 96.

Deschenaux, ii. 274.

Des Enclaves, Père, i. 202.

Desliettes, in command in the Illinois country, i. 336 ; proposes to exterminate the Outagamies, i. 336 ; joins Lignery's expedition, i. 338.

Desligneris, ii. 185, 190.

"Despatch," the, i. 173.

Destonnel, Mr., ii. 330.

D'Estournel, Vice-Admiral, see Estournel, Vice Admiral d'.

Destrahoudal, M., ii. 166, 167.

Des Ursins, La Loire, i. 329.

Detroit, important location of, i. 22 ; ii. 57 ; occupied by Du Lhut, i. 22 ; Livingston urges the occupation of, i. 22 ; its rivalry with Michilimackinac, i. 23 ; Cadillac's plans for, i. 23 ; proposed restriction of the beaver-trade to, i. 23 ; Cadillac lays the foundations for, i. 28 ; in the hands of the company of the Colony of Canada, i. 29 ; is given over to Cadillac, i. 32 ; the

Indian population at, i. 275 ; Dubuisson in command at, i. 279 ; its loss of strength in the departure of La Mothe-Cadillac, i. 327.

Detroit, fort, i. 279.

Detroit River, the, i. 29.

Dièreville, i. 131.

Dieskau, Baron, flotilla of, ii. 237.

Dion, ii. 289, 291.

Doddridge, i. 51.

Dominique, Father, i. 190.

Doolittle, Rev. Benjamin, ii. 222 ; on the defence of Number Four, ii. 229 ; sketch of, ii. 232 ; his sudden death, ii. 233 ; his famous narrative, ii. 233, 234.

Dorchester, joins the expedition against Port Royal, i. 126 ; i. 150.

Dorman, Ephraim, ii. 215.

Doty, ii. 249.

Doucette, at Annapolis, i. 196.

Douglas, Dr., on the plan to attack Louisbourg, ii. 64, 86, 112, 118 ; on the attack on the Island Battery, ii. 122 ; on the life at Louisbourg after the conquest, ii. 149.

Dover, attacked by French and Indians, i. 95, 99.

Downing, Joshua, killed by Indians, i. 52.

"Dragon," the, i. 136, 147, 151.

Dragonades, the, i. 4.

Drake, S. G., ii. 234.

Drowned Lands, the, ii. 237.

Dubuisson, Sieur, in command at Detroit, i. 279 ; dangerous visitors, i. 280 ; timely succor, i. 282 ; attacks the camp of the Outagamies, i. 285 ; the siege, i. 286 ; overtures from the enemy, i. 287 ; renewed hostilities, i. 290 ; wavering allies, i. 291 ; the